LEGAL CASES, NEW RELIGIOUS MOVEMENTS, AND MINORITY FAITHS

Ashgate Inform Series on Minority Religions and Spiritual Movements

Inform is an independent charity that collects and disseminates accurate, balanced and up-to-date information about minority religious and spiritual movements. The Ashgate Inform book series addresses themes related to new religions, many of which have been the topics of Inform seminars. Books in the series will attract both an academic and interested general readership, particularly in the areas of Religious Studies, and the Sociology of Religion and Theology.

Legal Cases, New Religious Movements, and Minority Faiths

Edited by

JAMES T. RICHARDSON
University of Nevada, Reno, USA

and

FRANÇOIS BELLANGER
Université de Genève, Switzerland

ASHGATE

Published by
Ashgate Publishing Limited
Wey Court East
Union Road
Farnham
Surrey, GU9 7PT
England

Ashgate Publishing Company
110 Cherry Street
Suite 3-1
Burlington, VT 05401-3818
USA

www.ashgate.com

British Library Cataloguing in Publication Data
A catalogue record for this book is available from the British Library

The Library of Congress has cataloged the printed edition as follows:
 Legal cases, new religious movements, and minority faiths / edited by James T. Richardson and Frangois Bellanger.
     pages cm.—(Ashgate inform series on minority religions and spiritual movements)
 Includes index.
 Includes bibliographical references and index.
 ISBN 978-1-4724-2874-5 (hardcover : alk. paper)—ISBN 978-1-4724-2875-2 (ebook)—ISBN 978-1-4724-2876-9 (epub)
 1. Religious minorities—Legal status, laws, etc. 2. Cults—Law and legislation I. Richardson, James T., 1941– editor of compilation. II. Bellanger, Frangois, editor of compilation.
 K3242.L439 2014
 342.08'52—dc23

2014002728

ISBN 9781472428745 (hbk)
ISBN 9781472428752 (ebk – PDF)
ISBN 9781472428769 (ebk – ePUB)

Printed in the United Kingdom by Henry Ling Limited, at the Dorset Press, Dorchester, DT1 1HD

Contents

List of Contributors

François Bellanger, PhD, Professor of Law (University of Geneva), Attorney at Law, has been a legal expert on cults for the Department of Justice of the Canton of Geneva (Switzerland) and is one of the authors of the official report on illegal sectarian practices published in Geneva in 1997 ("Audit sur les dérives sectaires"). He has published several articles on cults and religious freedom, and is the President of the Information Center on Beliefs in Geneva.

Claire Borowik has served as the international director of public affairs for the Family International since 2006. She also managed legal and media affairs for the organization in South America for four years, and in North America for 10 years. She has served in several countries of Central and South America for 20 years, and was imprisoned during the 1993 raids of Family communities in Argentina, where she served as the Family spokesperson and liaison for legal affairs. She is the codirector of the nonprofit web-based WorldWide Religious News Service, providing religious news to the academic and legal communities.

Henri de Cordes was the parliamentary assistant of the Member of Federal Parliament Antoine Duquesne, author of the report of the investigation committee of the Belgian House of Representatives on the illegal practices of cults (1996–1997). In April 1999, he was appointed vice president of the Information and Advice Center on Harmful Cultic Organizations (Brussels, Belgium) established by the law of 2 June 1998 following a recommendation of the investigation committee. On 9 June 2005, the House appointed him president for a six-year term. He is the author of *L'Etat belge face aux dérives sectaires* (*The Belgian State Faced with Cultic Deviations*), which describes how the Belgians addressed the cult issue during the period 1997–2006.

Massimo Introvigne is managing director of CESNUR, the Center for Studies of New Religions, established in 1988 and headquartered in Turin, Italy. He is also the secretary of APSOR, the Piedmont Association for the Sociology of Religion, and he served in 2011 as the OSCE (Organisation for Security and Co-operation in Europe) Representative for combating racism, xenophobia, intolerance and discrimination against Christians and members of other religions. In 2012 he was appointed as chairperson of the Observatory of Religious Liberty instituted by the Italian Ministry of Foreign Affairs. Dr Introvigne is the author or coauthor of sixty books in the field of sociology of religion and religious pluralism, including the award-winning *Encyclopedia of Religions in Italy*, whose third edition was published in 2012.

Philip Katz QC obtained his MA in Jurisprudence from University College, Oxford (1971–74) and then worked for a short period in the advertising industry. He soon returned to the Inns of Court School of Law to study for the barristers' professional examinations and was called to the Bar in 1976. He joined the Chambers of Rt Hon. Sir Arthur Irvine QC, MP as a pupil and has practiced in criminal law from those Chambers (now known as 9–12 Bell Yard) ever since. In 2000 he was appointed Queen's Counsel and also a Recorder of the Crown Court. In 2008 he was elected Head of Chambers, a role which he performed until recently. He continues to practice in criminal law and regularly appears for the Prosecution or the Defence in high profile and serious criminal trials.

Valerie A. Lykes, MA is a Doctoral Student in the Interdisciplinary Social Psychology Program at the University of Nevada, Reno. Her main research focus is the influence religion has on politics, aging, and the environment. She has published on minority religions in the justice system.

Evelyn M. Maeder received her PhD from the University of Nebraska-Lincoln, and her MA of Legal Studies from the University of Nebraska College of Law. She is currently an Assistant Professor in the Institute of Criminology and Criminal Justice at Carleton University in Canada, where she also holds a cross-appointment to the Department of Psychology. She is the director of the Legal Decision-Making Laboratory at Carleton, and her research has been funded by the Social Sciences and Humanities Research Council of Canada and the American Psychology-Law Society. Her primary research interests include the effects of extralegal characteristics on juror decision-making, as well as juror decision-making in, and public perceptions of, the Not Criminally Responsible on Account of Mental Disorder defence (Canada's version of the insanity defence).

Jean-François Mayer received his doctorate in history from the University of Lyon in 1984. From 1987 to 1990 he was in charge of a research project of the Swiss National Science Foundation on alternative religious groups in Switzerland, during which time he encountered and researched the Order of the

Solar Temple. Between 1991 and 1998 he worked as an analyst in international and security affairs for the Swiss Federal Government. In 1994 he was invited to take part as an expert in the Swiss police investigation of the Order of the Solar Temple. Since 1999 he has worked as a consultant and advisor to various academic projects. Between 1999 and 2007 he taught at the University of Fribourg as a lecturer in religious studies. In 2007 he founded the Religioscope Institute and is the editor of the website www.religion.info.

Monica K. Miller is an Associate Professor with a split appointment between the Criminal Justice Department and the Interdisciplinary PhD Program in Social Psychology. She is also an adjunct faculty at the Grant Sawyer Center for Justice Studies and a faculty associate in Women's Studies. She received her JD from the University of Nebraska College of Law in 2002 and her PhD in Social Psychology from the University of Nebraska-Lincoln in 2004. Her interests involve the application of psychological theories and justice principles to laws and policies. Her publications include *God in the Courtroom: Religion's Role at Trial* published by Oxford University Press in 2009, as well as numerous articles in professional journals and law reviews.

Alastair Mullis is a graduate of King's College London (1984) and Downing College Cambridge (1985). He is a Professor and Head of School at the University of East Anglia Law School. His main research and teaching interests lie in the areas of the law of defamation, international commercial law and torts. He has published widely in these areas and is the general editor of *Carter-Ruck on Libel and Privacy* (LexisNexis Butterworths), now in its sixth edition.

Susan J. Palmer is a Canadian sociologist whose primary research interest is new religious movements. She teaches in the Religious Studies departments at Concordia University and at Dawson College in Montreal and is an Affiliate Member of the Religious Studies Faculty at McGill. She is the author of 10 books in new religious movements, notably *Moon Sisters, Krishna Mothers, Rajneesh Lovers: Women's Roles in New Religions* (Syracuse University Press, 1994), and *Aliens Adored: Rael's UFO Religion* (Rutgers, 2004). She has engaged in field research with at least 30 different groups on topics ranging from apocalyptic activity, prophecy, charisma, communalism, childrearing, racialist religions, to research ethics and methods in studying new religions. Her most recent book, *The New Heretics of France* (Oxford University Press), explores the state-sponsored persecution of religious minorities in France.

Jeffrey E. Pfeifer is an Associate Professor of Forensic Psychology at Swinburne University of Technology in Melbourne, Australia, and has been teaching and researching in the areas of jury decision-making, policing, and correctional psychology for over 15 years. Dr Pfeifer has published a number of articles on the social perceptions of cults and New Religious Movements, especially with regard to the activation of negative stereotypes in jurors. In addition to his research Dr Pfeifer has also been involved in over 30 program evaluations on a variety of initiatives related to gambling, mental health, public safety, policing, and corrections and also conducted numerous workshops on police training and professional standards for a variety of organizations including the *Royal Canadian Mounted Police*, the *Ontario Provincial Police*, the *Western Australia Police Service*, the *Anti-Corruption Commission of Zambia*, the *Singapore Airport Security Service*, the *Sharjah (UAE) Police Service*, and the *Durban (South Africa) Police Service*. He has published over 35 peer-reviewed articles as well as two books.

James T. Richardson, is Professor of Sociology and Judicial Studies at the University of Nevada in Reno, and also a lawyer. He directs the Grant Sawyer Center for Justice Studies, as well as the Judicial Studies graduate degree program for trial judges at the University. His latest books include *Regulating Religion: Case Studies from around the Globe* (Kluwer, 2004) and *Saints under Siege: The Texas Raid on the Fundamentalist Latter Day Saints* (with Stuart Wright, New York University Press, 2011). He has published over 250 articles and book chapters, and has written or edited 10 books, mostly on new and minority faiths. In recent years his focus has been on legal aspects of social control of religions. He is currently president of the Society for the Scientific Study of Religion.

Andrew Scott is an associate professor in the Department of Law at the London School of Economics and Political Science. He is a graduate of Queen's University, Belfast (LLB Hons, MPhil) and the University of Wales (PhD). He held a senior lectureship at Norwich Law School, UEA before taking up a post at the London School of Economics in 2006. His research interests lie primarily in the fields of media law and regulation, and constitutional law. His current research agenda includes projects on the law of defamation, the interplay between defamation and religious faith, corporations and the public sphere, and the regulation of journalistic newsgathering practices. He is the co-author – with Gavin Millar QC – of a forthcoming book on Newsgathering: Law, Regulation and the Public Interest (Oxford University Press).

Jennifer Shoemaker holds an MA in Social Psychology from the University of Nevada, Reno and an MA in Professional Counselling from the Illinois School of Professional Psychology. Her research interests include religious motivation, growth and management of religious-based non-profits, and cultures of world religions. She currently teaches in the social and behavioural sciences department at Joliet Junior College in Joliet, Illinois, and in the humanities department at Northwestern College in Naperville, IL.

Hardeep Singh is a freelance journalist and broadcaster, and Press Secretary for the Network of Sikh Organisations. He has written for the *Guardian*, *Telegraph*, *Independent*, *Legalweek* and has appeared on BBC Radio 4, 5 Live and various BBC local stations. In 2011 he successfully defended the libel case *His Holiness v Singh*. He is one of 52,000 signatories at www.libelreform.org/.

Preface

Eileen Barker

Inform (Information Network Focus on Religious Movements, www.Inform.ac) was founded in 1988 with the objective of providing enquirers with information that was as objective, reliable, and up-to-date as possible about minority religions, in particular 'new religious movements' (NRMs) and those groups and movements that are sometimes referred to as 'cults' or 'sects'. Since then Inform has successfully accomplished its initial goal of helping to inform societal authorities, the mass media, scholars and members of the general public about all sorts of the smaller and new faiths that have attracted both adherents and the attention of others in society.

Over the years since 1988, Inform has found new ways to accomplish its initial goal and mission as well. This volume and a number of others being published in the Ashgate Inform series (see listing of series books included herein) are important examples of Inform's expanded role, as it continues to make readily available the scholarship being produced concerning NRMs and other minority religions. A brief recounting of the history of Inform will make it clear why this new development fits well with the long-term goals of Inform.

Throughout the 1970s and 1980s there had been a growing concern in some quarters that there was an unnecessary amount of suffering due to ignorance and misinformation about NRMs that had emanated from the media, the movements themselves and their opponents. Although there had been a considerable quantity of relevant work carried out by scholars, their conclusions were rarely communicated beyond the bounds of academia. The idea behind Inform was to draw on this material and, relying on the methods of the social sciences, attempt to assess the flood of often conflicting reports from other sources in order to be able to provide more reliable descriptions of the various religions and of the so-called 'cult scene' in general.

Based at the London School of Economics, Inform was established as an independent educational charity. It now has three full-time and four part-time staff as well as two honorary research fellows, all the research staff having post-graduate degrees in the sociology of religion. As its name suggests, Inform relies heavily on its international network, which consists of hundreds of professionals, other experts, and people with personal experience of minority religions. Although it has concentrated mainly on the religious scene in Europe and North America, Inform has by now accumulated material about over four thousand religious organisations around the world. From its beginnings, it was given, and continues to enjoy, the support of the British government and mainstream churches.

Inform's main tasks are to collect, assess and disseminate information. Over the years, it has responded to tens of thousands of enquiries. In the early days the largest minority of enquirers were concerned relatives, but requests for information are now more likely to be from government and other official organisations from throughout the world. Further enquirers include the media, academics, clergy, a variety of professionals and interested members of the public. From the very beginning, Inform has held day-long seminars twice a year that have focussed on a wide range of issues related to NRMs, examples being the law, children, women, the media, violence, prophecy, possession and money (see http://www.inform.ac/node/51 for a listing of the 50 or so topics).

A distinctive feature of these seminars has been the diversity of people who are invited to present papers. Frequently these have included members, former members and relatives of a wide range of religions, together with academics and other specialists such as lawyers, medical practitioners, social workers, representatives of the media, the government and the police. The audiences have also been widely diversified, giving all the participants the opportunity to hear and discuss issues with those who approach the topic from a very different perspective from their own.

In 2010 it was agreed that Ashgate would publish a series of volumes emanating from Inform Seminars which would, like the Seminars, include contributions not only from academics, but also from others with their own particular perspective. For some, this has been a controversial decision as not all contributors approach the topic with the kind of systematic rigour and objectivity that might be expected of a scholarly volume. However, Inform and the editorial board of the series are of the opinion that these non-academic chapters can add both insights and life to some of the tensions and controversies that abound in the field of minority religious movements. The present volume follows this pattern by including, along with academic scholars, professional lawyers and others who have played a role as actors in legal cases. That their perspectives are occasionally at variance with each other is considered by those of us involved in the series to be not a problem but an advantage.

Eileen Barker
Professor Emeritus of the Sociology of Religion
London School of Economics
Founder and Chair of Inform's Board of Governors
Editor, Ashgate Inform Series on Minority Religions and Spiritual Movements

Acknowledgements

We would like to thank those who have assisted with this project, including the authors of the chapters, who shared sometimes very personal stories of their encounters with the legal system. We are also grateful to those associated with Ashgate, particularly Sarah Lloyd, whose patience and advice was much appreciated. Eileen Barker, the series editor for Ashgate, has offered helpful comments throughout the project. Her support has been very important to its successful completion. David Shirley and Alex Limon, staff members at the University of Nevada Sawyer Center for Justice Studies, have worked many long hours making certain that the submissions met standards for proper format and style and that the index was done properly. Their help was essential and greatly appreciated. We are grateful as well to our families for their patience as we worked to make this project successful.

PART I
Controversial Religious Groups and the Legal System

Chapter 1

Courts, Crusaders and the Media: The Family International

Claire Borowik

Introduction

The emergence of new religions throughout the second half of the twentieth century predicating alternative lifestyles and values, challenging the status quo and operating outside the mainstream has been met over time with a range of reactions from curiosity and tolerance to consternation and disapprobation. Throughout the second half of the 1970s and the 1980s, a social milieu of intolerance developed; the convergence of pressures brought to bear by countermovements, former member crusaders, and stigmatizing media culminated in some extreme attempts at social control through incidents of government intervention. These interventions were conducted on the grounds that the belief system and practices of the minority religion posed a danger to members and their children, as well as to the larger society. Consequentially, such interventions have placed the legal system in the precarious position of judging the beliefs and practices of new religions while weighing in the balance constitutional guarantees of freedom of religion.

During the early 1990s, dozens of communal residences of the Family International (originally known as the Children of God) on three continents were subjected to internationally publicized military-style raids, resulting in lengthy court proceedings. Hundreds of children were taken into state custody and subjected to rigorous physical, psychological and educational evaluations. Notwithstanding the initial prejudice and presumption of guilt that fuelled these state interventions, in the final accounting the higher courts on all three continents upheld the rights of individuals to their religious beliefs and affirmed that the children were not at risk due to the unconventional beliefs and lifestyle of the movement. At the heart of these cases has been the well-being of children, an incontrovertible concern and responsibility of any society.

In their zealousness, however, authorities often overstepped the bounds of their authority, resulting in the rights of members being infringed upon and the very children they sought to 'rescue' being placed at risk. The trauma children have suffered from brutalizing raids, parental ruptures, the stigmatization of the media, and invasive psychological and medical procedures has rarely received serious reflection in the aftermath of such incidents.

The favourable outcomes of the Family International's legal proceedings in the face of vexatious opposition have resulted in significant judicial precedents and provide hope for the future of religious tolerance in the legal forum. The rulings of courts in several countries in Family cases indicate that the legal protections and constitutional guarantees in democratic countries, if punctiliously observed, can serve to protect the rights of marginalized religious minorities. These protections and guarantees can provide the necessary balance between religious freedom and concerns for the well-being of children in the legal realm and uphold the religious rights of individuals insofar as these do not impinge on societal imperatives. The debate, however, has moved into cyberspace, with the public serving as jury, as popular media, crusaders and activists compete to claim ownership of public opinion and construct narratives that will ultimately define new religions. Doubtless, this new dimension of the religious debate portends to have a significant impact on the ability of new religions to successfully develop beyond their radical roots and controversial beginnings to take a place in the religious marketplace.

Historical Background

Born in the heat of the counterculture movement of the 1960s, the Children of God emerged as a large millenarian, world-rejecting communal movement at the moment in time where the Holiness Movement met the Psychedelic Movement (Bainbridge 1997: 219). While it came into being as an integral part of the Jesus People, the Children of God developed radical innovative beliefs that separated it from the movement early on (Richardson and Davis 1983). Subsequently, the Children of God would be considered the most controversial of the communal groups to emerge from the Jesus People movement (Miller 1999: 96). Despite never exceeding 10,000 adults in its 45-year history, its members zealously established communes and carried out evangelistic activities in over 90 countries (Davis and Richardson 1976).

The roots of the Family International can be traced to the Pentecostal revival of post-World War II. Both its founder David Berg (1919–94) and his wife and successor, Karen Zerby, were raised in evangelical Pentecostal churches. David Berg became disenchanted with organized religion and established churches, which he dubbed 'churchianity', and in his writings he often excoriated their accommodation to the world. He contended that the churches had been overtaken by the secularization of modern society to the point that modern denominational Christianity had little in common with the radical message and impassioned commitment of the early church that he sought to resurrect.

Berg embraced the anti-establishment message that resonated amongst the counterculture youth that were his target audience, which he referred to as the 'lost generation' (Berg 1973). His teachings berated the 'System' for its corruption and declared that its destruction was imminent. Revolutionary language was adopted, with Jesus being cast as the true revolutionary of all time and the Bible the handbook to spiritual revolution (Cowan and Bromley 2008: 123). With its sackcloth vigils and message of 'Woe to America', from its earliest days the Children of God was no stranger to controversy. The movement's communal lifestyle, its radical message with anti-establishment themes and its unconventional doctrines and practices sparked opposition and negative media profiling from its earliest days. The Children of God is also credited with giving rise to the first 'cult watch' group, FREECOG (Free our Children from the Children of God), which would serve as the prototype for future anti-cult organizations (Shupe and Bromley 1994: 5).

Beginning in the mid-1970s, Berg's writings challenged conventional sexual mores and taboos with the postulation of the 'Law of Love' doctrine and the subsequent development of liberal antinomian sexual practices. According to this doctrine, individuals were freed from the strictures of the Mosaic Law, inclusive of biblical prohibitions of adultery and sexual immorality, through faith in Christ. As such, heterosexual relations between consenting adults, regardless of marital status, were deemed lawful in God's eyes to the extent that others affected by these actions were not hurt or offended (Richardson and Davis 1983). The development of the Law of Love doctrine led to a period of extensive theological exploration of sexual themes and experimentation, including the introduction of the controversial practice of 'flirty fishing'. Flirty fishing, discontinued in 1988, was a form of evangelistic outreach that encouraged members to frequent clubs and recreational places to meet and proselytize members of the opposite sex, with allowance for members to engage in sexual intimacy as a tangible manifestation of God's love.

During this period (1978–85), David Berg's most polemical statements and speculations were published, challenging traditional moral boundaries for sexual relations, including those relating to minors, which ultimately led to incidences of adult/minor sexual interaction. In 1986, during the first Family international teen gathering, grave complaints were made by several teenage women of sexual misconduct by adult men. Subsequently, an early draft of a child protection policy was published, followed in 1989 by an excommunication policy for those found guilty of child abuse. An official policy statement was published in 1992 with strong denunciations of child abuse and exploitation, renouncing previously published literature at variance with this position. This policy was ratified in 1995 in the Family International's *Charter of Rights and Responsibilities*, which would serve as the organization's constitution.[1]

From 1989 to 1994, the leadership worked to systematically expunge and remove from circulation any writings that could be construed to approve of aberrant practices, particularly relating to the sexuality of minors (Melton 1997: 55). In 1994, in compliance with a court stipulation in a custody hearing in England, acknowledgement was made by Karen Zerby of David Berg's responsibility in predicating a sexually liberal doctrine while failing to institute necessary protections for minors.[2] In 2006, a series of internal documents entitled *Family History, Doctrine, and Practices Regarding Sexuality* candidly examined the Family International's sexual history and made definitive statements regarding past errors in the interpretation of the Law of Love doctrine, culminating with a public apology to second generation members and former members.

We acknowledge that some of David's writings misapplied the Law of Love to sexual contact between adults and minors, and as such were the direct cause of

---

[1]   First instituted in 1995, the Charter was updated to reflect sweeping institutional change introduced into the organization in July 2010. The current version of the Family International's Charter can be viewed at: http://tficharter.com.

[2]   In 1992, the mother of a Family member filed a case with Lord Justice Ward in England, requesting the custody of her unmarried daughter's child. The grounds presented by the mother for the removal of the custody of her grandchild were her daughter's membership with the Family International. Although this case was strictly a custody case involving a Family member and her mother, Justice Ward devoted several years to hearing both former and current member testimony, as well as scholars of religion. He also studied Family literature and ordered social services to evaluate the condition of local Family communities in England before pronouncing his decision. After three years of rigorous investigative work, in November, 1995, Justice Ward emitted a lengthy ruling, in which he leveled some harsh criticisms of past eras of the movement's history, requiring assurances of changes made in years past, while also concluding that the Family International had undergone reformative changes. He concluded that he was satisfied that the movement provided a safe environment for children raised within the group and consequently awarded the mother care and control of her infant child (Bradney 1999: 217–18). See Richardson (1994) for a book chapter based on his testimony in this major case in the UK.

any misconduct that occurred at that time. This was rectified in 1986, when any sexual contact between adults and minors was banned. We regret that this policy was not in place during the earlier years of the Family to protect minors from hurt or harm. Sadly, because such rules were not in place, some of you experienced inappropriate sexual contact with adults, and we acknowledge that abusive actions occurred (Zerby and Kelly 2008).

As the public had gained a greater awareness of child safety and child protection concerns throughout the 1980s, the Family International had concomitantly undertaken measures to eradicate doctrine or practices that could place minors at risk and had begun retrenchment efforts to domesticate the sexual liberality of the late 1970s and early 1980s. By the early 1990s, the movement was approaching a relatively more conventional view on sexuality (Melton 1997: 11). In 2010, the application of the Law of Love doctrine to sexual relations between adults was ratified in principle at the Family International's most far-reaching restructuring to date, known as the 'Reboot'. However, the practice itself was significantly de-emphasized; in summarizing the current position, Zerby stated, 'Applying the doctrine of the Law of Love to sex is no longer something that we will promote or encourage members to practice' (Zerby 2010).

Notwithstanding the great pains taken in the late 1980s to address the errors of the past, these would have far-reaching consequences in the official investigations the Family International would face in the early 1990s. Family members would find themselves vulnerable to claims-making by counter-movements and detractors, in particular the claim that children in certain groups were being harmed 'just by being in a group that adheres to certain beliefs and practices thought by some to be harmful to children' (Richardson 1999: 175–6). Its communalistic lifestyle and home schooling of children, coupled with past sexually liberal doctrines and practices, and a relatively high degree of tension with the greater society would render the Family International susceptible to such collective claims. In the brief description of the cases that follows, it becomes evident that these concerns were elemental in instigating authorities to investigate and take action against Family communities. In the early 1990s, anti-cult organizations and detractors would collaborate to make grave claims of institutional child abuse, mobilizing authorities to take intrusive and draconian measures under the guise of concern for the well-being of Family children.

Brief Analysis of Governmental Interventions

From 1989 to 1993, predawn police raids were launched at dozens of Family International communal residences in Spain, Australia, France, and Argentina. Although there are significant differences in the development and resolution of each of these cases, more striking are the commonalities. Despite the variances in local culture, legal systems, geographical divides and constitutional expressions of freedom of worship, a similar pattern emerged in the investigations and subsequent legal proceedings.

The raids in Australia, France, and Argentina featured hundreds of heavily armed police officers forcibly entering communes in the dead of night (in some cases violently breaking down doors), accompanied by child protection agencies at the ready to take all the children into care. The media, previously alerted to the pending actions, were present to capture and broadcast images of the raids, which were accompanied by lurid sensationalistic headlines denouncing the group as a 'sinister cult' culpable of any number of pernicious acts. Self-proclaimed anti-cult 'experts' were consulted by examining magistrates and law enforcement and were interviewed by the media from the earliest stages. Their analyses of the movement, although lacking in empirical knowledge and parroting generalized popular rhetoric on 'cultic' groups came to be the primary source of information for law enforcement, as well as to inform the media's reporting of the incidents and consequently public opinion.

Adult members were arrested and incarcerated on non-specific charges, and considered guilty by association without having been individually charged with any misdeeds. Traumatized children, having been aggressively whisked away to detention centres by child protection agencies, in some cases were not permitted to contact their parents for several days after the raids. Regardless of the outcomes of medical and psychological evaluations, social welfare authorities were determined to place the children as wards of the state or to appoint custody to relatives outside the organization (Richardson 1999: 178). Due to the lack of evidence to substantiate the complaints filed by anti-cult organizations and ex-members from which the raids originated, officials scrambled post-intervention to produce corroboratory evidence to justify their actions. In each of the cases, after examining, interrogating and observing the 'rescued' children, no evidence was found to support their actions or claims that the children were victims of neglect or abuse.

> What was the net result of all these separate investigations following the terrorizing of large numbers of children and adults, mass arrests, imprisonments,

custody placements, invasive examinations, and breakup of households? Not a single case against Family adults was upheld in courts of law within the various countries involved. Not one of the more than 600 children examined by doctors and psychologists in these countries was found to have been abused. In every country, in every case, parents and children were released from custody for lack of evidence and eventually reunited. (Shepherd and Shepherd 2011: 238)

An analysis of the Family judicial proceedings suggests that the concerted claims-making of anti-cultists and ex-members, coupled with a stigmatizing media, ultimately created a clime of 'moral panic'.[3] The resultant pressure brought to bear on the authorities by these convergent claims galvanized the authorities to respond disproportionately and to exceed the limits of their authority.

Argentina

In October 1989 commando-style raids were staged on two Family communal residences in Buenos Aires by scores of heavily armed police under the direction of examining magistrate Alberto Piotti.[4] Twelve adults were detained for two weeks, while their 18 children were placed in state custody. The media had been alerted and were present for the initial stages of the raids, and broadcast images of officials throwing the movement's religious literature on what looked to be a pyre for burning on the front yard. A custody dispute was at the heart of the intervention; an estranged husband, the father of two children residing in the community, sought the assistance of Argentine journalist, Alfredo Silleta, an activist committed to alerting the public to the dangers of what he referred to as the 'invasion of the cults'. Silleta would later go on to found the Argentine anti-cult association FAPES (*Fundacion Argentina para el Estudio de las Sectas* – Argentine Foundation for the Study of Sects) in 1990. Based on the joint allegations of the estranged husband and Silleta, local police and social services officials were commissioned to launch the raids.

These proceedings formed the basis for three separate court actions: drug charges, child neglect, and corruption of minors. Considering the group's

---

[3]   The concept of 'moral panic' was developed in the 1970s to explain how some social problems generate exaggerated fears, often characterized by a reaction in the media and in political forums out of proportion to the actual threat (Richardson and Introvigne 2001: 143).

[4]   Alberto Piotti would later become a congressman in 1991, only to abruptly resign six years later due to allegations of having obstructed the investigation of the Jewish Community Centre bombing of 1994.

historical disapprobation of the use of drugs, the presiding magistrate summarily dismissed the drug charges (Moldes 1990). The Minors Court judge returned the custody of the children to their parents, convinced that the children were healthy and not at risk or in need of intervention. In her ruling, she stated that it was her 'sincere conviction that the minors found themselves in an environment fit for their physical and moral development; therefore the extreme conditions required for the court to intervene were not present' (Mercedes 1989). The third case, addressing charges of corruption of minors was also dismissed in May 1990 (Korvez 1990). Social workers and physicians had found no evidence of abuse in the course of their examinations. The children had been required to take state examinations to ascertain their educational development and all passed these tests with high marks, impressing the judicial authorities and teachers, who went on record stating their satisfaction. Court officials who visited the homes also issued positive reports about the living conditions and the care afforded the children (Richardson 1999: 178).

Notwithstanding the positive results of these investigations, the third case (corruption of minors) would be reopened three and a half years later by federal magistrate Roberto Marquevich. A minor from the previous case (16 years old at the time of the 1989 case) claimed to have testified falsely under duress and reversed her testimony, making claims of widespread abuse of minors (Prack 1996: 18). Three embittered apostates, who played a role in instigating similar official interventions in other countries joined forces with José Maria Baamonde, the head of the Argentine counter-cult organization SPES (*Servicio para el Esclarecimiento en Sectas* – Service for the Elucidation on Sects) to file similar claims. Once again, the local chapters of the Family International found themselves under investigation.

For several years, the Argentine public had been alerted by the media to the threat 'the proliferation of the cults' represented; the stage was set for the largest action against Family communities to occur. The political stakes were high, as the lessening of registration requirements for non-Catholic churches and religious movements was under heated debate in both the congress and the senate. There was noted resistance to this proposal from the Catholic Church, which had enjoyed a privileged position in the Argentine religious marketplace (Rosas 1993). Within this context, in September 1993, police staged predawn raids on five Family residences in the greater Buenos Aires area. Twenty-one adults were incarcerated on a pretrial basis for three and a half months, and 137 children of Family members were seized. This represented the largest number of children from a religious group ever taken into government custody in Argentine history. News of the raids and the litany of allegations, which included illegal association, kidnapping, child trafficking, prostitution, slavery, and child abuse, made lurid headlines around the world.

The Family children were held in dubious conditions in lice-infested government buildings. Due to concerns that members had been pre-emptively evacuating the region in anticipation of the raids, the government had advanced its time frame considerably. This resulted in social services being ill-prepared to undertake the care of over 130 children for the 104 days they remained in state custody. The children, who had not been permitted to bring their clothes or personal belongings, underwent multiple psychological evaluations, as well as invasive and degrading medical and gynaecological examinations. A psychologist from a counter-cult organization affiliated with the conservative sector of the Catholic Church (SPES) headed up the psychological evaluations of the children (Frigerio and Wynarczyk 2004: 456; Prack 1996: 18). It would later come to light in the Appeals Court ruling that the psychologist had falsified drawings and planted a textbook drawing of an abused child in one of the children's files, resulting in her losing her license to practice.

During their interrogations, several of the incarcerated men reported an angry Judge Marquevich, visibly out of control, demanding to know whether the accused believed in the Virgin Mary. This, coupled with the children not being allowed religious literature inclusive of the Bible, served to confirm Family members' conviction that they were the victims of religious persecution, on trial for their religious beliefs and not for actual infractions of the law. Marquevich's case quickly unravelled due to its lack of evidentiary basis, despite the claims he personally made in the international media of having substantiated the charges against members. He had the Family residences searched reiteratively in the hopes of turning up new evidence to justify the magnitude of the intervention. In the process, what personal belongings of Family members had not been confiscated in the initial raids were pilfered and never recovered.

In a show of solidarity, Family members staged peaceful protests outside Argentine embassies, consulates, trade centres and airline offices in major cities around the world to draw attention to the plight of their members (Richardson 1999: 179). In Argentina, members launched a vigorous media and legal campaign, including an appeal demanding the dismissal of all charges and the immediate release of the adults and children (Frigerio and Wynarczyk 2004: 470–71). Four of the spokespersons who presented themselves for this task were subsequently incarcerated by Judge Marquevich and added to the list of the accused. One mother's children were spirited away to an undisclosed location and were not discovered for several weeks. Such actions would stir the conscience of a segment of the Argentine public that was unwilling to witness the revival of the authoritarianism that had led to the atrocities of the 'Dirty War'. Journalists began questioning the actions of the courts and expressed concern at the overstepping of authority (Ruiz Nuñez 1993). Former judges and members of the Federal Bar Association of Buenos Aires, led by its then president, Carlos Cichello, responded by launching a petition for Judge Marquevich's impeachment. An Argentine ecumenical human rights organization also made a public statement protesting what they deemed the 'religious persecution of Family members' (*Página/12* 1993).

On 13 December 1993 the Federal Appeals Court declared Marquevich legally incompetent to rule in the case (Prack et al. 1993). The Court ordered the immediate release of the incarcerated adults and the return of the children to the custody of their parents. In their 200-page majority ruling, the magistrates methodically rejected and disproved each of the charges brought against the members of the Family International, while criticizing severely the magistrate and the career apostates from outside the country who had initially set in motion the investigations. The Court of Appeals also had harsh words for Judge Marquevich's discriminatory handling of the investigation, concluding that it was an illegal investigation and arbitrary use of penal power: 'This panorama puts in evidence an anachronistic continuation of the most severe Inquisitional system, one in which people were summoned only to confess their sins, being considered "witches" or "heretics"' (Prack et al. 1993).

A later analysis by Justice Prack of the proceedings and how these were reported by the media revealed glaring disparities between the media's reporting, claims made by former members and anti-cult organizations, and the actual findings of the court (Prack 1996: 15–16). The ruling of the Court of Appeals was subsequently upheld by the Supreme Court in 1995, resulting in the definitive closure of the case in July 2004. The ruling was handed down little over a month after Judge Marquevich had been impeached for misconduct in an unrelated case and removed from office.

Spain

In July 1990, two former members, a Spanish cult awareness organization, and local religious leaders claimed to authorities that Family children were being systematically abused. Consequently, the regional authorities in Barcelona raided a Family communal residence, smashing down the front door and taking 21 children into state custody. The parents of the children were charged with illegal association, operating an illegal school, inflicting mental damage on their children, and fraud. Although no evidence of abuse or neglect emerged after repeated medical and psychological evaluations, the children were forced to remain in state custody for nearly 12 months. They were not allowed any contact with their parents for the first two months. Subsequent parental visits were supervised and parents were not permitted to read the Bible or leave Bibles with their children (Richardson 1999: 179). As was the case in the Argentine state interventions, the children's psychological examinations were performed by an anti-cultist, in this case posing as a psychiatrist even though his degree was in dermatology. The children were placed in the care of hostile social workers who at times physically struck them and generally neglected them (Melton 1997: 34).

In May 1992, the Catalonian authorities filed for a permanent separation of the children from their parents, which was summarily rejected. In the Court's ruling, custody was awarded to the parents in no uncertain terms, while the competency and motives of the welfare agencies responsible for the apprehension of the children were strongly questioned. The Court found that the psychological testing of the children was 'designed rather to justify the operation than to describe any intellectual anomalies, which are completely non-existent' (Oubiña et al. 1992). The judges deemed the government's intervention to be 'reminiscent of the Spanish Inquisition' and the 'concentration camps of those former empires that ceased to be so when human dignity brought down the Berlin Wall'. They concluded that the parents 'are perfectly free to live with their children in whichever country they consider best and to orient them towards whatever moral, religious, or philosophical convictions they believe to be appropriate'.

In October 1994 the Constitutional Court found that the constitutional article guaranteeing education for minors did not inherently disallow parents to provide this education privately in accordance with their religious and moral convictions, thereby allowing the children to be home-schooled (Rodriguez-Pinero et al. 1994). On 29 June 1993, the parents were acquitted of all charges, a ruling which was subsequently upheld by the Supreme Court of Spain in October 1994, thus ending a difficult chapter of the Family International's history in Spain. In his analysis of the proceedings, Spanish jurist Motilla applauded the resolve of the courts to reject anti-cult definitions of terms in favour of legal definitions:

> In the criminal proceedings against the group ... the Court rejects, with good reason in my opinion, the reliability of the subjective conclusions reached by law enforcement, based on the influence of two psychologists who labelled the group as a destructive cult, or debates in the public forum by the media. Only that

which is tried and found by the courts can be considered proven and affirmed. The Court's objectivity and evenhanded judgment of the group's conduct within judicial and penal definitions led it to reject the series of socially disseminated allegations regarding the behavior of the so-called cults. (Motilla 1993: 97)

Australia

In May 1992 over 150 police and some 200 officials from the Community Services department in New South Wales and Victoria staged elaborate synchronized predawn raids on six Family residences in Sydney and Melbourne, taking 153 children into state custody. Authorities stated that former members and anti-cult organizations had reported that widespread sexual, physical, and psychological abuse of minors was occurring at the residences. After a week of medical and psychological examinations revealed no evidence of sexual or psychological abuse, the children in Sydney were ordered returned to the care of their parents (Levine 1992). The Department of Community Services (DOCS), however, continued to pursue the case in the courts.

Hearings to determine the validity of charges against the parents received continual press coverage for over six months, until a mediated settlement reached in October 1992 stayed the case for a year (Shepherd and Shepherd 2011: 247). The agreement stipulated that the care applications for the children would be withdrawn upon completion of a 12-month period of socialization activities, conducted at the expense of the DOCS. The department also withdrew their allegations that the children had been subjected to inappropriate sexual behaviour (settlement mediated by Sir Lawrence Street in 1992). In Melbourne, the Supreme Court of Victoria also ordered that all Family children in custody be returned to the care of their parents after the first week, pending a decision on the protection applications sought by Community Services (H&CS). Regardless of the precedent set by the mediation agreement reached in Sydney, Melbourne's Community Services department was not amenable to mediation. After 23 months of pursuing the protection applications, under pressure from the state government, Community Services finally agreed to mediation.

These cases became a source of embarrassment for the government, as media reports claimed that millions of dollars of taxpayer money were being invested in cases where ultimately the police had found no evidence of criminal wrongdoing. Estimates were made that the New South Wales action had cost nearly $3.5 million (USD), while the Victoria case was estimated by *The Melbourne Age* to have cost taxpayers as much as $10 million (Messina 1994;

Richardson 1999: 180–81). The actions of the police and Community Services came under fire in New South Wales Parliament in November 1993 when the former Police Minister produced evidence that the raids were conducted unlawfully. Subsequently, 62 Family children initiated a civil action against the Community Services department in Sydney.

In March 1999, the Supreme Court found that 'in entering the relevant premises, searching for and removing the various plaintiffs, the defendant's servants [officers of police and Community Services] and agents were not acting under any authority conferred by the warrants but wrongfully and contrary to the law' (Dunford 1999). The police department and Community Services sought to settle for damages, and an agreement was reached. Although the terms of the settlement were confidential, the Australian media reported 'huge compensation payoffs'. While this represented a victory for the Family International, nevertheless, the pain and personal and financial costs for Family members were also huge (Hutch 1994: 370).

France

From 1991 to 1993, law enforcement officials in France conducted an extensive covert investigation of Family members residing in France. The investigation originated in allegations levelled by the primary French anti-cult organization ADFI (Association for the Defence of the Family and Individual). ADFI had drawn attention to the court proceedings then underway in Spain in an effort to instigate public disapproval and to pressure law enforcement to take action on members residing in France. Despite the failure of police surveillance to reveal illicit activities, the examining magistrate ordered raids of the local communities based on the information provided by ADFI and the testimony of a small number of ex-members (Inchauspé 2001: 5).

In June 1993, approximately 200 heavily armed police, brandishing axes and machine guns, conducted raids on two Family communities in Eguilles and Lyon, injuring and brutalizing a number of Family members (none of whom resisted arrest). Media representatives were on hand to cover the efforts to 'rescue' children from what they dubbed a 'sex cult'. Authorities arrested 22 adults and placed 80 children in state custody. An exhaustive search of Family residences produced no evidence of wrongdoing.

The authorities, working closely with ADFI throughout the proceedings, appointed an ADFI psychiatrist to interview and evaluate the children (Melton 1997: 36). Court-appointed doctors detected no signs of neglect or abuse after thorough examination of the children. The adult members were released 48 hours after their apprehension; five days later the 33 children taken in custody in Lyon were returned to their parents. The prosecuting attorney appealed this decision, requesting that the custody of the children be retained by the state. The Appeals Court upheld the lower court's decision, and by the end of September 1993 the case had been dismissed for all the families residing in Lyon (Penaud 1993).

After 51 days of separation, the children from the Eguilles community were released to their parents in July 1993. A provisional ruling by the Minors Court of Aix-en-Provence stated that the Family children were not at risk, but nonetheless required them to engage in court-supervised weekly socialization activities for a 12-month period, subsidized by the state. No restrictions were imposed on the parents regarding their missionary activities and education of their children at home. The criminal investigation had produced no evidence of wrongdoing and the proceedings were officially closed in January 1999, acquitting Family members of all charges. The closure of this case in favour of Family members was deemed a serious blow to ADFI:

> Six years after the raids, the Justice Court of Aix-en-Provence has vindicated the Family. All defendants have been found not guilty and acquitted. The decision is a major embarrassment for ADFI and the French anti-cult milieu.... But we do not hear apologies for the unnecessary suffering caused to adults, teenagers, and children in the brutal 1993 raids (CESNUR 1999).

An appeal was promptly lodged by ADFI, which was subsequently rejected by the courts on 24 February 2000, bringing a definitive end to these proceedings. In his legal analysis of the case, French jurist Inchauspé concludes:

> Justice, manipulated by anti-cult movements and the pressure of the media, is reassessing its approach. To date, these cases have been met with intolerance in a society that boasts of its tolerance. They rest, in fact, on a lack of understanding of convictions, strongly held and religious in nature, in a society that is lacking in both. (Inchauspé 2001: 10)

Judging Crime, Not Religion

The government interventions and court proceedings Family communities have endured raise troubling questions as to how law enforcement, social welfare officials, and the public become desensitized to the point of tolerating the intolerable in the treatment of children in religious groups. These proceedings serve as a case in point of the critical role the media and countermovement crusaders play in manipulating and instigating fear and suspicion to create moral panics (Frigerio and Wynarczyk 2004: 457). Once a clime of collective fear and anxiety has been fomented through claims-making and narratives that paint a sinister and pernicious picture of marginal religions, the justification has been constructed for actions that ultimately prove to be detrimental and injurious to the children (Wright 1997: 105).

Clearly there exists a precarious balance between protecting the rights and well-being of children and protecting freedom of belief and conscience (Homer 1999: 187). Court cases involving Family communities have provided a test case for courts on several continents. The courts have been faced with the confluence of extreme allegations based in part on controversial literature and practices previously renounced. These have gained further momentum due to pejorative labelling and stereotyping promulgated by ex-member crusaders and the press, and political pressure from conservative elements and advocacy groups to take action against the movement. In a clime where collective abuse claims are made and guilt is presumed in media reporting, one would expect negative outcomes for the members of unpopular minority religions, more so in the case of the Family International, which has been stamped by controversy since its inception.

Magistrates in Family cases at the Appeals Court and Supreme Court levels have shown their ability to withstand such pressures and not allow discrimination or bias to colour their final judgments or taint the legal process. Nonetheless, throughout the process members have found themselves in a fierce uphill battle to disprove generalized allegations and anti-cult stereotyping. The underlying premise has been the ironic presumption that 'in a process one is not presumed innocent, one becomes innocent' (Inchauspé 2001: 1). As two Argentine academics lamented, 'anti-cult leaders achieved ownership of the problem and their interpretive framework became hegemonic' (Frigerio and Wynarczyk 2004: 457).

Lamentably, the children were victimized in many cases, as social welfare and law enforcement had become desensitized by 'brainwashing' and 'cult' stereotypes, and acted with very little consideration for the traumatizing effects of the proceedings on the children. While damages were sought and successfully brokered for the children in Australia, members did not have the financial means to undertake such costly proceedings in other countries. In such cases, they had to be contented with their vindication by the courts, scant though the media coverage of final outcomes has been in such cases.

When do authorities cross the line from exercising their authority in protecting the best interest of children to intolerance and persecution of religious minorities? Court cases of the Family International provide some legal precedents that may serve to demarcate the boundaries of law enforcement and the courts in upholding their legal responsibilities, without obstructing the rights of parents to raise their children according to their religious convictions. In his article *Judges Shouldn't Judge Sins*, Argentine journalist and human rights specialist Ruiz Nuñez deemed the Appeals Court resolution in favour of Family members a 'valuable judicial tool, reaffirming respect for minorities and rebuffing the use of the penal system to persecute such groups'. He also warned that 'the penal code is not a book of catechism and sin is not synonymous with crime. To confuse the boundaries of these areas and to meddle with the application of these standards is not only unacceptable, but is socially dangerous' (Ruiz Nuñez 1993).

The justices of the Supreme Court of Spain expressed a similar sentiment: 'Judges cannot enter into the sanctuary of personal beliefs, except when external behaviours originating from a particular ideology negatively affect legally protected rights' (Vadillo et al. 1994). Australian magistrate Gregory Levine (1993) further warned against using child protection laws as a pretext to harass small religious movements:

> In my view, it was not envisioned by the legislature that all such groups, organizations or sects should have their children made the subject of protection applications as a form of class action. It must be of concern that this form of inquiry may set a precedent for the bringing of protection applications in relation to other sects whose practices and beliefs do not appear to accord with mainstream thinking.

Argentine magistrates also made a resounding statement regarding the importance of respecting free exercise of belief and religious practice:

> By adopting intolerant attitudes based exclusively on ethical perfectionism, we allow penal punishment to enter the realm of individual privacy and open the door to a subtle form of authoritarianism; especially when freedom of belief and the liberty to express that belief are restricted. By no means can a judge meddle in the evaluation of that which is thought to be correct morally, politically and/or religiously. (Prack et al. 1993)

Conclusions

The magnitude of the government interventions in the case of the Family International and the convergence of pressures brought to bear by apostates, crusaders, and the media serve to highlight the challenges prevalent in the debate regarding unconventional new religions. The precarious balancing act of upholding the rights of the individual to religious belief and practice while fulfilling society's responsibility to protect the rights of children emphasizes the role the courts play in this narrative. Clearly it would behove new religions with unconventional practices and beliefs to be cognizant of the limits of religious freedom in the form of their societal and legal responsibilities. During their formative periods, religious movements may not foresee the need to institute protections for their members, or calculate the long-term consequences of the radical beliefs and practices that gave birth to the movement but are necessarily modified over time.

In the case of the Family International, the movement made significant reforms in the 1980s to guarantee the rights and protection of individuals and children. The courts for their part upheld the rights of members to their beliefs and practices in the absence of wrongdoing. However, the impact of the raids on the evolution of the movement and the human cost in the lives of its members cannot be understated. The government interventions necessitated the diverting of the movement's limited resources to defensive efforts. The movement had to adjust its priorities and alter its course to deal with such pervasive external pressures (Richardson 1999: 181). The self-examination process prompted by these proceedings led to the creation of the Family International's *Charter*, which served to codify practice and doctrine and uphold the rights of members. The organization became more cognizant of the importance of fostering constructive relations with the larger community and adopting a policy of greater openness regarding the life and practices of its communes. Family members also initiated reconciliation endeavours with former members and made strides in becoming more involved in their local communities, in particular through developing charitable works to serve needy sectors.

Having left behind the raids and court cases of the 1990s, the Family International has faced new challenges with the 'Internet wars'. This new frontier has provided an open forum for anti-cultists, apostates and infotainment-driven media to promulgate negative stereotypes and to stigmatize new religions and their members. The impact of court verdicts upholding and defining the free exercise of religion for new religions may be greatly lessened over time, as the debate becomes firmly entrenched in the courts of public opinion. In this venue, crusading cyber-activists may play a pivotal role in the public profiling and stigmatization of the movements, hindering the ability of new religions to develop and find their place within the greater society.

Unconventional new religions may be left with little defence in cyberspace due to the monetary resources and manpower required to mount an adequate response and the permanence of and ease of access to information indiscriminately posted on the Internet. The religious debate, as it now continues in the realm of cyberspace, has repositioned itself on a new and unregulated frontier. New religions, in their quest for religious tolerance and the free exercise of their religion, portend to continue to test society's ability to accommodate, or at least to tolerate, novel religious expressions and innovative lifestyles that challenge contemporary society and culture.

> How are we to understand radical religious movements that depart from the traditions of the ordinary churches and challenge the deadness of secular society? Are they, as their opponents would have us believe, pathological collections of abnormal individuals and conspiracies based on fraud and deception? Or are they shining examples of honest religious dissent? (Bainbridge 2002: xi)

References

Bainbridge, William Sims. 1997. *The Sociology of Religious Movements*. New York and London: Routledge.

Bainbridge, William Sims. 2002. *The Endtime Family: Children of God*. Albany: State University of New York Press.

Berg, David. 1973. *Bye, Bye, Pie. Mo Letter 232*. Zurich: The Family International.

Bradney, Anthony. 1999. 'Children of a Newer God.' In *Children in New Religions*, edited by Susan Palmer and Charlotte Hardman, 210–23. New Brunswick, New Jersey, London: Rutgers University Press.

CESNUR. January 1999. 'The Family Vindicated by French Court – "Catastrophe" for the Anti-Cult Movement, ADFI and the Government Mission to Fight Cults'. Retrieved from www.cesnur.org/testi/Aix2000_eng. htm.

Cowan, Douglas E. and David G. Bromley. 2008. *Cults and New Religions*. Oxford: Blackwell Publishing.

Davis, Rex and J.T. Richardson. 1976. 'The Organization and Functioning of the Children of God'. *Sociological Analysis* 15(4): 323–37.

Dunford, J. 1999. *Hartnett v. State of New South Wales.* New South Wales Supreme Court. 265. Sydney, Australia, 31 March.

Frigerio, Alejandro and Hilario Wynarczyk. 2004. 'Cult Controversies and Government Control of New Religious Movements in Argentina, 1985–2002'. In *Regulating Religion: Case Studies from around the Globe*, edited by James T. Richardson, 453–76. New York: Kluwer Academic/Plenum Publishers.

Homer, Michael. 1999. 'The Precarious Balance between Freedom of Religion and the Best Interests of the Child'. In *Children in New Religions*, edited by Susan Palmer and Charlotte Hardman, 187–209. New Brunswick, New Jersey, London: Rutgers University Press.

Hutch, Richard. 1994. 'The Uses and Misuses of Attribution Theory'. *Journal of Religion and Health* 33(4): 365–71.

Inchauspé, Dominique. 2001. *L'innocence judiciaire.* [*Judicial Innocence*]. France: Editions Litec.

Korvez, Alejandro de. 1990. 'Judgment in Case No. 34,269'. Provincial Court of San Isidro, Province of Buenos Aires, Argentina, 23 May.

Levine, David. 1992. 'Judgment in Stuart Hartingdon and 28 Others v. The Director General of the Department of Community Service.' New South Wales Supreme Court, Common Law Division. Sydney, Australia, 2 November.

Levine, Gregory. 1993. 'Applicant Director General of Community Services Victoria (on behalf of Senior Constable Linda O'Sullivan, the "Protective Intervener") v. Children Asher, Virginia, Adam, Renee, Clare, Karen, Daniel and Stephen BUCKLEY'. Melbourne Children's Court. Melbourne, Australia, 27 April.

Melton, J. Gordon. 1997. *The Children of God: "The Family."* Signature Books.

Mercedes Fernandez de Zingoni, Eleonora. 1989. 'Judgment in Case No. 17,142, Cavazza, Nicola, Maria Victoria and Others'. Minor's Court of San Isidro, Province of Buenos Aires, Argentina, 19 December.

Messina, Alex. 1994. 'Children of God May Sue'. *The Melbourne Age*, 23 April.

Miller, Timothy. 1999. *60s Communes: Hippies and Beyond.* Syracuse, New York: Syracuse University Press.

Moldes, Leónidas. 1990. Federal Court of San Isidro, Province of Buenos Aires, Case No. 81/89. Argentina, 11 January.

Motilla, Augustín. 1993. 'Grupos Marginales y Libertad Religiosa: Los Nuevos Movimientos Religiosos ante los Tribunales de Justicia' [Marginal Groups and Religious Liberty: New Religious Movements and the Courts]. *Anuario de Derecho Eclesiástico del Estado* Spain: EDERSA IX: 89–151.

Oubiña, Adolfo Fernandez , Jesus I. Perez Burred, and Jose Ma. Bachs Estany. 1992. "Judgement in Cases 0160/92-E, Dannis Edward Molinsky vs. Children's Welfare Department." Provincial Court Barcelona. Barcelona, Spain, 21 May.

Página/12. 1993. '50 Abogados contra Marquevich: Juicio politico en familia' [50 Lawyers against Marquevich: A Family Impeachment]. 8 October: 13. Buenos Aires, Argentina.

Penaud, J.J. 1993. "Ruling Concerning Educational Assistance in Case No. 114/93." Minors Court of Appeal, Lyon, France, 23 July.

Prack, Horacio Enrique. 1996. 'El Caso de los Niños de Dios' [The legal case of the Children of God] in *Jueces y Periodistas: Como se infórma y cómo se juzga* [*Judges and Reporters: How They are Informed and How They Judge*], edited by Hector Ruiz Nuñez, 14–62. Argentina: Fundación Poder Ciudadano.

Prack, Horacio Enrique, Alberto Mansur, and Daniel Mario Rudi. 1993. 'Judgment in Case 81/89'. Federal Appeals Court of San Isidro, Province of Buenos Aires, Argentina, 13 December.

Richardson, James T. 1994. 'Update on the Family: Organizational Change and Development in a Controversial New Religious Group'. In *Sex, Sin, and Slander: Investigation of the Family/Children of God*, edited by James Lewis and Gordom Melton, 27–40. Stanford, CA: Center for Academic Publication.

Richardson, James T. 1999. 'Social Control of New Religions: From 'Brainwashing' Claims to Child Sex Abuse Accusations' in *Children in New Religions*, edited by Susan J. Palmer and Charlotte E. Hardman, 172–86. New Brunswick, New Jersey, London: Rutgers University Press.

Richardson, James T. and Rex Davis. 1983. 'Experiential Fundamentalism: Revisions of Orthodoxy in the Jesus Movement.' *Journal of the American Academy of Religion* LI(3): 397–425.

Richardson, James T., and Massimo Introvigne. 2001. 'Brainwashing Theories in European Parliamentary and Administrative Reports on Cults and Sects.' *Journal for the Scientific Study of Religion* 40(2): 143–68.

Rodriguez-Pinero Bravo-Ferrer, Miguel, Fernando Garcia-Mon Gonzalez-Regueral, Carlos de la Vega Benayas, Vicente Gimeno Sendra, Rafael de Mendizabal Allende, and Pedro Cruz Villalon. 1994. 'Decision in Appeals 1561, 1562, 1563, 1564, 1565, 1566 and 1567/1992.' First Courtroom of the Constitutional Court. Madrid, Spain, 3 October: 1.

Rosas, Faustino. 1993. 'Trasfondo Político y Conflicto Religioso por el Desarrollo de las 'Sectas' Cristianas' [Political Backdrop and Religious Conflict due to the Development of Christian 'Cults']. Argentina: *El Informador Publico*, December 1993: 14–15.

Ruiz Nuñez, Hector. (1993). 'Los Jueces No Deben Juzgar Pecados' [Judges Shouldn't Judge Sins]. Argentina. *Revista Humor*, 22 December edition: 27–8.

Shepherd, Gary and Gordon Shepherd. 2011. 'Learning the Wrong Lessons: A Comparison of FLDS, Family International and Branch Davidian Child-Protection Interventions'. In *Modern Polygamy in the United States: Historical, Cultural, and Legal Issues*, edited by Cardell Jacobson, Cardell and Lara Burton, 237–58. New York: Oxford University Press.

Shupe, Anson and David G. Bromley. 1994. *Anti-cult Movements in Cross-Cultural Perspectives*. New York and London: Garland Publishing Inc.

Street, Sir Lawrence. 1992. "Mediated Settlement." Sydney, Australia, 27 October.

Vadillo, Enrique Ruiz, Jose Antonio Martin Pallin, and Justo Carrero Ramos. 1994. 'Verdict number 1669/94.' Supreme Court Two. Verdict number 1669/94. Madrid, Spain, 30 October.

Wright, Stuart A. 1997. 'Media Coverage of Unconventional Religion: Any "Good News" For Minority Faiths?' *Review of Religious Research* 39(2): 101–15.

Zerby, Karen. 2010. *Applying God's Law of Love*. The Family International. http://www.thefamilyinternational.org/.

Zerby, Karen and Steve Kelly. 2008. *An Open Letter of Apology from Maria and Peter*. The Family International. http://www.myconclusion.com/apology-to-second-generation.

Chapter 2

Scientology in Italy:
Plagio and the Twenty Year Legal Saga

Massimo Introvigne

On October 5, 2000, the Church of Scientology won in Milan the mother of all its court cases in Italy, a case that had troubled the Church for some twenty years. This chapter offers a review of the facts leading to the Milan decision, perhaps the most significant in Italy about a new religious movement, and an analysis of the decision itself. In order to understand the Italian legal context, however, it is necessary to start from a short summary of an Italian Constitutional Court decision dating back to 1981 (Corte Costituzionale 1981), which exerted an important influence on the Scientology case.

The *Plagio* Constitutional Precedent

The Italian expression *plagio* is often used as a translation for the English "brainwashing" although a literal translation of "brainwashing" *lavaggio del cervello*, is also used. We hear, for example, that such and such a person was subjected to plagio by cults. This use of the expression plagio is rooted in the old article 603 of the 1930 Italian penal code that, under the heading plagio, mandated a jail term of five to fifteen years for anyone who subjected an individual to his own will, so as to reduce that individual to a total state of subjugation.

The word *plagio* is not of recent coinage, being derived from Roman law, where it was called *plagium* in Latin. Already in ancient Rome in the third century B.C., *plagium* denoted the crime of someone who took illegal possession of a free man and made him his slave, or someone who stole someone else's slave. After slavery was outlawed, the crime of plagio was retained, with the exact legal meaning of reducing a person into slavery, now always illegal. By extension, in the nineteenth century, the word was also used to indicate the forced recruitment of soldiers into a foreign army. The first Italian penal code, published in 1889, used the traditional meaning of the term in its article, 145, which punished with twelve to twenty years of jail anyone who reduces a person into slavery or other similar status. The new penal code of 1930, still in force today, made a distinction between slavery as a legal status and slavery as a factual condition. Anyone reducing a person to a condition of slavery (legal status)— for example, by bartering or selling that person in countries where slavery was not abolished—was to be punished pursuant to article 600. And anyone who subjected a person to his or her own power so as to reduce that person in a total state of subjugation, thus reducing her into slavery (factual condition) but without representing that person as technically a slave, or without intending to barter or sell the victim, was to be punished under article 603. With the latter article, even though they were largely unaware of it, the 1930 Italian legislators, for the first time in the world, were treating as a criminal activity what later would be called brainwashing.

Until the 1960s, however, no effects followed the introduction into the Italian penal code of article 603. In the first 40 years of its existence, there were very few plagio trials, for the most part dealing with seductions of a sexual nature, and all ended either in acquittals or in defendants found guilty on grounds different from article 603 (Usai 1996). All changed in 1968, when the Rome Court of Assizes sentenced Aldo Braibanti in a case that became notorious. A self-taught communist philosopher and gay activist, Braibanti had taken into his home two young men to work as secretaries and had confined them to small rooms, wearing them out (according to the prosecution) by not feeding them properly and by depriving them of sleep and of contact with the outside world, until he had brought the two disciples to a state of homosexual subjugation. On July 14, 1968, Braibanti was found guilty of plagio by a jury; the Court of Appeals of Rome (again in a jury trial) upheld the judgment on November 28, 1969, and the Supreme Court (i.e. the Court of Cassation, which is not to be confused with the Constitutional Court, Italy's highest court which deals only with questions of constitutionality) did the same on October 21, 1971. The trial gave rise to the Braibanti case, which led major Italian left-wing intellectuals such as the novelists Alberto Moravia (1907–90) and Umberto Eco, and a large number of attorneys and psychiatrists, to petition for the abolition of the crime of plagio, regarded as a non-existing crime which was easily used against politically or socially unpopular figures.

So famous was the Braibanti case in Italy that many are convinced today that it was the case of the gay philosopher that brought the Italian Constitutional Court to declare the illegitimacy of the article on plagio, deleting it from the

Italian penal code. But that was not the case. The Constitutional Court never reviewed the Braibanti case. It did, however, review the case of Father Emilio Grasso, a Catholic priest and the head of the independent charismatic movement later called Redemptor Hominis Community, a movement which was officially recognized by the Catholic Church in the same year of the decision, 1981, and still exists today. Father Grasso was accused of driving a wedge between his young followers and their families, and promoting a cult of his own personality. In a November 2, 1978, ruling, the Court of Rome raised the issue of constitutional legitimacy of article 603. On June 8, 1981, the Constitutional Court decision number 96 declared article 603 unconstitutional. The decision included a broad historical review of the matter, and essentially accepted the objections that the total state of subjugation called for in article 603 could not be achieved with mere psychological methods. In any case, the Constitutional Court said, the opinions within the academic community of psychiatrists and psychologists were so contrasting as to prevent a judge from finding a safer ground for his or her conclusions. The resulting danger was that such state of ambiguity could lead to decisions based on the degree of popularity or acceptance of the ideas instilled by the alleged plagio.

Although the 1981 ruling was certainly influenced by the fact that Charismatic Catholic priests like Grasso were more socially accepted than gay philosophers such as Braibanti, the decision had a crucial influence on the attempts to prosecute a number of new religious movements, including Scientology. Basically, the Constitutional Court had ruled that brainwashing is an imaginary crime, and that mainline science does not sustain the idea that it is possible to place a person in a state of total psychological subjection by the use of mind control techniques. Constitutional Court decisions are binding for all courts in Italy. The Parliament may try to change the situation determined by a Constitutional Court decision by passing a new law, and several unsuccessful attempts to reintroduce a provision similar to the defunct article 603 have been made throughout the years. But any new law will likely be declared unconstitutional by the Constitutional Court if it is regarded as not compatible with the principles of the 1981 decision. That decision had, inter alia, the involuntary effect of greatly helping the Church of Scientology in Italy.

The Great Milan Scientology Trial

Scientology opened its first Italian mission in Milan in 1978. Almost immediately, reports about the alleged brainwashing practices of Scientology, in part influenced by foreign controversies, appeared in the Italian media. The Milan police and prosecutors quietly started an investigation in 1980, before the Constitutional Court plagio decision of June 1981. The Constitutional Court effectively eliminated the possibility of prosecuting Scientology for plagio, i.e. for putting its followers in a state of psychological subjection through 'mind control' techniques. This almost stopped the Milan investigation of Scientology. It was slowly continued, however, while the prosecutors tried to find grounds other than plagio for characterizing what they perceived as illegitimate and hard-pressure techniques used by Scientologists in order to sell their services. The first vocal ex-members and anti-cult activists, in the meantime, insisted that Scientology should be prosecuted.

Finally, after a lengthy investigation which had extended beyond Milan to all Scientology missions in Italy, the Milan prosecutor decided on October 3, 1988, to indict the main leaders and several members of the Italian Church of Scientology for fraud, conspiracy to commit fraud, and other crimes. The prosecutor, however, lost his case. On July 2, 1991, Judge Piero Pajardi (1926–94) of the Court of Milan decided that the operations of the Church of Scientology in Italy were not illegal per se. There was no fraud, only the operation of a very idiosyncratic and typically American religion, which was however still protected by the broad Italian concept of religious liberty. Those Scientologists who were found guilty of crimes, particularly because of pressures exerted in selling their services to particularly weak 'customers,' Pajardi concluded, went beyond the instructions of the Church, which was not responsible for their behavior. Pajardi's decision was not complimentary to Scientology. He found its ideology quite crude and vulgar, but concluded that allowing even such unpalatable organizations as Scientology to operate freely is the price to be paid in order to protect democracy and religious liberty. It is worth noting that Pajardi had extensive experience with religion. He was an active Roman Catholic, and an amateur but gifted writer of Church history.

The prosecutor appealed, insisting that Pajardi's decision rested mostly on religious liberty. But since, according to the prosecutor, Scientology was not a religion, any argument deriving from religious liberty was not applicable to the defendants. On November 5, 1993, the Milan Court of Appeal sided partially with the prosecutor, finding a large number of Scientologists guilty of a variety of crimes, including conspiracy to commit fraud. Whether Scientology was a religion was not really decided by the 1993 decision. However the Italian Supreme Court, on February 9, 1995, annulled the Milan 1993 decision, considering the question of whether Scientology was indeed a religion quite relevant and asking the Court of Appeal to reconsider it.

On December 2, 1996, the Court of Appeal of Milan complied, but maintained that Scientology was not a religion. The Milan appeal judges noted that in Italy "there is no legislative definition of religion" and "nowhere in the Italian law there is any useful element in order to distinguish a religious organization from other social groups" (Corte d'Appello di Milano 1996: 30). However, among a number of possible definitions derived not from the law but from social sciences, the Milan judges selected one defining religion as a system of doctrines centered on the presupposition of the existence of a Supreme Being, who has a relation with humans, the latter having towards him a duty of obedience and reverence (Corte d'Appello di Milano 1996: 31). Additional criteria based on the case law of the Italian Constitutional Court were considered, but these remained clearly ancillary to the main definition.

Theoretically, the reference to a Supreme Being may be interpreted in a non-theistic sense. This, by the way, was the interpretation of the U.S. Supreme Court in the *Welsh* case when discussing the Universal Military Training and Service Act of 1948, which also included in its definition of religion a reference to a relation to a Supreme Being (U.S. Supreme Court 1970). The Milan judges, however, interpreted Supreme Being in a theistic sense. As a consequence, they excluded the non-theistic Scientology from the sphere of religion.

On October 8, 1997, the Supreme Court annulled also the Milan 1996 decision, again with remand, meaning that another section of the Court of Appeal of Milan shall reexamine the facts of the case. The Supreme Court regarded the Milan theistic definition of religion as "unacceptable" and "a mistake" because it was "based only on the paradigm of Biblical religions" (Corte di Cassazione 1997: 28). As such, the definition would exclude inter alia Buddhism, whose main Italian organization, the Italian Buddhist Union, had been recognized by Italian administrative authorities as a religious denomination since 1991. Buddhism, according to the Supreme Court, certainly does not affirm the existence of a Supreme Being and, as a consequence, does not propose a direct relation of the human being with him. Yet, few in Italy would doubt that Buddhism is a religion.

It is true, the Supreme Court observed, that the self-definition of a group as religious is not enough in order to recognize it as a genuine religion (Corte di Cassazione 1997: 32). The Milan 1996 decision quoted the case law of the Italian Constitutional Court and its reference to the common opinion in order to decide whether or not a group is a religion. The relevant common opinion, however, according to the Supreme Court, is the opinion of the scholars rather than the public opinion (Corte di Cassazione 1997: 34). Media, in particular, were regarded as not particularly relevant. The "public opinion," the Court said, is normally hostile to religious minorities and, additionally, is quite difficult to ascertain: one wonders, the Supreme Court noted, from what source the Milan judges knew the public opinion of the whole national community (Corte di Cassazione 1997: 35). On the other hand, most scholars—according to the Supreme Court—seemed to prefer a definition of religion broad enough to include Scientology and, when asked, would conclude that Scientology is in fact a religion, having as its aim "the liberation of the human spirit through the knowledge of the divine spirit residing within each human being" (Corte di Cassazione 1997: 35). The 48-page decision of the Supreme Court also examined some of the arguments used by critics (and by the Milan 1996 judges) in order to deny to Scientology the status of religion. Five main arguments were discussed.

First, critics object that Scientology is syncretistic and does not propose any really original belief. This is, the Supreme Court argued, irrelevant, since syncretism is not rare among genuine religions, and many recently established Christian denominations exhibit very few original features (Corte di Cassazione 1997: 35) when compared to older churches.

Second, it is argued that Scientology is presented to perspective converts as science, not as religion. The Supreme Court replied that, at least since Thomas Aquinas (1225–74), Christian theology claims to be a science. On the other hand, science claiming to lead to non-empirical results such as "knowledge of God"—or perhaps, in the case of Scientology, of human beings as gods—may be both bad science and inherently religious (Corte di Cassazione 1997: 36).

Third, critics make reference to ex-members, mostly militant apostates. The Court of Appeal decision of 1996 explicitly mentioned apostates John Atack (1990) and Gerald Armstrong, who claimed that Scientology is not a religion but only a facade to hide criminal activities. The Supreme Court asked how we may know that the opinion of these disgruntled ex-members is representative of the larger population of former Scientologists. Other ex-members in fact appeared as witnesses for the defense, and at any rate, the number of ex-members of Scientology appears to be quite large. The opinion of two and even twenty of them, thus, according to the Supreme Court, was hardly representative of what the average ex-member believes.

Fourth, texts by L. Ron Hubbard (1911–86), the founder of Scientology, and by some early Italian leaders, were quoted by the prosecution to imply that Scientology's basic aim is to make money. Such texts' interest in money appears, according to the Supreme Court, excessive, but perhaps appears much less excessive if we consider how money was raised in the past by the Roman Catholic Church (Corte di Cassazione 1997: 44). The Supreme Court quotes the story of Ananias and Sapphira in the *Acts of the Apostles*, who died because they kept for personal use a part of what they obtained from the sale of their property and lied to the bishop, rather than giving everything to him. It also mentions late Medieval controversies about the sale of indulgences, and the fact that until very recently Italian Catholic churches used to affix at the church's door a list of services offered (Masses and similar) with the corresponding costs (Corte di Cassazione 1997: 44–5). This, according to the Supreme Court, confirms that quid pro quo services are more widespread among religions that the Milan 1996 judges seemed to believe.

Concerning Scientology, the Supreme Court went on to observe that the more disturbing texts on money quoted by the prosecution and by disgruntled ex-members are but a minimal part of Hubbard's enormous literary production, including about 8,000 works; and that they were mostly circular letters or bulletins intended for the officers in charge of finances and the economic structure, not for the average member (Corte di Cassazione 1997: 43). Finally, even if one should take at face value the crude comment included in a technical bulletin of Scientology—not written personally by Hubbard, however—that the only reason why L. Ron Hubbard established the Church was in order to sell and deliver Dianetics and Scientology (Corte di Cassazione 1997: 43), this would not necessarily mean, according to the Supreme Court, that Scientology is not a religion. What is, in fact, the ultimate aim of selling Dianetics and Scientology? There is no evidence, the Supreme Court suggested, that such sales are only organized in order to assure the personal welfare of the leaders. If they are intended as a proselytization tool, then making money is only an intermediate aim. The ultimate aim is proselytization, and this aim could hardly be more typical of a religion, even if, according to the strategy of the founder (Hubbard), new converts are sought and organized through the "sale and delivery" of Dianetics and Scientology (Corte di Cassazione 1997: 43).

A fifth objection discussed by the Supreme Court is that Scientology is not a religion since there is evidence, in the Milan case itself, that a number of Scientologists were guilty of fraudulent sales techniques, or abused particularly weak customers, when selling Dianetics or Scientology. These illegal activities, the Supreme Court comments, should be punished, but there is no evidence that they are more than occasional deviant activities of a certain number of leaders and members within the Milan branch, with no general significance (Corte di Cassazione 1997: 46) concerning the nature of Scientology in general. On this point, the Supreme Court in 1997 basically reverted to Judge Pajardi's assessment of 1991.

The Decision of October 7, 2000

On October 5, 2000, the Court of Appeal of Milan, deciding to remand for the third time the same case, finally closed the 20-year-old saga, ended its feud with the Supreme Court, and found in favor of the Scientologists. The appellate judges noted that this judgment had been already widely written by the two decisions of the Supreme Court (Corte d'Appello di Milano 2000: 21). It is true that in the 2000 case the prosecutor tried to switch strategy at the last minute, claiming that perhaps Scientology was a religion, but the 33 defendants (of the Milan case) had formed up, inside Scientology, a separated conspiracy (Corte d'Appello di Milano 2000: 21–2) which was criminal rather than religious. This was not what the prosecution claimed at the beginning of the saga. Initially, the target of the Milan Prosecution Office was the Church of Scientology in itself, not a group of rogue Scientologists which, by misunderstanding the religious nature of Scientology and unbeknownst to the international leadership, established a separated criminal conspiracy (Corte d'Appello di Milano 2000: 28) within the Church in order to make money through repeated fraud.

The 2000 decision answered that the new prosecution strategy was simply too inconsistent with the initial attitude of the Milan Prosecution Office, which indeed was based on the thesis of Scientology's criminal character and insisted that Scientology per se, not a group of renegade Scientologists, was a criminal group (Corte d'Appello di Milano 2000: 23). The judges in 2000 regarded as by now (i.e. after two decisions of the Supreme Court) inescapable (Corte d'Appello di Milano 2000: 25) the conclusion that the whole prosecution case rested or fell with the claim that Scientology is not a religion. And, in fact, the Supreme Court had been especially peremptory (Corte d'Appello di Milano 2000: 25) in requiring the appellate judges to apply certain criteria for defining what is, and is not, a religion.

Once again, the judges of the 2000 decision repeated what these criteria were all about by stating that there are nine passages in the journey toward deciding whether Scientology is or is not a religion. The first is to recognize that, under Italian law, the religious character of an association could not be ruled out by expressing personal, one-sided opinions on the tenets of their beliefs. For example, the lack of a concept of salvation of the soul through the connection of humans with God could be claimed to violate a number of precise constitutional precepts forbidding one to identify how a religion is recognizable as such only by comparing it to existing or intervening religions (Corte d'Appello di Milano 2000: 26).

Second, an important criterion for deciding whether a group is religious is "public recognition." However, public recognition does not mean recognition by the media, nor by elusive public opinion. The opinion of scholars is more important. And even if one wanted to read "public recognition" as meaning "recognition by the people," the judges would have to explain why the statements made by thousands of followers (who are part of the people), the opinions of experts, and the conclusions of other court decisions (which, in deciding, normally avail themselves of the tenets of common experience and of known facts) should not be considered as an important part of recognition by the people (Corte d'Appello di Milano 2000: 26).

Third, the texts of Scientology, by mentioning a path to liberation which includes both bodily techniques and other means in order to achieve a particular experience of the spiritual world, in fact placed the association (Scientology) in an area which is shared by other denominations that have been recognized (as religious) without any problem (Corte d'Appello di Milano 2000: 26).

Fourth, there is no reason to consider the opinion of single disgruntled ex-members such as Atack and Armstrong as particularly authoritative. Certainly, it is not more authoritative than the opinion of credentialed academic scholars.

Fifth, there is nothing in the documents of Scientology denying that it is a religion.

Sixth, the fact that Scientology does not have a creed (Corte d'Appello di Milano 2000: 27) or a theology compared to these found in the Catholic Church is irrelevant. As mentioned earlier, using similarity or dissimilarity with mainline religions for deciding the religious nature or otherwise of newer movements was regarded by the Supreme Court as constitutionally unacceptable.

Seventh, the unordinary and somewhat disturbing interest in money by Hubbard does not exclude per se that Scientology is a religion.

Eighth, "proven crimes were not found to have happened in the standard operational basis, but they were found to be occasional deviations from general rules of conduct" (Corte d'Appello di Milano 2000: 27). The lengthy Milan investigation found indeed a few instances of deviation, but these were not generalized nor derived from instructions by the international headquarters of the Church (Corte d'Appello di Milano 2000: 27).

Ninth, the fact that these "instances of deviation" (Corte d'Appello di Milano 2000: 27) were mostly concentrated in Milan does not prove that the Milan branch of Scientology had become somewhat different from the international Church of Scientology, i.e. a non-religious criminal organization. Rather, it proved that at a certain stage some Milan Scientologists came to operate in a peculiar set of conditions which induced them to behave in a certain (illegal) way.

Perhaps they were driven by a "spirit of emulation" (Corte d'Appello di Milano 2000: 29) toward those of them who, by going beyond what was both lawful under Italian law and mandated by the Church itself, had obtained particularly good proselytization results.

The Court of Appeal concluded that, by applying the two binding Supreme Court decisions and using their criteria, Scientology should be recognized as a religion under Italian law. This protects most of the activities performed by Scientologists in Italy under the statutes on religious liberty. Most but not all. However, those activities which were regarded as illegal were regarded as the fault of individual Scientologists and did not change the general evaluation of the activities of the Church of Scientology as legal in Italy.

Aftermath

The 2000 decision stated that Scientology is a religious organization but left open the question whether all or some of Scientology's activities were taxable. The judges made it clear that not all activities of a religious organization are inherently religious, and those which are not religious are taxable. A string of court cases followed, whereby the Italian Tax Office tried to limit the number of tax-exempt activities performed by Scientology. In these cases, Scientology was not always successful, and activities such as its drug rehabilitation program Narconon were eventually regarded as non-religious and taxable. While Scientologists often complain that these tax decisions are unfair and derive from anti-cult prejudices, it is also the case that the Italian Tax Office, particularly in recent years when its revenues and strategies have been affected by the economic crisis, has tried to limit the scope of tax exemptions of all religious organizations, including the Roman Catholic Church.

The success achieved by Scientology at the end of the long Milan saga remains quite significant. The Church of Scientology was recognized as a religious organization, and its worldview and structure were defined as typical of a religion, after one of the most detailed discussions of the issue among the growing body of international case law about Scientology.[1] As for whether its proselytization techniques are lawful in Italy, the 1981 Constitutional Court decision on plagio largely prevented the judges from discussing allegations of brainwashing or mind control. In order to prosecute Scientology for undue influence, new

---

[1]   See James T. Richardson (2009) for discussion of major cases involving Scientology in other countries.

statutes more or less similar to the old article 603 should be reintroduced into Italian law. Anti-cult activists produce on average one proposal each year in this field, but none of these has even reached the floor of the Parliament because of obvious concerns that any such law would violate the principles established by the 1981 plagio decision and will thus be declared unconstitutional. Perhaps strong anti-cult feelings in Italian society at large may induce the Parliament to challenge the Constitutional Court, in the hope that the latter will revisit its 1981 decision. So far, however, these feelings are not widespread.

The Milan Court of Appeal decision of 2000 was based on the Supreme Court decision of 1997. Together, these two decisions include one of the most important discussions, not only in Italy, of how courts may apply existing laws apparently requiring them to decide whether a specific group is, or is not, a religion. The Supreme Court argued that the non-existence of a legal definition of religion in Italy (and elsewhere) is not coincidental. Any definition would rapidly become obsolete and, in fact, limit religious liberty. It is much better, according to the Italian Supreme Court, not to limit with a definition, always by its very nature restrictive, the broader field of religious liberty (Corte di Cassazione 1997: 29). Religion is an ever-evolving concept, and courts may only interpret it within the frame of a specific historical and geographical context, taking into account the opinions of the scholars. The Scientology precedent, thus, opened the way to a quite liberal attitude of Italian courts on the issue of whether new religious movements should be regarded as genuine religions

References

Atack, John. 1990. *A Piece of Blue Sky: Scientology, Dianetics, and L. Ron Hubbard Exposed.* New York: Carol Publishing Group.

Corte Costituzionale (Supreme Constitutional Court). 1981. *In re Grasso*, decision no. 96 of June 8, 1981. Giurisprudenza Costituzionale 1, 1981: 806–34.

Corte d'Appello di Milano (Court of Appeal of Milan). 1993. *In re Segalla and others.* Sezione III Penale (Third Criminal Section), decision no. 4386 of November 5, 1993, case number RG 1144/92.

Corte d'Appello di Milano (Court of Appeal of Milan). 1996. *In re Bandera and others.* Sezione IV Penale (Fourth Criminal Section), decision no. 4314 of December 2, 1996, case number RG 1315/95.

Corte d'Appello di Milano (Court of Appeal of Milan). 2000. *In re Bandera and others*. Sezione I Penale (First Criminal Section), decision no. 14780 of October 5, 2000, case number RG 4291/1997.

Corte di Cassazione (Supreme Court of Cassation). 1995. *In re Segalla and others*. Sezione II Penale (Second Criminal Section), decision no. 163 of February 9, 1995, case number RG 30971/1994.

Corte di Cassazione (Supreme Court of Cassation). 1997. *In re Bandera and others*. Sezione VI Penale (Sixth Criminal Section), decision no. 1329 of October 8, 1997, case number RG 16835.

Richardson, James T. 2009. "Scientology in Court: A Look at Major Cases from Various Countries." In *Scientology*, edited by James Lewis, 283–94.Oxford: Oxford University Press.

Tribunale di Milano (Justice Cour of Milan). 1991. *In re Segalla and others*. Sezione I Penale (First Criminal Section), decision of July 2, 1991, case number RG 4159/88.

U.S. Supreme Court. 1970. *Welsh v. United States*. 398 U.S. 333.

Usai, Alessandro. 1996. Profili penali dei condizionamenti psichici. Riflessioni sui problemi penali posti dalla fenomenologia dei nuovi movimenti religiosi. Milan: Giuffré.

Chapter 3

The Order of the Solar Temple: From Apocalypse to Court

Jean-François Mayer

Introduction

Few people join a religious group for the purpose of breaking the law or expecting to come into conflict with the state. But a spiritual quest sometimes takes unexpected turns. In the 1980s I visited a Hindu-based religious group whose leader, Swami Okarananda Saraswati (1929–2000) had been jailed in Switzerland during several years. As I was visiting the ashram, I was led through an office where I noticed a wall covered with thick bound volumes. Without looking closer, I asked my guide: 'Have you collected and bound all the discourses of the guru?' He answered: 'No, those are our legal books.' For years, the group had attempted to get the sentence overturned and their leader exonerated, pursuing this struggle for redress even after he was released. I realized that several disciples had turned into legal experts and were spending most of their time immersed not in meditation, but in law books – an unusual kind of spiritual practice, but one that could probably be interpreted by a Hindu group as a service (*seva*).

For a researcher as well, studying religious movements can have unexpected consequences. It can be quite a shock to discover that the group one is studying has carried out criminal activities – and even more traumatic if a scholar has whitewashed a group that is actively engaged in such activities, as happened to some Japanese researchers in relation to the Aum Sinrikyo case (Watanabe 2001: 99–101).

My own experience with what has become known as the Order of the Solar Temple[1] was different. I had conducted research on the group for a few months

---

[1] While always below the threshold of 1,000 members, the group used a variety of names, some of them simultaneously, to describe various types of activities or subgroups, as well as to attempt to relaunch activities under different, supposedly more attractive guises. For the sake of clarity, I will mostly use 'Order of the Solar Temple' as a label, since it has become generally known under that name.

in 1987 as part of a wider project on the history and developments of alternative religious movements in Switzerland (Mayer 1993). During the following years I had further occasional contacts either with the group or with people who were familiar with it. From the early 1990s I had no opportunity to monitor the movement or participate in its activities. But I had published a research article on some aspects of the group, based on my 1987 field research work, in a small French bulletin on religious movements (English translation: Mayer 2006). When the news of 53 murders and suicides broke in October 1994, it surprised me as much as everybody else. I later discovered that these events resulted from developments that had started after I lost contact with the group; moreover, only a core group of members was privy to what took place.

A number of victims lost their lives on the territory of the Swiss canton of Fribourg, where I reside. The judge in charge of the case invited me to take part in the investigation as an expert. This gave me a privileged insight into the case and the investigative work conducted by the police officers, with whom I spent most of my waking hours during the first three weeks of the investigation, while also interacting frequently with them later. My duties as an expert involved both sorting and examining documents, on the one hand, and being present at key interviews with people interrogated by police officers, on the other hand.

In this chapter, besides reconstructing how the Solar Temple came into conflict with the law, I will share my observations derived from my position as an expert in the case. Obviously, at the time I was doing this work, I did not reflect on the questions raised in this volume. Retrospectively, however, thinking about them can hopefully throw more light not only on that specific case, but on others as well.

History of the Oder: On Their Way to Suicide and Murder

The history, practices and beliefs of the Order of the Solar Temple have been told elsewhere (Mayer 1999a; Mayer 1999b; Lewis 2006). The original core group was made up of French people who had been active in the esoteric subculture; several of them had belonged to the Ancient Mystical Order Rosae Crucis (AMORC). After starting around 1973 as a small spiritual commune on French territory close to the border with Switzerland, the group moved to Switzerland in 1978, where the Golden Way Foundation was created and would remain at the heart of the group's activities undertaken over the ensuing years. Substantial donations allowed the buying of a property in a suburb of Geneva. A nucleus, known as the Fraternity, led a communitarian life, while other activities reached a broader range of people.

Prominent among ideological references were the Rosy Cross and Templar Knights, through the channel of neo-Templar organizations (Caillet 1997), while borrowings from Free Masonry were also present in the background (Bogdan 2006). This universe of beliefs was related to the occult subculture that had developed in the West since the nineteenth century in the Theosophical lineage. Formulas such as Alice Bailey's 'Great Invocation' were used in some rituals, pointing to roots in the cultic milieu. Despite the Christian references evoked by the Templar reference, the content and rituals had little to do with Christianity and much more with the legacy of the 'Masters' of Theosophical legacy:

> The Cosmic Christ is a highly evolved being who accepted the mission to guide the evolution of the Earth to the level determined by Cosmic Intelligence. The Christ is the sum total of all evolution which has taken place within our solar system. His body could be regarded as consisting of vibrations stepped down from the vast powerhouse of the Father or Universal Consciousness.... Periodically, whenever a new evolutionary impulse was required on the planet, the Cosmic Christ would ensoul certain individuals to various degrees (Delaforge 1987: 24).

The beliefs of the group included a strong concern about destructive forces that were carrying the planet downwards and destroying the environment. On the other hand, there was an acknowledgement of positive forces associated with aspirations to a New Age, although these were deemed to be insufficiently structured in the spiritual lives of seekers. The lectures of one of its leaders, Luc Jouret (see below) often included warnings about impending catastrophes linked to environmental deterioration. A global disaster was threatening, but it could be staved off, or at least there might be enough survivors 'to carry the species toward the evolutionary blueprint intended for mankind' (Delaforge 1987: 133). There was a survivalist component in the order's beliefs, evidenced by the creation of farms seen as 'survival centers' and by the publication of two volumes on the topic 'surviving the year 2000' (Cahiers de Sarah 1986). So in the 1980s there seemed to be little about the group pointing toward a wish to leave this life or take ones' own life.

From the beginning, the key figure of the group was a French citizen, Jo Di Mambro (1924–94). He had joined AMORC as early as 1956; at that time, it was a growing, accessible organization for people seeking esoteric teachings. A jeweller by training, he was twice accused of having defrauded business associates, once in the 1950s and again in the 1960s (Bédat 2000: 56, 65–6). In 1972 he was given a suspended six-month sentence in France after writing bad cheques and abusing people's trust. Apparently, these experiences reinforced his already existing tendency to behave in a secretive way and avoid the limelight. While not an impressive or charismatic figure in the eyes of outsiders – just the opposite, in fact – he was seen as an exceptional being by his followers, some of whom associated with him from the late 1960s and 1970s until the end. In 1992 one devoted order member confided to a fellow 'Knight' that Di Mambro 'was beyond doubt the most powerful entity currently living on this planet' (Delorme 1996: 56).

However, a decade later, in the thriving Geneva-based community of the early 1980s, another figure who was very willing to go public appeared and joined the group: a Belgian homeopathic physician with a strong interest in various alternative healing techniques, Luc Jouret (1947–94). A charismatic and charming speaker, Jouret met Di Mambro in 1980 and came to settle at the Geneva centre in 1982. After the takeover of a pre-existing neo-Templar organization, the Renovated Order of the Temple, Jouret became its Grand Master and retained some of its members after a rupture took place. He also became the focus of the movement's public activities. An exoteric structure, called the Archedia Clubs, which served as an entry point for the order, was launched, with conference tours by Jouret across France and French-speaking Switzerland, and later in Quebec. The group also had a few isolated members in the United States.

The group cultivated high ambitions for growth and envisioned structures designed for a much larger movement. Jouret was a successful speaker, addressing audiences that reached hundreds of people and being invited onto radio programmes, but most listeners did not convert into followers, since they were a typical audience of spiritual seekers, most of them curious and open to a variety of messages, but not eager to commit themselves. The order probably never had more than five hundred followers at any one time.

Some of them were wealthy and donated generously: one of them, businessman Camille Pilet, seems to have given several million Swiss francs, which probably prevented the group from going bankrupt during its last few years. Much money was needed for paying Di Mambro's bills and supporting the core group, most of whom had no income; moreover, Di Mambro's financial management was far from rational or cautious. At the time of the 1994 events there was little money left in accounts linked to the order's leaders. This was one of several factors that created a crisis situation in the early 1990s. Not only had recruitment become more difficult, but several people who had been close to the core group left the group, including Di Mambro's own son. The impact of such defections on Di Mambro's mind should not be underestimated, since people such as him need followers as a way of confirming the plausibility of their message. Over the years, some people also started to complain about miraculous phenomena that had allegedly taken place during the order's ceremonies or even denounced them as having been faked. An atmosphere of dissent started to emerge, resulting in internal tensions and clans forming within the order.

In addition, while the order had not gone entirely unnoticed by anti-cult groups, it had not been mentioned prominently in their publications or in newspapers. In 1992, however, a former member of the order was invited by an anti-cult group to visit Martinique island in the French Caribbean, where the order had a following, and denounced it publicly, with media coverage, although this remained mostly confined to Martinique and Quebec. It was obviously only a matter of time until coverage would extend to France or Switzerland.

Another important episode took place in early 1993 in Quebec and caused further trouble. Jouret asked a trusted member to buy guns (with silencers) without going through legal channels. By coincidence, at that very time, the police were investigating anonymous terrorist threats from an unknown group. They were tipped off by an informer about an order member who had been attempting to buy guns with silencers. The police then put several members of the group under surveillance and thus discovered the existence of the order.

Canadian members involved in the attempt to procure weapons were arrested on 8 March 1993. The arrests were reported in Canadian media and extracts from wiretaps were made public, giving unwanted publicity to the order. The former member who had travelled to Martinique held a press conference on 10 March. A number of articles were published in the media about the 'doomsday cult' and the places where it gathered in Quebec. Former members revealed that the true leader was not Jouret, but Di Mambro. Moreover, after the media revealed that several members had been recruited at the state-owned Hydro-Quebec, the largest electrical company in Canada, and that Jouret had provided training seminars there, Hydro-Quebec launched an internal investigation, thus closing down further activities there. The member who had played a pivotal role for the order at Hydro-Quebec lost his job.

In June and July two members of the order and Jouret were sentenced to a year of unsupervised probation and a fine of a thousand Canadian dollars. The judge accepted the explanation that the men had wanted to buy the guns only for self-defence purposes and remarked that media coverage had badly penalized them, thus justifying the mild sentence. Some observers wondered, however, why silencers would have been needed for self-defence.

While media exposure receded, preparations by the core group of the Order for leaving this Earth proceeded. This led to a mixture of suicides and murders, since some people considered as 'traitors' were eliminated at the same time that the leaders and their trusted followers undertook what was called a 'transit'. In early October 1994 (in different events at three sites in Quebec and Switzerland), a total of 53 people perished: 5 in Morin Heights (Quebec), 23 in Cheiry (Canton of Fribourg, Switzerland) and 25 in salvan (Canton of Valais, Switzerland). A year later (December 1995), 16 more people – all identified as members of the order during the investigation after the 1994 events – lost their lives in another 'transit' in France (in a forest area of the Vercors Plateau, French Prealps). Finally, in March 1997 five people took their lives in Saint-Casimir, Quebec. This was probably the final act of the Order of the Solar Temple, since all its most devoted members had either died or been killed.

The Solar Temple and the Law before the 1994 Events: Roots of Violence?

The fiery end of the Order of the Solar Temple was not only a dramatic event; it also had a dramatic impact on the debate about 'cults' in French-speaking countries. Analysing the case thus bears an interest going beyond knowledge of a single event.

There have been scholarly discussions on the cause of violence in the case of the Solar Temple as well as other cases of violence linked to religious beliefs. The psychological mindset of the leaders of the Order of the Solar Temple definitely played a role in what took place, even if a doctrinal framework had to be built up in order to justify the actions. The tapping of Jouret's phone calls by the Quebec police in 1993 shows that a feeling of being persecuted mixed with a desire to escape from this world had already developed before the arrests. The calls indicate that Jouret was in a depressed mood at that time: he was sure that he and Di Mambro were under attack and suggested he was about to leave this Earth. This is confirmed by former members, who describe him at that time as paranoid, acting as if were living in a 'spiritual spy novel' and convinced of being the target of conspiracies, informing local groups about his visits using code words and conveying his message 'with the pathetic tone of a martyr' (Dauvergne 2008: 209–11). Internal documents recovered during the investigation show that the entire core group, starting with Di Mambro, had been immersed in a similar mindset. Perceiving themselves as victims of a mighty conspiracy from 'dark forces' represented at the same time a way of confirming the significance of their own mission. This would have consequences for the unfolding events.

Did the investigation in Quebec cause the drifting of the order toward the 1994 murders and suicides? Opinions regarding the exact nature and significance of the events are not unanimous. From the start of their investigation into the

1994 events, Quebec police officers were convinced that their intervention in 1993 had not hastened the fiery end of the Solar Temple, but, on the contrary, had prevented it from taking place earlier and had encouraged the leaders to move the operation to Europe. The first documents with clear allusions to the 'transit' were drafted in February 1993, around the time police in Quebec had started their surveillance. As we have seen, the arrests of the members involved only took place on 8 March 1993. Even if we were to believe comments implying that Jouret might have received word of the investigation before the arrests (in conversations a few days before, he claimed to be aware that his phone calls were being tapped, but this might merely reflect his paranoid mindset), a document found on a computer and the attempt to procure guns with silencers provide evidence that the first steps toward the 'transit' or other types of violent action had already been initiated before the group came into conflict with the law.

Beyond the psychological state of Di Mambro and Jouret, everything points to internal tensions as the primary cause of the initiative to leave this world. In Catherine Wessinger's typology (2000: 18–20), the Order of the Solar Temple clearly belongs to the type known as fragile groups: events such as opposition, which might just be seen as a nuisance by other types of groups,[2] are perceived by leaders of such groups as intolerable developments of a cosmic significance.

The 1993 events and accusations by former members would only confirm a pre-existing interpretive framework. Moreover, the suspicious behaviour of Di Mambro and his wife in terms of their way of life and frequent travels around the world, along with the fact that they repeatedly asked for new passports at different places, together with bank wires that were seen as suspicious, had attracted the notice of police agencies tracking money laundering, and an investigation was launched. When Di Mambro's wife did not succeed in getting a new passport from the French consulate in Montreal, she asked a lawyer she knew to help her, but he refused, writing to her in August 1994 that the passport problem was linked to a police investigation with legal and political aspects. This came as a clear vindication of the worst fears of the leaders of the Solar Temple.

---

[2]   Authorities had not played up the cult fears after the 1993 media reports on the 'doomsday cult' in Quebec: Public Security Minister Claude Ryan actually took a position against surveillance targeting 'cult members' and stated that, unless a cult uses the pretext of religious beliefs to induce people to break the law, there was no reason for police intervention: 'We should beware of any generalizations here. Religious sects are perfectly legal and principled. They have a right to exist as have all kinds of other associations' (*The Gazette*, Montreal, 11 March 1993). Along with the mild sentence received by Jouret, this moderate reaction shows there was no unbearable pressure put on the Solar Temple at that time.

While there is no certainty, converging pieces of evidence indicate that legal troubles were not at the root of the violent end of the order, but probably reinforced the preconceived commitment of the core group to leave this planet. Specific events added to the feeling of being besieged and cornered that the leaders had cultivated as the result of internal tensions and impending failure.

Di Mambro himself definitely did not see himself as a criminal, but as someone who was being persecuted by an unjust world and ungrateful apostates. This is clearly expressed in the manifestoes that were sent at the time of the 1994 events to a number of people, including the media and the author of this article: the word 'justice' is used several times, and the leaders of the order were clearly assuming the posture of victims. Strikingly, at the very time some members had already lost their lives and the leadership was about to take the same path in early October 1994, Di Mambro drafted a letter he intended to send to the public prosecutor, accusing a former member to whom he had already paid some money and who wanted more of blackmail. Di Mambro had obviously developed his own understanding of justice in a process that is typical of the narcissistic personality he assuredly was (Oakes 1997): he understood as just what was good for the order and himself. In a video recovered on a camera at his chalet at Salvan recording a discussion between a few members of the core group on 18 September 1994, one participant reports having seen in a meditation the word 'vengeance'. Di Mambro then explained that it was an equivalent of the phrase 'justice and sentence', allegedly expressing the same concept in impersonal terms.

Investigation Challenges after the Murders and Suicides

When two bodies were discovered in a fire in Quebec, and subsequently three more in the same charred house (those of a couple who had been killed along with their baby child and hidden in a closet), the local police at least had some previous knowledge of the Order of the Solar Temple, since they had conducted surveillance of it in 1993 and several former members had disclosed information to the media. For Swiss police, the situation was entirely different: police officers in charge of the investigation had no previous experience of dealing with religious movements, while this particular movement had attracted little police attention or negative media reports in Switzerland.[3]

---

[3]   In 1979 the mother of a member of the community had complained to the police in Geneva due to concerns about her daughter: the police then interviewed Di Mambro and another member, but nothing illegal was found. In 1985 an investigation on the activities of the group was conducted by the police in Geneva (apparently without the knowledge of

The issue of a lack of knowledge about the world of occult groups was probably not the main challenge facing the investigation[4]. After all, police are accustomed to penetrating hidden, unusual, secretive worlds, where criminals maintain a code of silence. There were several other issues, some quite specific to this case.

Firstly, the challenge was obviously to understand what could have led to the deaths of 53 people. The initial assumption of police officers – and mine too – was that somebody, or a small group of people, might have survived and would have gone into hiding or might still be on the hunt for critics or defectors. One should remember that practically no information was available then about the reasons for what happened. The bodies of the leaders had been badly burned and it would take some time to confirm their identities.[5] After a few days, based on documents that had been gathered and discussions with some surviving core members, it became obvious that most of the people involved had died. To this day, however, several investigators continue to suspect that three male members (two of whom were French policemen), who perished in the second event in 1995, might have visited the crime scene where 23 order members had died, but these suspicions could never be proved, despite lengthy interrogations of the three men, who did not confess.

---

the leaders of the order), but it could only find that members had been making substantial donations to the order, and that the sources of funding were opaque.

[4]   If I may recall a personal memory here, my first contact with a police officer working on this case was on the day following the discovery of the murders and suicides that had taken place in the small village of Cheiry, where 23 bodies had been found in a burning farmhouse. I was waiting for the investigating judge, who had asked to see me due to my earlier research on the group, while a police officer was perusing some files recovered from the farmhouse. Not really expecting an answer from me, he commented on the title of a document he had just opened: 'FARC; what does that mean?' I instantly replied: 'Frères Aînés de la Rose-Croix' (Elder Brothers of the Rose Cross). He retorted: 'No, it is written here: Ferme Agricole de Recherche et de Culture' (Agricultural Farm for Research and Culture). I explained: 'Well, it has two meanings: an exoteric one and an esoteric one'. Continuing to browse through the document, he found by chance exactly what I had told him and exclaimed: 'How could you know that? You might be helpful to us!' This led to my participation as an expert in the police investigation.

[5]   Their identities were established beyond doubt, including by DNA analysis in addition to the already conclusive results of autopsies. This was the right thing to do, since rumours alleging that Jouret was still alive circulated, including statements made in 1996 in front of a Belgian parliamentary commission. This did not surprise the forensic physician who had conducted the autopsies – he had expected that Luc Jouret would experience a fate after his death similar to that of Elvis Presley, sightings of whom have been repeatedly reported (*Tribune de Genève*, 12 December 1996).

The second challenge was the emerging awareness that the investigation would find no living culprit. This can happen with any investigation. But there were many victims, and thus also a number of relatives anxious to discover the truth and looking for culprits who could be held accountable for what had happened. Shocked by the realization that nobody would be brought to court, several relatives started to point to alleged flaws in police work, soon supported by media-friendly lawyers. This increased dramatically after the second 'transit' occurred.

Doubts were reinforced by investigative reports in media, sometimes of a sensationalist nature, at other times throwing up interesting pieces of information. This constituted a third challenge. Only somebody who has been part of an investigation can fully realize how media reports can shape a public environment toward police work, spreading doubts and uncertainties. Investigators are not supposed to leak information to the media or to correct media statements. As an expert, I was constantly approached by representatives of the media attempting to get insider information, since I had access to the ongoing investigation. I managed to speak with them without ever leaking any information, but I needed to be permanently on my guard and maintain my composure (even when suddenly presented with a confidential document in front of rolling cameras). I agreed to speak to the media about knowledge I had gained prior to the investigation, but not about knowledge gained during the investigation if it had not already been made public. It was especially difficult when questions were asked about people who were still alive: it was out of the question to comment on such people, even if they had played a significant role in the group. I realized how frustrating it can be for investigators and experts to bear the brunt of (sometimes inaccurate) criticism without reacting, even though they often had the knowledge to do so.

A fourth challenge was the fact that police are accustomed to dealing with criminals, i.e. people who know that they are criminals, even if they claim to be innocent. In the case of the Solar Temple, however, the people involved had no criminal records and did not feel like criminals – because they were not. They found themselves in a strange situation, somewhere between victims and accomplices. Either they were shocked, because they had never realized what was going to happen, or they were supportive of what happened, seeing it as a valuable mission by a spiritual elite, to the extent of explaining that they would have been willing to join if invited to do so. But how is it possible to protect a 'normal' citizen against him- or herself? This happened again during the investigation on the second 'transit' in 1995: a person interviewed by the police sometime after the events admitted that he might decide to follow the same path some day. He subsequently lost his life in Quebec in the last 'transit' in 1997.

Again, nothing could be done to prevent him: he had done nothing illegal, had set no date and had merely admitted it was an acceptable option for him.

After the Events: Doubts and Controversies around a Trial

At the time of the 1995 events, conspiracy theories, or simply alternative theories, flourished. They centred around two main topics. On the one hand, a number of people expressed doubts that the 'transit' had taken place in a closed circle and claimed there must have been some external intervention, e.g. a squad of killers. Such theories continue to circulate to this day, based on expert witnesses regarding the way the bodies of the victims were burned and other elements. On the other hand, there have been many allegations regarding a much more sinister background than just a movement led to its physical end by its leaders. According to these theories, connections with secret societies, such as some branches of French Free Masonry, as well as with shady rightist political circles should be taken into account in order to understand the unfolding of events.

The Swiss investigation had managed to stick to dry facts. Swiss investigators had found no reason to suspect a more sinister background and hidden structure over and above the order itself, although Di Mambro had attempted to convince his followers he had been only relaying the instructions of the secret 'Masters of Zurich'. While it is true that the pressure and questions had not been the same before the second 'transit' occurred, probably the French cultural context was more prone to suspicions about political manipulations than the Swiss one.

One should not underestimate the impact of narratives imposed by media, lawyers and advocacy groups, especially when dealing with an order that had cultivated esoteric teachings. Di Mambro and his associates had deliberately attempted to forge their own narrative of the end of the order through various documents they left behind. But far from shedding light on the events, these two types of narratives tended to obscure them, to the extent that it became difficult to sort out allegations from facts.

There was obviously a pressure on authorities to prevent the repetition of similar events: since a second 'transit' had taken place, could one rule out the possibility that further events might occur? The issue was a delicate one, since not only adults (both consenting and non-consenting) had been involved in the 1994 and 1995 events, but also children of followers, who lost their lives with their parents. In Geneva, there was a case of a mother whose eight-year-old daughter was temporarily entrusted to the care of her grandparents for her 'psychological and physical well-being' in mid-January 1996: the authorities did not want to take any chances, since the mother had belonged to the order. This was a quite unusual case of taking preventive measures, since no problem could be found with the mother beside the fact that she had been a member of the order. In early March the court in charge of tutelage decided that the child should be given back to her mother.

The French determination to have a court case was clear – stemming in part from the desire to make it an exercise about the danger of 'cults'. But who could be put in the dock, since there was no known survivor involved in the death of 16 people – unless one believed in the existence of a mysterious and unidentified squad of killers? One man was targeted: a conductor, Michel Tabachnik (b. 1942), who had been associated with Di Mambro since 1977 and had been quite involved in the activities of the order over the years, before moving away from it in the years immediately preceding the 'transits', but reconnecting with the group in the months just before they took place. He had been the keynote speaker at two private meetings organized by the order in 1994, and had taken part in a ritual during a gathering of a small group. Despite these links, Tabachnik had more or less escaped public attention after the events of 1994; he had been interviewed by Swiss police for many hours, but this had not been made public. At the time of the December 1995 events, his name made the headlines and his very unclever line of defence (minimizing his role and then being forced to admit that he had had closer relations with Di Mambro than he had first publicly admitted) made him look quite suspicious.

Still, there was no proof of Tabachnik's alleged criminal involvement in the 1994 events, and still less in those of December 1995, since he had had no relations with the people who perished then. Needing to put somebody on trial, on 11 July 2000 French judge Luc Fontaine decided there was enough evidence to send Tabachnik to court after an examination of texts he had prepared for the order, in addition to the fact that he had participated in a leading role at a gathering of the order's members on 24 September 1994, even if it could not be proved that he had any precise knowledge of what would follow.

Tabachnik's teachings delivered to the order's followers were written in an obscure style – in fact, on a video of a meeting of the order, people who had patiently listened to a talk by Tabachnik admitted that they had not understood what he had said. But according to the expert opinion of French psychiatrist (and anti-cult activist) Jean-Marie Abgrall,[6] these writings had contributed to

---

[6]   Not unsurprisingly, in the context of the heated debates on the interpretation of conversions to controversial movements, Abgrall's views have been criticized by several authors as 'pseudoscientific theories' (see Anthony and Robbins 2004).

the conditioning of some of the group by making them believe they belonged to an elite group and creating a 'homicidal dynamic' ('une dynamique homicide'). Thus, a kind of moral responsibility for what had taken place was attributed to Tabachnik (see Vuillemin 2011: 169–89).

These efforts were fruitless: after a trial, on 25 June 2001, Michel Tabachnik was cleared of criminal involvement, since it was hard to believe that his writings could have played the role attributed to them by the expert (who had actually nuanced his own assessment during the court hearings by stating that his interpretation of Tabachnik's writings was subject to discussion). Regarding the suggestion that Tabachnik had played a role in events that were part of the preparations for homicides and suicides, no conclusive proof could be found. Thus, the benefit of the doubt was given to the accused.

This was not to be the end of the matter, however. Several relatives of victims were not pleased with the outcome of the investigation. For some of them, the issue was not so much the role of Tabachnik as their belief that the events had taken place with outside agency. They denounced what they saw as inconsistencies, claimed that some pieces of evidence had not been duly considered and subsequently also attempted to prove that the bodies of the victims could not possibly have burned in the way reported by the investigation, but that a flamethrower was allegedly used. Similarly, the leading French cult-watching organization, the Union Nationale des Associations de Défense des Familles et de l'Individu Victimes de Sectes, was also dissatisfied with the court decision, but did not agree with the thesis of some kind of outside agency: it believed in Tabachnik's responsibility and wanted him condemned. With a different agenda, it felt that the external agency thesis was detrimental to the exemplary 'cult' dimension of the case. Thus the prosecutor of the magistrates' court decided to appeal the judgment so that the entire case (both civil and penal) could be examined again.

It took five years to reach a verdict. The case was first supposed to be heard in September 2003, then in June 2004 and later in June 2005. But different factors delayed it each time, including accusations against French experts of divulging confidential documents and requests for additional investigations by the relatives of victims.

Finally, the trial took place from 24 October to 30 October 2006. On 20 December 2006 the appeal court upheld the original verdict, as was to be expected. The personal consequences of this investigation and trial had been heavy for Michel Tabachnik: over 11 years he had lost most of his contracts as a conductor on the international circuit and had to put his career and income-earning capacity on hold, living only from some musical teaching in Denmark and with the help of faithful friends, he later reported. Around 2005 his career resumed and he is now fully active once more. That someone had to wait 11 years to be cleared of accusations of participation in criminal activities, with wide international media exposure associating him with a 'murderous cult', tells us something about the dramatic consequences that such cases can lead to – and not only when they relate to religious movements, although undoubtedly the peculiar nature of the case added to the problems Tabachnik experienced.

Thus the death of 74 people ended without anybody being convicted of the crime. This does not prevent some relatives from continuing to express doubts about the outcome. 'After all, there are 74 dead; somebody must be responsible', stated Alain Vuarnet, whose mother and brother had perished in 1995.[7] On a website about the process and in occasional interviews he continues to state his belief that his mother, his brother and their companions were 'assassinated by one or several persons still at large today'.[8] Over the years, other relatives have expressed their belief that there must have been a hidden puppet master (*L'Illustré*, 1 October 2007). While nobody disputes that a number of victims in both the 1994 and 1995 events were killed (starting with children), everything points to the fact that they were killed by fellow order members who then committed suicide: in both cases, some knew they would leave this world (while possibly not being aware of the methods to be used) and several left unambiguous farewell notes. The 1997 event involved only consenting adults. Nevertheless, some journalists continued to raise questions and doubts about the case (e.g. Fusier 2003, 2006, 2010). But unless an unidentified person who was involved suddenly appears or somebody confesses, it seems unlikely that new elements could radically revise the conclusions drawn by the police investigation.

Reflections on the Solar Temple Investigations and Trials

The Order of the Solar Temple sailed in the waters of esoteric doctrines, occult knowledge, and initiatory mysteries, and the whole discussion about it has come

---

[7]   'Il y a quand même 74 morts, il doit bien y avoir une responsabilité là-dedans' (*Agence Télégraphique Suisse*, 20 December 2006). Alain Vuarnet explained that his family had originally believed in the suicides thesis (or 'assisted suicides' by two members of the group who subsequently killed themselves, according to the conclusions of the investigation), but that they started to doubt it from 1996 due to deficiencies in the investigation (A. Vuarnet 2007: 229).

[8]   http://www.ots-proces.org, home page "Edito" (accessed 25 May 2014). Both Alain Vuarnet (2007) and his father, Jean Vuarnet (1996), have written books about their experience.

to reflect some of these characteristics. Even a novelist would have a hard time concocting a scenario such as the end of the Solar Temple, with two repeat 'transits'. As already mentioned, the leaders of the order had also attempted to suppress as much evidence as possible of what happened in the years and months before October 1994: beside consuming the corpses of those who lost their lives, this had certainly been one of the reasons for setting fire to key places associated with the Order, where documents were kept, including locations where nobody died (in several cases, the fire was started through remotely, phone-activated devices). The leaders had also attempted to craft their own narrative about an elite group of Knight Templars leaving this Earth to reach a higher dimension. It thus cannot come as a surprise that such peculiar events would give rise to all kinds of theories, either by the media or by distraught families. Fortunately, some ignition systems did not function properly and allowed investigators to gather a significant amount of informative material.

One cannot blame the victims' relatives, with their continuing suffering, since they have even heard experts suggesting that there was much that had not been disclosed, giving credence to accusations of manipulation around the case. They quote statements such as the one allegedly made in 2003 to the newspaper *Nice-Matin* by psychiatrist Jean-Marie Abgrall when asked about the Solar Temple: 'It is a truth beyond our reach, going up to [the level of] a state secret. I will speak some day. Like the judge, we all have official versions. There has been a lead cloak. There is too much at stake, too many interests at stake.'[9]

In any attempt to deal with such a case, one needs to keep a cool head, to avoid being distracted by all the 'polluting noise' coming from a range of sometimes problematic sources, and to focus not on conjecture, but facts. If something cannot be proved with a reasonable level of certainty, one should be cautious. This is what French courts managed to do in 2001 and 2006, but it is not a line easily followed, especially when judges, experts, and investigators come under media pressure and criticism for supposedly not doing their job properly and are dealing with topics that are by nature shrouded in mysteries. What, then, is true, and what are just appearances hiding the 'real' truth? Many people can no longer distinguish between the two. Especially in the years immediately after the 1995, there were far-fetched rumors linking the Solar Temple to all kinds

---

[9] 'C'est une vérité qui nous dépasse, qui va jusqu'au secret d'État. Je m'exprimerai un jour. Comme le juge, on a tous des versions officielles. Il y a eu une chape de plomb. Il y a trop d'enjeux, d'intérêts en jeu' (*Nice-Matin*, 15 February 2003; full text: http://www.prevensectes.com/rev0302.htm#15; acccessed 15 January 2012). To my knowledge, Abgrall has never explained what he meant, retracted his statement, nor claimed that he had been misquoted.

of criminal cases and other mysterious events that were duly reported by some media and books.[10]

When the French investigation started after the December 1995 'transit', there were expectations that French judge and police would do what the Swiss investigation had allegedly failed to do and uncover what had escaped the Swiss investigators. Tabachnik had exactly that feeling when he was first interrogated by French police: that they wanted to restart the investigation already conducted in Switzerland, in addition to that of the 1995 events (Tabachnik 1997). Soon the French investigation started to face criticisms similar to the Swiss one. In the end, the conclusions were essentially the same, and disappointed those who had expected fresh revelations. True, it brought to light additional details regarding historical aspects of the background and genesis of the Order of the Solar Temple in France in the esoteric and masonic milieu,[11] but this did not alter the interpretation of the final events themselves.

Since apparently all people responsible for the crimes have perished, question marks are bound to linger regarding such a case. There are 'black spots', i.e. questions that will probably never be answered – although none would radically change the interpretative framework of the events. For people who participated in the investigation, this remains frustrating. But it is much more so – and painfully so – for relatives who remain with their doubts and, in some cases, continue to believe that the investigation and court decisions have failed to reach the truth, possibly due to pressures of some kind and to a mysterious, unexplored background. The mother and grandmother of two of the victims of the 1995 events summarize their feelings in a way that expresses all the frustrations and doubts felt to this day by some of the families:

---

[10]   There has even been a book by a British psychologist and documentary filmmaker linking the Solar Temple to Grace Kelly and Prince Charles (Cohen 2004). The British author spoke to people who made quite surprising statements about the Solar Temple: over the years, he is not the only one who has come across dubious figures who have attempted to capitalize on the case by making sensational revelations, although no trace of any link they might have had with the order could be found during the investigations.

[11]   During the investigation in Switzerland, police and experts had been asked to focus on the events themselves: the history was deemed to be important only to the extent that it could explain the events of October 1994. When dealing with cases of such an impact and magnitude, however, it seems that an in-depth investigation of the history of the group in question is necessary – not that it would change anything regarding the final interpretation of the events, but because many critical questions can be expected, and investigating aspects not directly linked to the criminal activities themselves will help to prevent accusations of the investigation having neglected areas of possible interest. This is more than an academic exercise.

The sixteen people slaughtered in France lost their lives because they knew too much about the first massacre; they knew too much about the financial schemings.... I am convinced that, if the Swiss and all those in charge of the investigation on the first massacres had done their job properly, the one in Vercors could have been avoided. I am upset. Seventy-four people have been assassinated and nobody is able to find the culprits! (quoted in Jaton 1999: 160; my translation).

The culprits were identified: they had left this world with their disciples. While always remaining open to new evidence that might shed more light on the case, one can confidently state that the main conclusions of the Swiss and French investigations match reality, insofar as we base our analysis on available evidence. But this will not convince some of the victims' relatives who are left with sad memories of the tragic fate of their loved ones and feelings of helplessness that justice has not been done.

References

Anthony, D. and T. Robbins. 2004. 'Pseudoscience Versus Minority Religions: An Evaluation of the Brainwashing Theories of Jean-Marie Abgrall'. In *Regulating Religion: Case Studies from around the Globe*, edited by J.T. Richardson, 127–49. New York: Kluwer Academic / Plenum Publishers.

Bédat, A. et al. 2000. *L'Ordre du Temple Solaire: les secrets d'une manipulation*. Paris: Flammarion.

Bogdan, H. 2006. 'Death as Initiation: The Order of the Solar Temple and Rituals of Initiation'. In *The Order of the Solar Temple: The Temple of Death*, edited by J.R. Lewis, 133–53. Aldershot: Ashgate.

Cahiers de Sarah. 1986. *Survivre à l'An 2000*, vols. 1 and 2. Toronto: Editions Atlanta.

Caillet, S. 1997. *L'Ordre Rénové du Temple: aux racines du Temple Solaire*. Paris: Editions Dervy.

Cohen, D. 2004. *Diana: Death of a Goddess*. London: Century.

Dauvergne, C. 2008. *Vingt ans au soleil du Temple*. Paris: Desclée de Brouwer.

Delaforge, G. 1987. *The Templar Tradition in the Age of Aquarius*. Putney: Threshold Books.

Delorme, H. 1996, *Crois et meurs dans l'Ordre du Temple Solaire*. Saint-Alphonse-de-Granby: Editions de la Paix.

Fusier, M. 2003. *Des mots qui font des morts: le procès Tabachnik et le Temple Solaire*. Bursinel: Pandora Publishing.

Fusier, M. 2006. *Secret d'Etat? Ordre du Temple Solaire, 10 ans après le drame du Vercors*. Brignais: Editions des Traboules.

Fusier, M. 2010. *O.T.S.: l'impossible procès*. Brignais: Editions des Traboules.

Jaton, R. 1999. *Ordre du Temple Solaire: en quête de vérité*. Geneva: Editions Slatkine.

Lewis, J.R. (ed.) 2006. *The Order of the Solar Temple: The Temple of Death*. Aldershot: Ashgate.

Mayer, J.-F. 1993. *Les Nouvelles Voies Spirituelles: enquête sur la religiosité parallèle en Suisse*. Lausanne: L'Age d'Homme.

Mayer, J.-F. 1999a. 'Our terrestrial journey is coming to an end': the last voyage of the Solar Temple. *Nova Religio: The Journal of Alternative and Emergent Religions*, 2(2): 172–96.

Mayer, J.-F. 1999b. 'Les chevaliers de l'Apocalypse: l'Ordre du Temple Solaire et ses adeptes'. In *Sectes et Démocratie*, edited by Françoise Champion and Martine Cohen, 205–23. Paris: Seuil.

Mayer, J.-F. 2006. 'Templars for the Age of Aquarius: The Archedia Clubs (1984–1991) and the International Chivalric Order of the Solar Tradition'. In *The Order of the Solar Temple: The Temple of Death*, edited by J.R. Lewis, 7–17. Aldershot: Ashgate.

Oakes, L. 1997. *Prophetic Charisma: The Psychology of Revolutionary Religious Personalities*. Syracuse: Syracuse University Press.

Tabachnik, M. 1997. *Bouc émissaire: dans le piège du temple Solaire*. Paris: Editions Michel Lafon.

Vuarnet, A. 2007. *Ma rage de vivre: un destin dans la tourmente de l'Ordre du Temple Solaire*. Monaco: Editions du Rocher.

Vuarnet, J. 1996. *Lettre à ceux qui ont tué ma femme et mon fils*. Paris: Fixot.

Vuillemin, F. 2011. *La Robe et l'Epée. Récit autobiographique*. Paris: L'Harmattan.

Watanabe, M. 2001. 'Opposition to Aum and the Rise of the "Anti-cult" Movement in Japan'. In *Religion and Social Crisis in Japan: Understanding Japanese Society through the Aum Affair*, edited by Robert J. Kisala and Mark R. Mullins, 87–105. New York: Palgrave.

Wessinger, C. 2000. *How the Millennium Comes Violently: From Jonestown to Heaven's Gate*. New York: Seven Bridges Press.

PART II
Specific Legal Cases Involving Minority Religious Groups

Chapter 4
The Mohan Singh Case:
What Is the Price of Confidentiality?

Philip Katz QC[1]

Introduction

In the summer of 2010, following two lengthy trials on indictment, a defendant named Michael Lyons (also known as 'Dr Mohan Singh') was convicted by a north London jury of one offence of rape and one offence of sexual assault by penetration. At his first trial in 2009 the jury was unable to reach any verdicts and a retrial was ordered. At his retrial in 2010 the second jury acquitted Lyons of some similar sexual offences and was again unable to reach verdicts in relation to others. For the two offences of which he was ultimately convicted Lyons was sentenced to a substantial term of imprisonment.

This chapter concerns some of the 'disclosure' issues which typically arise in this type of case and the tension, which was apparent at one stage during these proceedings, between the duty of disclosure and the right to confidentiality. The word *disclosure* crops up in different contexts in our police procedure and criminal law, but the context in this article is that of the fair trial in our adversarial system. In this context disclosure refers to the duty to hand over (disclose) material which is held by the prosecution or by a third party and which might be of legitimate use to the defence. This chapter is written with the clear and specific intention of avoiding any personal opinion on the facts or issues in the Lyons case. Furthermore it cannot hope to do more than give a very rough sketch of the rules and legal principles involved.

The Case

Lyons was at the centre of a large group of friends who claimed to be interested in Buddhism, natural healing, positive thinking and healthy living. The overwhelming majority of his friends were women although there were some men involved with the group. The group included models, actresses, successful businesswomen, exotic dancers and brilliant students. A very large number of

---

[1]   Barrister-at-law, 9-12 Bell Yard, London.

friends of both sexes were called as witnesses for the defence in both trials, as were healers of various sorts from around the world.

Most of these witnesses gave evidence that Lyons possessed extraordinary powers of healing and many claimed to speak from experience. One woman said on oath that Lyons could cure cancer over the phone. Others claimed that he had cured a variety of serious conditions by minor adjustments to the spine, encouragement to eat healthily and exhortations to 'take care'. He was obviously revered, not merely for his alleged powers of healing but also for his apparent connections with important personages in the world of Buddhism. One university student met Lyons while she was travelling in India during a break from her studies. Quite soon after meeting him she wrote in her diary that she was finding it difficult to decide who to follow as her 'master' – Lyons, Osho (the well-known twentieth-century 'sex guru') or Jesus.

Lyons' own business card carried a colourful image of himself robed in the fashion of a Lama, standing next to a genuine and eminent Lama. The pair of them appeared to be floating on a cloud in a heavenly blue sky. Beneath their feet was the motto, embossed in gold, 'DHARMA, DRAMA, KHARMA'.

The prosecution's case was that whatever his friends were interested in, Lyons himself was interested in sex. One complainant (in respect of whose allegations he was acquitted) gave evidence that Lyons claimed to have an organic penis. Organic or not, it was his penis that got Lyons into trouble. A number of women gave evidence in the two trials alleging sexual assaults committed on them by Lyons over many years, often under the guise of treatment. The complainants had met or been introduced to Lyons as a healer or guru figure and were often lulled into a false sense of security by the fact that he was surrounded by a group of apparently friendly women. The prosecution argued that some of Lyons's inner circle of women friends cynically helped to recruit new members to the group, knowing perfectly well what was likely to happen to them.

Whether Lyons and his group of friends qualified as a minority religion or a new religious movement is not an appropriate subject for me to discuss in this article. The prosecution suggested that there was a much darker side to the activities of the group, and it was labelled it as a cult.

INFORM became involved in these proceedings because of its neutral liaison role between complainants, witnesses and police.[2] For over a decade women had been speaking to INFORM about Lyons and his friends. As the

---

INFORM was established by Eileen Barker, Professor of Sociology at London School of Economics over a quarter century ago. Its major goal has been to collect objective information on minority religions and to make this information available to anyone desiring to learn more about such groups. Since its inception INFORM has amassed a huge data set on thousands of religious groups, and it possesses perhaps the largest such collection of such information in the world. See Barker (2001, 2006) and Beckford (2008) for more

years passed by, quite apart from women who made complaints of various sorts about the group, the estranged parents of some of Lyons' younger friends, exit counsellors and investigators also had contact with INFORM and eventually the police were involved.

The defence case, as outlined in their pretrial Case Statement, was to the effect that Lyons was not guilty of any sexual assaults. It was asserted on his behalf that insofar as he had touched any of the complainants it was in the context of treatment and was always done with their consent. During each of the trials many defence witnesses gave evidence that Lyons was celibate and not interested in sex. It had been suggested by Lyons in his own interviews under caution with the police, and by numerous defence witnesses in court, that the entire prosecution case was a wicked conspiracy to destroy an innocent man and a wonderful healer.

This conspiracy was said to be masterminded by the Jewish parents of a highly educated, young American woman who had become a friend of Lyons. She gave evidence for the defence in the first trial during which she claimed that her father had sexually abused and raped her when she was a child. She alleged that her mother knew of the abuse but had determined to support her husband rather than her daughter. She said that her parents were seeking, pre-emptively, to undermine their daughter's credibility should she ever report the abuse to the authorities in U.S. The parents were alleged to be doing this by organising a malicious internet campaign designed to discredit Lyons and his friends by falsely branding the group as a cult whose members had been 'brainwashed'.

During one hearing at the pretrial stage of the court proceedings, the defence floated the suggestion that INFORM might also have been a party to this conspiracy. During the first trial that suggestion was downgraded to an allegation that INFORM had been unwittingly involved. I shall return to this aspect of the case.

The prosecution's position was that this alleged, so-called 'conspiracy' was no more than the actions of two loving and desperate parents who were trying to restore relations with their estranged daughter, and who were doing everything they could to achieve this end by helping to bring Lyons to justice for his crimes.

I have referred to this alleged conspiracy as the defence case but the drama which played out in Court was something entirely different. To understand what happened, it is necessary to remember that in an English criminal trial the burden of proving the defendant's guilt remains on the prosecution from first till last, and the prosecution will only have proved its case if it has made the jury sure of guilt.

Thus, in order to prove that any sexual assaults had taken place it was necessary for the prosecution to prove, inter alia, not only that the *sexual* activity described

---

on the fascinating history and activities of INFORM, and also visit the INFORM website at http://www.lse.ac.uk/sociology/research/inform/home.aspx.

by the complainants had actually happened but also that, as a fact, it had been without their consent. When hands-on treatment and healing are involved, the issue of consent can become complicated. Some of the complainants had indeed consented to treatment from Lyons. The prosecution's case was that even in those cases where there had been an element of consent to treatment of one sort or another, Lyons' conduct went beyond any kind of legitimate treatment and became aggressively sexual. As such, it was done without the women's consent.

Of course, neither Lyons nor his lawyers were advancing a *positive* case that there had been sexual activity with consent. The basic defence case was a total denial of any sexual activity at all. Further, Lyons himself chose not to give evidence in either trial. However, his lawyers were perfectly entitled to 'put the prosecution to proof' of the consent element in the crime – in other words to require the prosecution to prove that the complainants had not consented to what they said had happened to them. We shall never know what, if any, findings of fact the second jury made in relation to the offences charged on the indictment upon which it acquitted or was undecided. Similarly in relation to the non-charged offences which were adduced as 'bad character' evidence[3]. But it was undoubtedly the jury's duty to acquit on any particular count unless it was sure firstly, that the alleged sexual activity had occurred, secondly that it had been without the complainant's consent, and thirdly that Lyons did not reasonably believe that the complainant was consenting. For obvious reasons the credibility of the complainants was the central issue.

Submissions and comments about the consistency and inconsistency of witnesses' evidence are a common feature of criminal trials. Consistency is regarded as a good indicator of a witness's reliability and truthfulness. In very general terms the prosecution cannot automatically adduce a witness's previous consistent statements to demonstrate that the witness's evidence in court is true. The reverse position is different for the defence. Demonstrating inconsistency is a permissible and effective way for the defence to establish unreliability and therefore doubt. Cross-examination on previous inconsistent statements by witnesses happens in most trials. Predictably therefore in the Lyons trials the complainants were each subjected to searching cross-examination by the defence on previous statements they had made describing the alleged offences, whether it was when they had spoken to therapists, doctors or police or when they spoke to or emailed friends. A small minority had contributed to internet sites about Lyons, and a few had spoken to INFORM. Some had kept diaries. In the second trial some of the complainants were even cross-examined by the defence using transcripts of their evidence in the first trial.

---

3   Criminal Justice Act 2003, S. 101.

The first point to make is that the defence had possession of and used most of this material legitimately. In fact a considerable proportion of it was made available to the defence by the prosecution, pursuant to its duty of disclosure. How did that happen?

As far as material emanating from police enquiries is concerned, investigating officers are well used to keeping records of contact with potential witnesses. Notebooks and contact sheets are maintained and retained. Interviews with some important witnesses are videotaped and often used as the witness's evidence-in-chief in court. Formal written statements, with signed perjury warnings, are taken from most witnesses. In sexual assault cases there will often be statements from witnesses to whom complainants made a 'recent complaint'. All of this material is routinely available to the defence and it is often used in court, as it was in the Lyons trial. Material emanating from the internet can be searched for, downloaded by either side and, if admissible, it can be used in court as it was in these trials.

As far as conversations with doctors, therapists and other professionals are concerned, full case notes will usually have been taken and kept. It is not unusual for such notes to be used in court. Some professional witnesses will have a great deal of experience of using their notes to draft their formal witness statements and of being cross-examined on them. INFORM's files were obviously not compiled with such forensic scrutiny in mind, but even some of the material in their files was made available to the defence and used by them in court.

The second point to make concerns the confidentiality of those who speak to an organisation like INFORM or to doctors or other professionals. In many such situations the complainants will speak in confidence. They may have been promised the confidentiality by the professional or expected it due to the circumstances in which the conversation was taking place. Further, there are many reasons why a complainant may want or expect confidentiality, and in any event, their right to privacy is protected by Art 8 ECHR. In the Lyons case, quite apart from those who eventually became prosecution witnesses in the trial, some individuals who had no intention of ever becoming witnesses had spoken to INFORM. Some were genuinely afraid for their safety or the safety of others.

Obviously confidentiality can be waived by the patient/client. But what about cases where there is no waiver? Can such confidential material end up being handed over to the defence?

Disclosure

Over the years there have been problems with the processes of disclosure in a number of high profile UK criminal cases. Seen from the prosecution perspective it has become something of a fashionable stick with which to beat the police and prosecutors. However, from the defence perspective, fair and proper disclosure is an important part of the guarantee of a fair trial.[4] The judge, as always the arbiter in relation to such matters, will have that guarantee at the forefront of her mind.

There has been a recent and comprehensive review of disclosure in criminal proceedings headed by Rt Hon Lord Justice Gross, a judge of the Court of Appeal.[5] The report from that review sets out the history of disclosure in English criminal law as well as giving a brief but valuable insight into the procedures of some foreign jurisdictions. I shall not attempt to summarise that review, but I can thoroughly commend it to anyone interested in the subject. Following that review (and a further review in November 2012) a new Judicial Protocol[6] was issued in December 2013. Since one theme of this article is 'confidentiality versus disclosure' it is necessary for the reader to have a very basic outline of the disclosure processes as they apply to a major prosecution such as the Lyons case. Essentially there are two categories of material to be considered: prosecution material and third party material.

Prosecution Material

Prosecution material has a statutory definition[7] but for present purposes can be roughly divided into two types. Firstly there is material which is created or generated internally by the investigation process itself. When police investigate serious crime they must record what they plan to do and what they actually do. All of these records must be retained and maintained. In a substantial investigation all actions taken, messages sent and documents created during the investigation are retained and scheduled. Although issues of sensitivity may arise, as well as issues to do with material which attracts immunity from disclosure by reason of some greater public interest (often police intelligence), confidentiality of the type being discussed in this article will not often arise in relation to this type of internal, police material.

Secondly there is what might be called the fruits of the investigation. When the police investigate crime they are duty-bound to be open-minded. They must pursue all reasonable lines of enquiry, whether these point towards or away from the suspect.[8] Thus at the end of the investigation there will often be a great deal

---

[4]   *R v. H and C* [2004] UKHL 3.

[5]   Review of Disclosure in Criminal Proceedings: September 2011. http://www.judiciary.gov.uk/publications-and-reports/reports/crime/review-disclosure-criminal-proceedings-september-2011.

[6]   Judicial Protocol on the Disclosure of Unused Material in Criminal Cases: December 2013.

[7]   See Criminal Procedure and Investigations Act 1996, S. 3 and S. 8.

[8]   Criminal Procedure and Investigations Act 1996 (Code of Practice) 2005 Order, para. 3.5; see also CPS Disclosure Manual, chap. 4.

of material: witness statements, exhibits, interview recordings of various sorts, transcripts and so on, some of it helpful to the prosecution, some of it not.

The prosecution (police and lawyers) will assemble its evidential case from all of this material. All material which comes into the hands of the police during an investigation will either be used by the prosecution as part of its evidential case (and served on the defence as such), or if not used by the Prosecution then the material is called 'unused material'. The police have been given guidance[9] as to what should be retained by them for possible disclosure of unused material.

Unused Material is scheduled by the nominated disclosure officer and those schedules will be inspected by a lawyer at the Crown Prosecution Service – the organisation which actually brings criminal proceedings to court – who must apply the standard disclosure test (see below). With the exception of sensitive material (usually 'intelligence' material) which is scheduled separately, the schedules themselves and a copy of any item contained in them which passes that standard test must be given to the defence. This process should be straightforward for a lawyer, and in cases of doubt, the original material, rather than just the schedule, will be inspected. The police are not lawyers but their procedures have been framed and developed with this duty of open disclosure in mind.

The defence can, and often do, request access to or copies of items of scheduled Unused Material. If the prosecution objects to the disclosure of material which has been requested by the defence, then there is a relatively simple procedure[10] which involves the judge deciding the issue.

The standard test for the disclosure of Unused Material in the hands of the prosecution is whether it is 'material which might reasonably be considered capable of undermining the case for the prosecution against the accused or of assisting the case for the accused'.[11] In applying the standard test, the prosecution and the judge are helped as to the disclosability of unused material by the contents of the defence case statement[12] which is required to be served pretrial. This document should set out the nature of the defence case and identify the factual and legal issues.

So, if an organisation such as INFORM speaks to the police investigating a crime and voluntarily hands over its files, the defence will get to see anything in them which is used by the prosecution as part of its evidential case. However, the chances are that even if the files are treated as Unused Material by the prosecution, the defence will also see anything in them which passes the standard disclosure test. In deciding whether to hand over its files voluntarily, the organisation will

---

9   Code of Practice issued under s23 of the 1996 Act, para. 5.4.
10   Criminal Procedure and Investigations Act 1996, S. 8.
11   Criminal Procedure and Investigations Act 1996 (as amended), S. 3.
12   Criminal Procedure and Investigations Act 1996, Ss. 6 and 6A.

obviously be able to take into account any issues of confidentiality which may arise. We shall see below what happens if the organisation refuses to hand over its files voluntarily to either side.

Third Party Material

The other principal category of disclosure material is third party material. Unsurprisingly this refers to material which is not and never has been in the hands of the prosecution. For historical and not very convincing reasons, disclosure of this type of material is treated differently, and it is here that the tension with confidentiality is likely to be most apparent.

By way of illustration, I have said that at an early stage of the Lyons court proceedings, the defence began to suggest that the so-called conspiracy against the defendant might have included INFORM itself. This occurred well after the main police investigation and well after Lyons had been charged. To a large extent, the prosecution had assembled its evidential case. The court proceedings were at the pretrial case management stage. At that point the prosecution had no intention of calling any witnesses from INFORM, and none of its files had been seen or seized by the police. INFORM was thus a third party and its files remained in its own possession. In those circumstances, when the defence started to point the finger at INFORM, the prosecution (in accordance with its duty to be open-minded and fair[13]), had to make a decision whether to seek access to the files. On the other hand the police had no duty to take speculative enquiries.

Early indications were that, for very understandable reasons, INFORM was not going to hand over its files voluntarily to anyone. If the defence believed that there was material in the hands of a third party which they wished to see, and might possibly have used, then they could have started by trying to persuade the police to approach the third party on their behalf. In the real world, the practicalities are that Third Parties are more likely to respond to a request from the police than from the defence. If the police do obtain the material, then time and money can be saved, and the prosecution can also avoid nasty surprises. So, as we have seen already, if the third party voluntarily hands its files over, then the issue of disclosure becomes routine.

If the police decline to help either because they consider the enquiry to be purely speculative or because they are refused voluntary cooperation by the third party, or if the defence themselves have got nowhere by asking nicely, then there is a rather cumbersome procedure[14] by which either side can apply to the judge to order the third party to produce the material. The third party (or any person

---

[13]   Attorney General's Guidelines (2005), para. 51 and 52.
[14]   Criminal Procedure (Attendance of Witnesses) Act 1965 (as amended), S. 2(2).

to whom the information relates has a right to be heard on any such application) will be able to defeat the request if the material in question is not likely to be 'material evidence'.[15] These words are significant because they exclude from disclosure any material which is not capable of being legally admissible evidence. This test is obviously not the same as the standard test for disclosure. Another refinement of this procedure is that, even in a case where the material is likely to be material evidence, the procedural rules explicitly require the judge to take into account any issues of confidentiality which arise.

Thus the judge must balance the right of the defendant to a fair trial with competing interests such as the third party's right or duty of confidentiality or the rights of a person to whom the information relates under Article 8 of the European Convention on Human Rights. For reasons which I shall explain, the judge in the Lyons case never had to decide the matter.

The Trial

In the Lyons case, as in most cases of serious sexual assault, many of the complainants had given their accounts to police in video-recorded interviews. There is official guidance[16] as to how such interviews should take place. In some trials (not the Lyons case) the recording can be used as the witness's evidence-in-chief.[17] Breaches of the guidance can lead to the recording being excluded from evidence.

Whilst not in breach of the guidance, the interviews in this case were lengthy and numerous. The interviewing officers went into minute circumstantial detail with the complainants, often repetitiously. Because the investigation stretched over many years, some complainants were interviewed in this way on different occasions and by different officers. All of these interviews were recorded, transcribed and disclosed to the defence.

More questions mean more answers, which means more scope for inconsistency. As I have explained, previous inconsistent statements may provide valuable ammunition for the defence. Whether, in the end, any particular inconsistency is important or not is a matter for the jury to decide, but from the defence viewpoint, the more versions the merrier. I think many prosecutors and judges would agree that over-elaborate police interviewing can be counterproductive. Quite apart from being tedious for everyone concerned, such interviewing can end up confusing the witness. Anxious complainants

---

[15] Criminal Procedure Rules 2013, Part 28.7.

[16] Achieving Best Evidence in Criminal Proceedings: Guidance for Vulnerable or Intimidated Witnesses, including Children 2002 (www.cps.gov.uk).

[17] Youth Justice and Criminal Evidence Act 1999, S. 27.

describing intimate events may find it difficult to concentrate for hours on end and to be as precise about detail as the officer might wish. It is common for complainants in sex cases to feel they are themselves to blame in some way for what happened to them. All the more so if, as in the Lyons case, some had consented to 'alternative treatment' and only realised what was really happening to them after it had started.

Further, complainants will often be interviewed well before anyone knows what line the accused will take. The police are not to know whether or not a defendant will answer questions in police interview under caution or whether he will ever give evidence at his trial. Either way they will not know how his defence case is going to be presented in court. As it turned out, the basic case presented on behalf of Lyons was a denial of any sexual activity at all. But he might just as easily have decided to present a positive case of consent rather than the 'putting to proof' exercise which in fact occurred. So, during the initial investigation the police were obliged to cover the question of consent with the complainants from every conceivable point of view. However in such situations, the police ought to be well aware that all of these interviews may end up being analysed in court, word by word. Brevity is a virtue.

In the same way, if anyone else receives from a complainant an account of a sexual assault, it must be appreciated that the account given may end up being scrutinised in court. If a note of the conversation has been taken and is handed to the police, then that note itself may well be disclosed and used. This applies as much to helpers at organisations such as INFORM as to anyone else, and it is no real solution to avoid taking a note since other difficult problems will then arise.

At the early stage when it was still being suggested that INFORM might be a party to the alleged conspiracy, the defence wished to explore whether there was any third party material in the hands of INFORM which might support this line of defence. They indicated that they wanted to see any and all records of contact between INFORM and many other individuals involved in the case. INFORM had indicated they would not voluntarily hand over their files to the police, so it was highly unlikely they would hand them to the defence. On this basis alone, it seemed easier and quicker for the prosecution to set in train the cumbersome court procedure for obtaining third party material.

There was the possibility that within INFORM's files there were notes of previous inconsistent accounts from complainants. When, in due course, leading prosecution counsel (me) personally examined the files, it was discovered that they contained no such material, but even the possibility added to the need for a proper examination of INFORM's files with the likely issues at trial in mind. The duty to consider the disclosure of Unused Material is not a once and for all paper exercise by the CPS lawyer on the schedules. The duty to review disclosure is continuous throughout the trial,[18] and the primary duty to manage that process on a day to day basis is that of prosecution counsel. A similar principle applies when considering whether to seek third party material. What may seem a fanciful line of defence or a 'fishing expedition' at the start may turn out to be a beast with legs. What is not thought to have any relevance may suddenly acquire it.

In the Lyons case, the CPS drafted the necessary written applications to the court but unfortunately did so without sufficient specificity in the request as to what was being sought. It was an unduly wide request. It had not been fully appreciated that there were people who had spoken to INFORM but who were not, and never intended to be, witnesses. INFORM was understandably alarmed by the very widely drafted request for 'blanket' disclosure. They obtained legal advice and resisted the application, probably not fully appreciating that this request was in reality being made by the prosecution trying to be helpful to the defence and in pursuance of its duty to be fair.

Counsel privately instructed by INFORM undertook an initial trawl of the files, but he could only decide what might be relevant using the necessarily limited insight he had as to the issues in the case. Further, the duty to review disclosure cannot be assumed by anyone other than prosecution counsel.

When the duty to keep disclosure under review was fully explained to INFORM and when an undertaking was given that the confidentiality of non-witnesses would be preserved, INFORM did agree to voluntary disclosure to the prosecution. The CPS then withdrew its application to the court. Unfortunately INFORM had already incurred the costs of its legal advice, and naturally it sought to recover those substantial costs. In the end the public purse had to pay.

Confidentiality

In all of these situations, it must clearly be understood that confidentiality has its limits. It will be trumped by the need to secure a fair trial. If confidential material is prosecution material (used or unused) then issues arising from the confidential nature of the material will hopefully already have been taken into account by the party handing it over to the prosecution. There will probably have been a waiver by the person entitled to confidentiality. If the third party material court procedure is being used, the judge must take the issues of confidentiality and Article 8 ECHR rights into account but the exercise is still a balancing of competing interests.

Now an organisation such as INFORM cannot be expected to act as an investigator. Nor can it be expected to create, maintain and retain its records

---

[18]   Criminal Procedure and Investigations Act 1996, S. 7A.

with a view to later scrutiny by the courts. Its work may be hampered it if has to warn informants that there is always a possibility that what they say will not remain confidential. On the other hand, INFORM acknowledges its duty to report crime to the police. If such an organisation does become involved in the trial process then it needs to be prepared. It would be well advised to have a clear policy and procedure in place as to how to deal with requests for access to its files from either side. Whether this means that it should warn informants of what might, in truth, be a remote possibility of confidentiality being set aside is not for me to say, but it is better to think about the problem and to plan for it rather than to wait for it to arise and be taken by surprise. It might also be cheaper. Had INFORM fought and lost the disclosure battle in court, it would have had to bear its own costs. For a charity this would have been serious.

Over the years, these practical difficulties have arisen in other similar situations, notably in relation to files held by local authority social services departments in cases of alleged sexual abuse of children. Local protocols operate in various court areas which set out in detail the steps which all of the parties are expected to take so that unnecessary delays and wasted costs are avoided. In 2006 the first national Protocol was published, in effect, by the senior judiciary, which covered the whole area of disclosure in the Crown Court but which included specific guidance in relation to third party material. That has now been replaced by the new Protocol (referred to above) issued in December 2013.[19]

The approach of our law to confidentiality is different to that, for example, in France where the disclosure of confidential information 'information à caractère secret' by a person entrusted with it, either because of his position or profession, or because of a temporary function or mission, is a crime, and the person breaking the confidence can be fined or sent to prison.[20]

In the most general terms our law is that, even where there has been no waiver, a professional can break the confidentiality of a client or patient and can do so subject only to his own professional rules and possibly to the civil law. It may result in the professional being struck off or sued, but it will not be punished by the state as a crime. Whether or not the material which the professional passes on in breach of confidence will be usable in court brings us to the issue of admissibility.

Admissiblility

We have seen that when considering whether to order that third party material should be handed over to a requesting party, the judge will refuse the application

---

[19]   Judicial Protocol on the Disclosure of Unused Material in Criminal Cases: December 2013, paras. 44–50.

[20]   Art. 226-13 of the French Criminal Code ("Code Pénal").

unless the material in question is likely to be 'material evidence'. This means, in effect, that the material in question must, prima facie, be admissible into evidence. There is some academic debate and conflicting legal authority as to exactly what this means in practice, but there is no need to explore those technical issues in this chapter.

We have also seen that the application of the standard test for disclosure of unused prosecution material may well result in the material being disclosed to the defence. Once the material has been handed over, inevitably the next question is whether the material can be used in court.

In our law there is one, overarching test for admissibility – relevance. If evidence is not relevant, then it will not be admissible. If it is relevant then, prima facie, it will be admissible.

Ironically there will be material in respect of which there is no duty to disclose which may still be relevant and admissible. Putting aside questions of legal professional privilege, some communications between lawyers and clients and communications with experts could conceivably be used in court. The same is true for material disclosed in error, even if the party seeking to use it should not normally have seen it. In criminal cases, by virtue of the special procedure used for material which attracts immunity from disclosure by reason of some greater public interest (PII), the judge may see the material, decide that it is relevant and order it to be disclosed. The only remedy for the prosecution if they do not wish to comply with the judge's order is to abandon the case.

Commercially sensitive material will certainly be admissible provided it passes the appropriate test. Even evidence which has been unlawfully obtained will not necessarily be inadmissible.

In the first Lyons trial the American father, himself an attorney, came to London and gave evidence for the prosecution in order to try to rebut the 'conspiracy' allegation. He explained that he had come to London because he hoped just to see his daughter with whom he had not had any contact for many months. He came into court knowing that his daughter was claiming he had raped and abused her. He was prepared for that accusation to be made to his face. What he was not prepared for was to be cross-examined by the defence using a file which he maintained had been previously stolen from the family home in Florida. The file contained the results of a great deal of research into Lyons and his friends, and it was something which was of obvious interest to the defence. The daughter in due course admitted on oath that she had paid others to obtain the file illegally. The father expressed astonishment that his private file, which he had last seen months ago in his home (and the theft of which he had reported to the police in the U.S.), suddenly appeared in the hands of Lyons's defence lawyers in London being used in order to try to show how determined he was to destroy Lyons. He was finally rendered speechless when, during further cross-examination, he was shown and asked about printouts of emails, and he realised that in order for the defence to have these documents, someone had hacked his and his wife's private email accounts.

Conclusion

It should therefore come as no surprise that, depending on the issues in the case, confidential material such as INFORM's files, whether it has been given to the prosecution voluntarily or obtained by means of the third party court procedure, may well be both disclosable and usable in an English criminal trial. Repeatedly I have referred to the concept of 'the fair trial' which has been central to English jurisprudence for centuries. It did not take the Human Rights Act nor Article 6 of the European Convention on Human Rights to make our legal system aware of this fundamental right. The duty of disclosure has long been recognised as an integral part of the guarantee that an accused will be fairly treated by the State. On the other hand, although it has often been said that a criminal trial is not a game of cricket, it might be thought unfair that when a victim of rape speaks in confidence about her experience to a friend, a doctor, a therapist, or an organisation like INFORM, both she and her audience need to be alert to the possibility that months or years later the conversation itself and any records of it will be picked apart in front of a jury by experts in the use of words and the art of persuasion.

References

Barker, Eileen. 2001. 'INFORM: Bringing the Sociology of Religion to the Public Space'. In *Frontier Religions in Public Space*, edited by Pauline Cote, 21–43.

Barker, Eileen. 2006. 'What Shall We Do about the Cults? Policies, Information, and the Perspective of INFORM'. In *The New religious Question: State Regulation or State Interference?* edited by Pauline Cote and Jeremy Gunn, 371–94. New York: Peter Lang.

Beckford, James A. 2008. 'Cults Need Vigilance, Not Alarmism'. *Church Times*, June 18. http://www.churchtimes.co.uk/articles/2008/20-june/comment/cults-need-vigilance,-not-alarmism, accessed November 14, 2013.

Chapter 5

The Resurrection of Religion in the U.S.? "Sacred Tea" Cases, the Religious Freedom Restoration Act, and the War on Drugs

James T. Richardson and Jennifer Shoemaker

Introduction

The United States Supreme Court issued a major ruling in 2005 in a case with significant ramifications for the role of religion in American life (*Gonzales v. O Centro Esp.*). The decision and its aftermath (discussed below) also could impact how the substance at issue in the case, hoasca tea (sometimes referred to asayahuasca), is defined in other nations around the world. Labate and Feeney (2011) note that religious organizations using this substance, which originated in Brazil, are now active in 38 countries around the world, and that the reception of those groups has varied considerably in those countries.

The unanimous opinion in the *Gonzales* case was written by Chief Justice John Roberts, adding to its gravity. With its reaffirmation that the Religious Freedom Restoration Act (RFRA) was applicable to all federal agencies, this ruling by the Roberts Court not only affirmed that religious considerations must be attended to in any federal governmental action, but the ruling also marked one of the first times that religious considerations have overcome the strong governmental interest in the several decade's long "war on drugs" in the United States.

This chapter will detail the events leading to litigation between the U.S. federal government and the religious organization *O Centro Espirita Beneficente Uniao do Vegetal* (UDV) from the District Court, all the way to the U.S. Supreme Court, which remanded the case back to the District Court for further proceedings. We start with a brief history of religious freedom jurisprudence in the U.S. and background information on the UDV, including on the hoasca tea which is at the heart of this issue. Following a presentation of highlights of the UDV's court battle, we discuss the Roberts Court and religious clause jurisprudence and offer an examination of the Court's posture toward religious freedom issues.

We then examine a second "tea case," involving The Church of the Holy Light of the Queen (CHLQ), a Santo Daime church in Ashland, Oregon. This group also faced legal difficulties regarding its use of Daime tea in its religious ceremonies (Daime tea also contains dimethyltryptamine—DMT, as does the UDV's hoasca tea).

In conclusion, we examine the ramifications that decisions in these two cases may have on public policy in the United States, particularly concerning the ongoing "war on drugs" in the United States.

Religious Freedom in the United States

The Religious Freedom Restoration Act (RFRA) was passed nearly unanimously by Congress in 1993 in reaction to a major shift in religious freedom jurisprudence announced in *Employment Div. v. Smith*. This was a case out of the State of Oregon in which the Court unexpectedly dismissed the "compelling interest" test that had been a major rule of law for decades in the area of religious freedom. RFRA prohibited the Federal Government from substantially burdening a person's exercise of religion, "even if the burden results from a rule of general applicability," except when the government can "demonstrat[e] that application of the burden to the person (1) [furthers] a compelling government interest; and (2) is the least restrictive means of furthering that ... interest" (*Gonzales v. O Centro Esp.*, par. 424). Prior to *Smith*, when one's religious freedom was to be impinged upon by governmental action, the government was required to demonstrate a compelling state interest in pursuing its chosen course of action, and that there were no other less restrictive means to accomplish the governmental interest.[1]

RFRA was originally applicable to all governmental actions, whether federal, state, or local in origin. However, in 1997 RFRA was overturned by the United States Supreme Court in *City of Boerne v. Flores* as to its applicability to state and local government actions. That case involved a dispute between a Catholic Church in Boerne, Texas, and city authorities over the expansion of a Catholic church which was designated a historic building in a historic district,

---

[1]   It is worth noting that the compelling interest test was often ignored in practice. Gedicks (1995) calls the test "illusory," and notes that it has seldom been enforced in cases involving minority faiths.

thus requiring governmental approval before any changes could be made in the building. Local zoning officials rejected a request for a building permit to expand the church, and the Catholic Bishop of San Antonio filed a suit against the city, claiming that the church's rights under RFRA were violated. The suit was lost at the District Court level, with the Court declaring RFRA unconstitutional. On appeal to the Fifth Circuit Court of Appeals, Bishop Flores prevailed, but then the City of Boerne appealed to the Supreme Court, which found RFRA unconstitutional as to local and state government and ruled in favor of the City of Boerne. However, *Boerne* left open whether RFRA remained applicable to actions of federal agencies.[2]

However, the U.S. Supreme Court ruled unanimously, with Chief Justice John Roberts writing the opinion, that RFRA was still the law of the land when federal agencies took action that impinged upon the religious freedom of individuals and groups in the United States, even if that religious freedom involved the use of banned substances. This quite significant ruling in *Gonzales v. O Centro Esp.*, demonstrated a possible new direction of the Roberts Court in cases dealing with religious freedom. We will present background information on the group involved, on the case brought by the group, tracing the many machinations of the case as it has evolved over the past decade in federal courts in the U.S., and examining the significance of this case in relation to the war on drugs. We also will examine implications of this watershed moment in church and state jurisprudence in America, including a new case from the State of Oregon which relies heavily on the precedent set by the *Gonzales* ruling.

Introduction to the UDV

UDV is a religion founded in Brazil, blending "Indigenous and Amazonian spiritual traditions within Christian theology" ("Press Summary"). While the history of this religion goes back hundreds of years, it was in 1961 that UDV emerged as a distinct religious practice. The UDV has approximately 7,000 members in Brazil, but the presence of the UDV in the United States is considerably smaller, with only a few hundred members. The Christian doctrine of the UDV includes a belief in Jesus Christ as the Son of God, and members are taught to love thy neighbor as thyself. Unlike mainstream Christianity, however, the UDV believes in reincarnation of the spirit in an evolution toward "Purification," or sainthood.

---

[2]   See Richardson (1999).

Translated, Uniao do Vegetal literally means "the union of the plants" ("Press Summary"). The UDV believes that the Amazon forest holds spiritual values, and therefore, protection of the environment is an important component of UDV's doctrine. Members strive to live in harmony with nature, which includes planting and managing mariri (*Banisteriopsis caapi*) and chacrona (*Psychotria sp*) (Alexander 2008), both of which are used to make hoasca tea, a central element of the UDV's religious ceremony.

Hoasca Tea and DMT

Hoasca tea used by UDV members is at the heart of legal battles with government authorities in the United States and elsewhere.[3] As part of their religious ceremonies, UDV members ingest hoasca tea, which they believe aids in mental concentration, necessary in order to "experience communion with God" ("Press Summary"). Hoasca tea contains dimethyltryptamine (DMT), which is categorized as a Schedule I hallucinogen in the Federal Controlled Substances Act.

The Controlled Substances Act was passed by the United States Congress in 1970 for the legal regulation of substances. Passage of the Act heralded the beginning of the "war on drugs" launched by the administration of President Richard Nixon. The Act contains five "sub-schedules," ranging from Schedule I, substances with a high likelihood of abuse, to Schedule V, substances with a low potential for abuse. Because DMT is a Schedule I drug, it is one of the most highly regulated substances under the Act (Chapter 1), and the government considers it illegal to be imported or distributed, including as an ingredient in hoasca tea. Because the UDV was importing and using the tea as part of religious ceremonies in the U.S., the government began investigating the organization, culminating in actions being taken to stop importation and use of hoasca tea by

---

[3]   Use of the substance hoasca (sometimes spelled ayahuasca) has been legal since 1992 in Brazil, but in some other nations in recent years the decisions are mixed. Arrests of practitioners have occurred in Germany, France, Spain, and the Netherlands, but most of those arrested have since been released after further investigation and court decisions affirming Santo Daime is a religion. The United Nations International Narcotics Control Board issued a report in 2001 that DMT, the active agent in hoasca tea is not subject to legal control. This UN report apparently played a major role in some decisions reached in European countries concerning use of hoasca tea. See www.erowid.org for more details on the chemical make-up of the tea and what has happened in other nations as well as the United States concerning its legal status. For excellent summaries of the international challenges faced in attempting to regulate the religious use of hoasca tea, see Labate and Feeney (2012) and Feeney and Labate (2013).

the UDV. This action resulted, perhaps inadvertently; in a major test of religious freedom considerations versus the "war on drugs" that has been an important part of American domestic and foreign policy for years.

Litigation

On May 21, 1999, U.S. Customs agents confiscated church records, computers, and hoasca tea from UDV national headquarters in Santa Fe, New Mexico. While the U.S. government did not press any charges against the UDV at this time, it did inform the UDV that it would prosecute in the future for any hoasca importation and/or possession. The plants that are used to make the tea do not grow in the U.S.; therefore, the UDV did not have access to hoasca after the confiscation and threat of prosecution. By denying the UDV access to and use of hoasca tea, the government was denying members supplies that UDV participants claimed were needed to practice the religion, thus allegedly impinging upon their religious freedom.

In December of 2000, the UDV filed a Complaint for Declaratory and Injunctive Relief against the U.S. government with the U.S. District Court of New Mexico. The UDV argument was based on five issues: The Equal Protection Clause of the Fourteenth Amendment to the United States Constitution, the Controlled Substances Act (CSA), The First Amendment of the United States Constitution, international law, and the Religious Freedom Restoration Act.

Outcome of the Original Motion and Subsequent Court Cases

In its decision on the complaint filed by the UDV, the District Court found that the defendants, the U.S. government, did not violate the Plaintiff's rights under the Controlled Substances Act (CSA), the First Amendment, or international law. However, the Court found that the Plaintiff's rights had been violated under RFRA, and therefore the preliminary injunction sought by the UDV was granted by the District Court. This injunction allowed the ritual use of hoasca to continue while the legal action was being resolved. The Court deferred ruling on the claims under the Equal Protection Clause because these claims referred primarily to the type of relief sought by the Plaintiffs.

In their motion, the Plaintiffs argued that the CSA is only applicable to pure DMT, and that hoasca tea is different enough from pure DMT that it should not be considered an illegal substance under the CSA. The District Court was not convinced by the Plaintiff's arguments, and concluded that hoasca, like pure DMT, is considered an illegal substance under the CSA. As a part of this argument, the UDV cited *Employment Div. v. Smith*, which allowed the Native American Church to use peyote, also a Schedule I hallucinogenic, in its religious ceremonies. Because church members are explicitly allowed to use peyote for religious purposes under the federal regulatory exemption, it would seem that the use of peyote by members of the Native American Church is not considered to be in violation of the CSA. The Court disagreed, stating that the CSA is a neutral, generally applicable law acceptable under *Smith*, and therefore the Court did not extend the "peyote exemption" to the UDV.

The motion was also denied based on the First Amendment. According to the First Amendment, "Congress shall make no law respecting an establishment of religion, or prohibiting the free exercise thereof." The plaintiffs argued that the CSA prohibits their free exercise of religion. Ingestion of hoasca tea is a fundamental practice to the UDV religion. Therefore, by preventing members from obtaining the tea, the government is causing members to be unable to participate in this fundamental religious practice.

The UDV also claimed, under RFRA, that their freedom of religion had been "substantially burdened." When a plaintiff brings a claim under RFRA, the plaintiff must first present evidence that his or her religious freedom has been substantially burdened by the government. Once the plaintiff meets "the threshold requirements by a preponderance of the evidence," then "the burden shifts to the government to demonstrate that the challenged regulation furthers a compelling state interest in the least restrictive manner" (*O Centro Esp. v. Ashcroft* 2002). The Court accepted the claim that the government's actions constituted a substantial burden on the UDV member's practice of their religion. Therefore, the burden shifted to the government to show that the confiscation of and ban on importing hoasca was the least restrictive means of fighting the use of controlled substances in the U.S. If the government cannot meet this burden, then the court must find a violation of RFRA.

The government contended that it had three compelling interests for its actions: (1) Adhering to the 1971 Convention on Psychotropic Substances, (2) preventing the health and safety risks posed by hoasca, and (3) preventing the diversion of hoasca to non-religious use. The District Court found that the government did not meet the burden placed on it; the government did not show that hoasca presented a significant health risk to UDV members, nor was there a significant risk of hoasca being diverted for non-religious use.

Regarding the government's concern about possible diversion of hoasca for non-religious use, testimony from both sides was again conflictual. The government presented expert testimony that the positive effects of hoasca ingestion, the recent rise in the use of hallucinogens in the U.S., rising internet interest in hoasca, and the vulnerability of international shipping of controlled substances would contribute to a high potential for diversion of hoasca. Conversely, the Plaintiff's experts maintained that potential for non-religious use of hoasca is minimal because demand for hoasca would be low based on its negative side effects, the availability of substitute drugs, the small amount of hoasca imported by the UDV, the minimal potential market for the tea, and the UDV's motivation for keeping the tea supply from being diverted (based on the belief that use of hoasca outside of religious ceremonies is sacrilegious).

The District Court concluded that the government did not meet the burden of demonstrating a "compelling interest." Therefore, the likelihood of the Plaintiff's success of their claim under RFRA was good, and the Court granted the Plaintiff's Motion for an injunction under RFRA.

In summary, the Court concluded that the UDV had met the standards required for preliminary injunctive relief:

1. The UDV demonstrated a likelihood of success with its RFRA claim.
2. UDV members will suffer irreparable harm to the freedom to practice their religion as a result of the government's actions.
3. The potential injury to the Plaintiffs outweighs injury to the defendants.
4. The public interest served by upholding UDV members' right to practice their religion favors granting the injunction.

Court of Appeal

The Justice Department appealed the District Court's decision to grant the preliminary injunction. The Court of Appeals for the Tenth Circuit Court upheld the District Court's decision to grant the preliminary injunction, agreeing with the District Court's analysis. However, one Justice (Murphy) filed a dissenting opinion, asserting that the Court erred in its decision that "the status quo here is not the need to enforce the CSA [Controlled Substances Act] but rather UDV's religious practice free from a governmentally imposed burden." (*O Centro Esp. v. Ashcroft* 2003). Murphy contended that the status quo is the enforcement of the CSA, a strong statement evidencing the deference given to the war on drugs in many court decisions in recent years. Additionally, Murphy argued that the U.S. Government did carry its burden to show that hoasca poses health risks to UDV members, and that there is potential for hoasca to be diverted for non-religious uses. Justice Murphy also denied that the UDV met its burden to demonstrate the third and fourth factors required for a preliminary injunction—the potential injury to the plaintiffs and the public interest served by upholding UDV members' right to practice their religion.

En Banc Review

The government's next step was to request an en banc review of the preliminary injunction (a review by all the Justices of the Appeals Court). This request was granted, and on November 12, 2004, Justice Seymour issued an opinion which was joined in whole by five judges and in part by two judges (*O Centro Espirita Beneficente Uniao do Vegetal v. Ashcroft* 2004). This opinion supported the prior decision that the potential injury to the plaintiffs outweighs injury to the defendants.

Justice McConnell issued a separate opinion which was joined in whole by one and in part by two other justices, stating agreement with Justice Murphy's concern regarding the status quo issue, and his concern that the UDV should be required to meet a heightened standard of justification, given the concern about drug use in American society. Unlike Justice Murphy, however, Justice McConnell's opinion concluded that the UDV had met this heightened standard. Justice Murphy issued an opinion in this case also, which was joined in whole by three justices and in part by three justices. Here he revisited the status quo issue, stating that the UDV did not meet a heightened standard of proof (which contradicts the aforementioned opinion in the case issued by Justice McConnell). This opinion also concluded that the preliminary injunction, which discounted the importance of the 1971 Convention on Psychotropic Substances, could be detrimental to the U.S. Government's ability to gain cooperation from other countries in controlling illegal drug trade.

Additionally, Justice Hartz wrote a dissenting opinion expressing his view that the UDV was unlikely to succeed with its RFRA claim based on the compelling interest of the government to uphold the Controlled Substances Act. This was another strong statement indicating the tradition of support for the government's efforts to control the use of substances deemed harmful under national law and in treaties. However, overall the *en banc* review resulted in the Court's denial of the government's request to stay the injunction granted by the District Court.

United States Supreme Court

In February 2005, the government petitioned for a Writ of Certiorari, which was granted on April 18, 2005. The question to be decided by the Supreme Court was whether the Religious Freedom Restoration Act of 1993, 42 U.S.C. 2000bb et seq., requires the Government to permit the importation, distribution, possession, and use of a Schedule I hallucinogenic controlled substance, where Congress has found that the substance has a high potential for abuse, it is unsafe for use even under medical supervision, and its importation and distribution would violate an international treaty ("Petition").

Thus the issue was clearly joined, and RFRA was pitted against the long-term efforts of the government in its "war on drugs."

The petition was based on the argument that enforcement of the preliminary injunction bars the government from enforcing the Controlled Substances Act and violates the 1971 Convention on Psychotropic Substances. In the Petition for a Writ of Certiorari, then Attorney General Alberto R. Gonzales stated that the decision to grant the preliminary injunction "is contrary ... to the decision of every other court of appeals to address similar religion-based requests for exemptions from the Nation's drug laws." The Supreme Court granted the petition, thus setting up a major test of the reach of the "war on drugs" in contemporary American society.

This case granted the Roberts Court a significant opportunity to take a strong stand on the role of religion in American society. The Supreme Court ruled in favor of the preliminary injunction, stating that "the Government has not carried the burden expressly placed on it by Congress in the Religious Freedom Restoration Act" (*Gonzales v. O Centro Esp.*). In part I of Chief Justice Roberts's opinion, the Court laid out the facts of the case, including an explanation of the Religious Freedom Restoration Act, the Controlled Substances Act, background of the UDV, and a summary of the case up to the present hearing. In Part II, Justice Roberts noted that the government conceded the fact that the UDV had established a *prima facie* case under RFRA regarding the burden to their religious freedom by application of the Controlled Substances Act. Additionally, the government failed to prove that prohibiting the importation and use of hoasca by the UDV would be justified by the asserted compelling interests. According to the Supreme Court opinion, RFRA places the burden on the government to prove a compelling interest, which the government did not do. Part III of the opinion dealt with the government's second line of argument, concerning the inclusion of DMT on the Controlled Substances Act of Schedule I drugs. The government argues that allowing the importation and use of hoasca will weaken the CSA, leading to further religious exemptions. The Court's response was three-fold.

First, the language of RFRA states that the compelling interest test be applied to each claimant, and therefore a ruling in one case does not necessarily mean the ruling will be the same in similar cases. Each case must be examined in light of the individual circumstances. Second, the Court dismissed the government's claim that the listing of DMT on Schedule I of the CSA should unquestionably prohibit the UDV's import and use of hoasca. This dismissal was based on the CSA's allowance for the Attorney General to make exceptions to the Act based on public health and safety findings. This allowance is what sanctioned the exemption made to the Native American Church for its use of peyote in its religious ceremonies (peyote also is a Schedule I substance). The third part of the Court's response addressed the government's claim that the CSA is "a closed regulatory system that admits of no exceptions under RFRA" (*Gonzales v. O Centro Esp.*). The government here was arguing for uniformity—that granting an exception to the UDV would open the door for more exemptions. However, the Court also refuted this argument by citing the peyote exception to the CSA.

Part IV, the final part to the Court's opinion, regarded the government's assertion that an exemption for the UDV would violate the 1971 United Nations Convention on Psychotropic Substances. The District Court had found that hoasca is different enough from DMT itself as to not be included as part of the Convention. On this point, the Supreme Court disagreed with the District Court, based on part of the Convention that specifically includes solutions or mixtures containing substances covered in the Convention. However, the government did not produce evidence demonstrating the "international consequences" of granting an exemption for hoasca. Therefore, the Court ruled that the government had not met the compelling interest test, and the Supreme Court affirmed the decision made by the Court of Appeals in favor of the UDV, upholding the injunction, and remanded the case to the District Court for further proceedings.

The Roberts Court and Religion Clause Jurisprudence

There have been few assessments of the Roberts Court's posture on religion cases, mainly because Justice Roberts's tenure on the Court began only a few years ago on September 29, 2005. However, a few commentators have offered some tentative assessments of the few rulings involving religion made by the Roberts Court so far. Douglas Kmiec, writing in the *Pepperdine Law Review*[4] examines the first two years of the Roberts Court, focusing on a case that may be telling of Roberts's posture toward religious jurisprudence. *Hein v. Freedom*

---

4   Also see Esbeck (2008).

from Religion Foundation involved an effort by a taxpayer to sue to stop the expenditure of significant funds controlled by the White House which were being used to promote President Bush's faith-based initiatives. Chief Justice Roberts joined the controlling plurality opinion by Justice Alito that upheld the major holding on standing from the famous *Flast v. Cohen*[5] case decided by the Warren Court but precluded standing as to the current action. Justices Scalia and Thomas wanted to overturn *Flast*, but this position did not prevail, and the actions of the Administration in support of faith-based initiatives passed constitutional muster.

In 2008 noted constitutional scholar Erwin Chemerinsky and Marci Hamilton, who successfully argued the *Boerne* case before the Supreme Court in 1997, presented a review of key Supreme Court cases, including the *Hein* case (Chemerinsky & Hamilton). Hamilton is clearly unhappy with the *Hein* decision that allows expenditures by the Executive Branch in support of religion to go unchallenged. She is complimentary of the organization that brought the suit (the Freedom from Religion Foundation), and critical of the limitation that the Court brought to the original *Flast* decision. Hamilton adds: "The bottom line is that the Executive Branch now knows that it cannot be challenged by taxpayers for expenditures ... such as funding religion."

The *Hein* decision may portend other rulings that favor a larger role of religion in public life in America. Noted constitutional scholar Erwin Chemerinsky has opined that this is the case, in an article assessing the Roberts Court's first year of operation. He says, among other things, that the addition of Justice Alito itself changes the Court's posture toward religion: "I read over 200 of Judge Alito's Third Circuit opinions, and the one area where he was less conservative than the Supreme Court was with regard to the free exercise of religion" (para. 551). After indicating that he does not yet think there are enough votes to overturn *Smith*, Chemerinsky then says:

> I think the place in religion where we are going to see the change is the Establishment Clause because I think here we now have five votes—Roberts, Scalia, Kennedy, Thomas, and Alito—to allow much more government aid to religion, to allow much more religious involvement in government, and to overrule the test that's controlled the Establishment Clause since 1971 (para. 552).

---

[5]   This 1968 ruling by the U.S. Supreme Court resulted in the Flast test, a two-part test to determine if a taxpayer had standing to sue the government in federal courts to prevent an unconstitutional use of taxpayer funds. In the ruling, the Court determined that the Plaintiffs met both nexuses of the test, and therefore the case would be heard.

Chemerinsky refers, of course, to the famous "Lemon test" from *Lemon v. Kurtzman.*[6]

Chemerinsky in the same review article also summarizes the UDV case and offers this conclusion:

> I think this case is important because it indicates that the Court does treat the Religious Freedom Restoration Act as constitutional when applied to the federal government. I also think it shows that the Court is using a very robust, traditional form of strict scrutiny under the law (para. 543).

2008 District Court Hearing

The remanded UDV case was heard on April 9, 2008, in Federal District Court in Albuquerque, New Mexico. The government claimed that the UDV lacked standing to bring a suit for injunctive relief. A plaintiff must satisfy two conditions in order to be in good standing to seek relief: (1) there must be "a good chance" that the defendant will injure the plaintiff in the future" and (2) "the relief requested is likely to prevent the injury from occurring" ("Plaintiffs' response"). Because the government has asserted that it will prosecute the UDV in the future if it continues to import and consume hoasca, the UDV asserted that it satisfies both conditions and therefore has standing to seek injunctive relief.

District Judge James A. Parker issued his opinion on the case June 16, 2008. He cited the complexity of the issues involved in the case, and on that basis, the Court addressed only part of the Defendant's Motion to Dismiss. The Court ruled that the Motion to Dismiss should be granted as to the plaintiff's free exercise, equal protection, and international law claims (Counts 6–8, respectively). However, the Court did not rule on the RFRA claim at this time, which led the two sides to begin the settlement negotiations that were eventually concluded in July of 2010.

---

[6]   A recent case, Pleasant Grove City, Utah v. Summum (129 S. Ct. 1125 (2009)) suggests that Chemerinsky may be correct concerning changes in Establishment Clause jurisprudence. In Pleasant Grove the Supreme Court ruled against an effort to place a monument displaying the "Seven Aphorisms of Summum" in a park in which a monument displaying the Ten Commandments was allowed. See Bartrum (2009).

Final Settlement

In July of 2010 the two sides finally reached a settlement which can be considered a major victory in the battle for religious freedom. While many details were addressed in the settlement agreement, the most important point is this: the UDV won the right to continue to import and ingest the hoasca tea without U.S. governmental interference (so long as the government has no reason other than the fact that hoasca contains DMT). Secondly, the U.S. Government must pay the legal fees and expenses that the UDV incurred as they fought eleven years for the freedom to practice their religion (an undisclosed amount). The UDV must comply with strict regulations, including accounting for all hoasca importation and use and disposal and maintenance of a Drug Enforcement Administration (DEA) registration by each UDV congregation importing the hoasca tea. However, these regulations seem reasonable given the considerable concerns raised by the international importation of a substance containing a Schedule I drug. The attorney for the UDV, Nancy Hollander said, "I would consider it a true win. The UDV members won the right to practice their religion and the government was forced to pay the legal fees and expenses that ten years of litigation costs to get there."[7]

Setting a Precedent: The Second "Tea Case"

In September of 2008, the CHLQ brought an action before the District Court in Oregon in a case with almost identical facts to that of the UDV case from New Mexico. This case involved Santo Daime, another Brazilian religion. The CHLQ is a Santo Daime church in Ashland, Oregon. In 1999, U.S. federal agents raided the home of Jonathan Goldman, a Santo Daime padronho (spiritual leader) and founder of the CHLQ. During the raid, agents seized Daime tea, which is identical to the hoasca tea used by the UDV. The Santo Daime use the tea in their religious ceremonies, and it is considered to be an essential sacrament of the religion. Claiming that the tea is an essential part of the practice of their religion, members of the CHLQ church asserted that by confiscating the tea, federal agents were substantially burdening members' practice of their religion.

After the raid by federal agents, CHLQ attempted to negotiate an agreement with the U.S. Department of Justice, which the Department refused to consider. However, the Oregon Board of Pharmacy did determine that the "CHLQ's

---

[7]   Personal communication, August 12, 2011.

religious use of Daime tea was a "non-drug," and therefore "not subject to state laws and regulations" (*Church of the Holy Light, et al. v. Mukasey, et al.*). CHLQ sought a permanent injunction to allow it to import and use Daime tea in religious ceremonies.

The arguments presented by both sides in this case were similar to those in the UDV case. On March 18, 2009, Judge Owen M. Panner of the Oregon District Court ruled in the case of *Church of the Holy Light, et al. v. Mukasey, et al.* that the Defendants had not presented evidence that met the compelling interest burden; the plaintiffs, however, *had* met their burden of proof. Therefore, Judge Panner issued a permanent injunction on behalf of the CHLQ (Panner 2009b). In his decision, Panner relied heavily on the decision of the U.S. Supreme Court in the UDV case from New Mexico. Judge Panner did impose rigorous conditions on the Holy Light group for their continued use of the sacred tea (Panner 2009a), but his ruling was a major victory for the group, and a significant loss for the government, not only in this second "tea case," but also in the continuing "war on drugs" that had gained such deference in other legal actions.[8]

It is worth noting that in the second tea case an expert statement was submitted on behalf of the defendants (the hovernment) by a noted scholar of new religions, Professor Lorne Dawson, from the departments of Sociology and Religious Studies at University of Waterloo, Waterloo, Ontario, Canada (Dawson). The 64-page statement critiqued the studies offered by the plaintiffs claiming that use of sacred tea substances in both the New Mexico and Oregon cases was not harmful to those involved. The thorough critique of those studies questioned the scientific merit of many of the studies submitted, raising a question about why motions were not made to exclude the studies under current evidence law in the United States which requires judges to assess the scientific validity of any such evidence proffered. However, this was not done, and the Judge apparently paid little attention to the critique, and instead considered the matter settled law after the ruling of the United States Supreme Court in the UDV case from New Mexico.[9]

---

[8]   See Judge Panner's findings in Panner (2009a, b), the latter of which lists a number of conditions on the continued use of the tea in religious ceremonies.

[9]   Current evidence law is governed by the Daubert trilogy (see Ginsburg and Richardson 1996) requiring judges to serve as "gatekeepers" who assess the scientific quality of proffered evidence before allowing it to be heard by a jury. The criteria used include (1) falsifiability (testability) of claims made, (2) error rate in applying theories; (3) general acceptance of methods and findings, and (4) whether the findings have been subject to peer review and published. Also, the Daubert series of cases includes a fifth criterion, that being whether the research was done specifically for the case at hand. If so, the research was to be discounted, if not totally disallowed. In the tea cases some of the studies cited by the plaintiffs

Implications of UDV for the "War on Drugs"

One other very important implication to note is that the original UDV case represents one of the first times that the nation's long-running "war on drugs," established through statute and governmental policy, has been forced to show deference to religious freedom concerns. This implication is not unrelated to the previous discussion of the possible growing interest of the Roberts Court in supporting more involvement of religion in American public life. Perhaps the decade's-long concern about drug use is being supplanted in part by concern about the role of religion in American society.

The "war on drugs," since its inception decades ago, has pervaded all areas of American life and has garnered considerable deference from the courts. We have seen a number of Bill of Rights provisions and federal statutes subjugated to enforcement of efforts to control drugs over the years. But many have declared the war a failure and have decried the disruptions it has brought to American society.[10] The "tea cases" may herald an important new chapter in the continuing battle between the effort to control drugs and other concerns for personal freedoms in the United States, including religious freedom. The fact that the Supreme Court would, even after being reminded by then Attorney General Gonzales that the Appeal Court decision in the New Mexico case granting the injunction "is contrary ... to the decision of every other court of appeals to address similar religion-based requests from the Nation's drug laws" ("Petition"), rule so firmly against the government is quite significant.

Until the *UDV* case, the only religious based exemption from the nation's drug laws was for peyote, which is used by members of the Native American Church (and which was the focus of the famous *Smith* decision of 1990 that led to passage of RFRA). Now there are two exceptions, with the second being hoasca tea used by the UDV and other Brazilian-based religious groups. A recent law review article by Mark Levine presses the case that the courts, after *UDV*, should also recognize marijuana use by the Rastafarians as another exemption to the nation's drug laws (par. 187). He is critical of the effort by the Court in the *UDV* case to focus on similarities that exist between religious uses of peyote and hoasca tea, while ignoring other cases involving use of marijuana, which is also a Schedule I drug, as a religious sacrament. Levine cites *Olsen v. Drug Enforcement Admin.*,

---

were done in preparation for litigation. However, all these criteria were ignored by the Judge in the Oregon case, who ruled in favor of the plaintiffs using the precedent of the UDV New Mexico case.

[10]   Among many assessments from major figures and media outlets in America, see Cronkite (2006) and Cardoso, Vaviria, and Zedille (2009).

where an effort of the Ethiopian Zion Coptic Church to gain an exemption to allow the use of marijuana in its rituals was rejected. He notes that there are more similarities between the Rastafarians and the hoasca tea imbibing religious groups than there are between the Native American Church and the UDV, and asked why the religious uses of marijuana were ignored by the Supreme Court.

Whether Levine's logic will prevail and yet another illegal drug will be added to the pantheon of those deemed acceptable by the courts remains to be seen. Levine himself seems doubtful, but whatever the outcome of his argument, it is clear that religious concerns have been raised to a new level in American society with the *UDV* decision, and the "war on drugs" has suffered a setback in the courts. This possible realignment of values could represent a major change in religion-based jurisprudence in America.

Conclusions

The United States Supreme Court's decision in the New Mexico "sacred tea case" has immense ramifications for public policy in the United States, and may well influence how other nations deal with religious groups using the substance as part of their rituals. While rejecting all other claims of the UDV, the Court affirmed strongly (via the unanimous decision authored by Chief Justice Roberts) in the UDV case that RFRA does apply to federal agencies, thus removing any lingering doubt resulting from the *Boerne* decision (see Richardson 1999). The strongly worded ruling in *UDV* requires any federal agency attempting to take an action that could arguably impinge on a group or person's religious freedom to pass muster under the compelling interest and least restrictive means tests required under RFRA. The impact of this holding already has been amply demonstrated in the second "tea case" from Oregon.

This affirmation of RFRA as applying to federal agencies may mark a quite different chapter in religious freedom jurisprudence in this country under the Roberts Court. This posture on such cases seems a major new development in the controversy over the role of religion and whether religious groups have too much power in American society, as some such as Marci Hamilton have argued.

One other very important implication to note is that the original UDV case represents one of the first times that the nation's long-running war on drugs, established through statute and governmental policy, has been forced to show deference to religious freedom concerns. The war on drugs has seen a number of Bill of Rights provisions and federal statutes subjugated to enforcement efforts to control drugs over the years. The "tea cases" may herald another chapter in the continuing battle between the effort to control drugs and other concerns for personal freedoms in the United States, including religious freedom. Whether this ruling will affect how other nations define and treat the use of hoasca tea or Ayahuasca remains to be seen.

References

Alexander, Steven. "Mariri (Banisteriopsis caapi) vine II" *Tropical Biodiversity— The Amazon*." E. Guinn, C. Barrigar, and K.K. Young. 1 May 2007. Web. 19 March 2008.

Bartrum, Ian. 2009. "*Pleasant Grove v. Summum*: Losing the Battle to Win the War." *Virginia Law Review in Brief* 95: 43–8.

Cardoso, F.H., C. Vaviria, and E. Zedille. 2009. "The War on Drugs is a Failure." *Wall Street Journal*, February 23.

Chemerinsky, Erwin and Marci Hamilton. 2008. "Nineteenth Annual Supreme Review: First Amendment Decisions." *Touro Law Review* 23: 756–7.

Chemerinsky, Erwin. 2006. "The Rookie Year of the Roberts Court and a Look Ahead." *Pepperdine Law Review* 34: 551–2.

Church of the Holy Light of the Queen, et al. v. Michael B. Mukasey, et al. 615 F Supp 2d 1210 (2009).

City of Boerne v. Flores. 521 U.S. 507 (1999).

Controlled Substances Act, Pub. L. 91-513. 84 Stat. 1236. October 27, 1970.

Cronkite, Walter. 2006. "Telling the Truth about the War on Drugs." *The Huffington Post*, March 1.

Dawson, Lorne. *Witness Statement of Lorne Dawson, Ph.D.* Filed in Federal District Court, Portland, OR: 2008. Available from first author.

Employment Division v. Smith, 494 U.S. 872 (1990).

Esbeck, Carl H. 2008. "What the *Hein* Decision Can Tell Us about the Roberts Court and the Establishment Clause." *Mississippi Law Journal* 78: 199–226.

Feeney, K. and B. Labate. 2013. "Religious Freedom and the Expansion of Ayahuasca Ceremonies in Europe." In *Breaking Conventions: Essays on Psychedelic Conventions*, edited by C. Adams, D. Luke, A. Waldstein, B. Sessa, and D. King, 117–28. London: Strange Attractor Press.

Flast v. Cohen. 392 U.S. 83 (1968).

Gedicks, Frederick Mark. 1995. "RFRA and the Possibility of Justice." *Montana Law Review* 56: 95–117.

Ginsburg, G.P. and J.T. Richardson. 1996. "'Brainwashing' Evidence in Light of *Daubert.*" In *Law and Science*, edited by Helen Reece, 265–88. Oxford: Oxford University Press.

Gonzales v. O Centro Espirita Beneficente Uniao do Vegetal. 546 U.S. 418 (2006).

Hamilton, Marci. 2005. *God vs. the Gavel*. New York: Cambridge University Press.

Hein v. Freedom from Religion Foundation. 127 S. Ct. 2553 (2007).

Kmiec, D. 2008."An Enigmatic Court? Examining the Roberts Court as it Begins Year Three." *Pepperdine Law Review* 35: 465–568.

Labate, Beatriz and Kevin Feeney. 2012. "Ayahuasca and the Process of Regulation in Brazil and Internationally: Implications and Challenges." *International Journal of Drug Policy* 23: 154161.

Lemon v. Kurtzman. 403 U.S. 602 (1971).

Levine, Mark. 2009. "An Opiate of the Masses: Religious Gerrymandering and Sacramental Intoxification." *North Carolina Central Law Review* 31: 177–97.

O Centro Espirita Beneficente Uniao do Vegetal v. Ashcroft. 282 F. Supp 2d (2002).

O Centro Espirita Beneficente Uniao do Vegetal v. Ashcroft. 342 F 3d 1170 (2003).

O Centro Espirita Beneficente Uniao do Vegetal v. Ashcroft. 342 F 3d 1170. "Petition for Writ of Certiorari." Filed Sept. 4, 2003.

O Centro Espirita Beneficente Uniao do Vegetal v. Ashcroft, 389 F.3d 973 2004

O Centro Espirita Beneficente Uniao do Vegetal v. Mukasey, CIV. No. 00-1647 JP/RLP. "Plaintiffs' Response to Defendants' Motion to Dismiss." (D.N.M. February 22, 2008)

Olsen v. Drug Enforcement Administration. 878 F.2d 1458. D.C. Cir. (1989).

Panner, O. 2009a. "Findings of Fact and Conclusions of Law." Filed March 18, 2009. In *Church of the Holy Light of the Queen, et al. v. Michael B. Mukasey, et al.* 615 F Supp 2d 1210 (2009).

Panner, O. 2009b. "Judgment." Filed March 19, 2009. In *Church of the Holy Light of the Queen, et al. v. Michael B. Mukasey, et al.* 615 F Supp 2d 1210 (2009).

"Press Summary." *Religious Freedom, the United States Supreme Court and the União do Vegetal*. Available at UDV website: http://www.udvusa.org/udvusa/summary.php.

Richardson, J.T. 1999. "The Religious Freedom Restoration Act: A Short-lived Experiment in Religious Freedom." *Religion and Law in the Global Village*, edited by D.E. Guinn, C. Barrigar, and K.K. Young, 143–64. Atlanta, GA: Scholars Press.

Chapter 6

Religion or Sedition?
The Domestic Terrorism Trial
of the Hutaree, a Michigan-based
Christian Militia[1]

Susan J. Palmer

Introduction

On March 27, 2012, the FBI launched a series of raids, targeting a small, obscure militia group that called themselves "Hutaree." Nine raids were executed simultaneously over five hours in Michigan, Ohio and Indiana. The agencies involved were the Department of Homeland Security and the Terrorism Task Force, who worked with local and state police to execute the search warrants.

The largest raid targeted a memorial service that was held in warehouse in Ann Arbor. Hutaree members had shown up without their guns, prepared to honor a deceased militiaman. The service was interrupted at 6:30 p.m. by 50 FBI agents who made a "dynamic entry" into the warehouse, handcuffed all the guests and arrested the Hutaree leader, his family and core group.

Two days later, nine members of the Hutaree were charged with plotting to wage war against the government, and with conspiring to use "weapons of mass destruction" (Zeskind 2009). They were also charged with planning a guerilla war against police officers using "trip-wired and anti-command detonated antipersonnel IEDs (improvised explosive devices)" (see Palmer 2010). Five Hutaree members were about to spend the next two years in prison.

Mug shots of the nine Hutaree in green prison suits appeared in hundreds of media reports, with headlines like, "Violent underbelly of arrested Hutaree militia members revealed" (Housley 2010). Activist Archie Cary writes:

---

[1]   An earlier version of this chapter was presented at the CESNUR conference, held at Chouaic Doukkali University in El Jadida, Morocco (September 20–22, 2012).

> The [media] ran hard with the story. Within 48 hours, the template was set: A
> "right-wing extremist Christian' militia group had been planning to wreak havoc
> by killing law enforcement officers as a way to engage a wider war against the
> government. Soon the MSM had the Hutarees tried, convicted and jailed." (Cary
> 2010)

The Southern Poverty Law Center used the occasion to highlight the "growing
threat of right-wing militia groups from America's radical right, where a pervasive
rage against the government has become red hot" (SPLC "Hatewatch" 2010).
SPLC spokesperson, Mark Potok, reminded journalists of his 2009 report, *Rage
on the Right*, which documented 512 antigovernment "patriot" groups and a
total of 75 domestic terrorism plots since the 1995 Oklahoma City bombing
(SPLC "Hatewatch" 2010).

Within a month, by May 2010, the Hutaree story had faded from the news,
leaving the public with the conviction that a violent plot had been "thwarted
by the FBI in the nick of time" (Cary 2010). But two years later, when the case
came to trial, a federal judge acquitted all the Hutaree members of all the charges
related to seditious conspiracy. They were released from prison on the same day,
on March 27, 2012.

The Hutaree militia stands out as the very first non-Muslim "domestic
extremist" group to be cast as the lead in what journalist William Grigg (2012)
calls "one of the Bureau's post-911 Homeland Security Theatre productions."
The FBI had first begun investigating Michigan's "white" militia movements in
2008, around the time of Obama's election, as part of the Homeland Security
project to monitor and control right-wing terrorist groups. The Hutaree was
similar to other U.S. militias, in that they saw themselves as defending the
Constitution. Unlike the majority of militias in Michigan, however, they were
religious in their orientation. Their training drills were a preparation for a cosmic
battle between Good and Evil, when Jesus Christ would return to overthrow the
satanic New World Order. They appeared to offer a convenient target for the
Department of Homeland Security and the Joint Terrorism Task Force, whose
agents were under pressure to demonstrate their knowledge and control over
right-wing militia "terrorist" groups after 9/11, at the time of the election and
inauguration of America's first African-American president.

The Hutaree incident is a fascinating story that raises serious questions about
how the U.S. Government, holding true to the Fourth Amendment, tolerates
private militia groups—and yet singles out a few examples of "extremism" and
"fanaticism" for punishment.[2]

---

[2]   When I presented this chapter at the CESNUR conference in Morocco, several
Moroccan scholars expressed their astonishment that the U.S. Government would tolerate
citizens who dressed up in army clothes and ran around in the woods shooting guns and

The FBI's handling of the case, which in retrospect can only be explained as a "sting operation," raises serious concerns about human and civil rights in the post-9/11 "war on terror." The trial of the Hutaree, who were accused of "conspiracy to commit sedition," hinged on the subtle distinctions between Free Speech and Sedition. Finally, the Hutaree story conveys a message about the relative integrity of federal law enforcement versus the U.S. judicial system, and the independence and power of federal judges to uphold the law.[3]

Hutaree, a "Christian Militia"

This relatively small militia group, whose numbers fluctuated between 50 and 150, was founded around 2007 by David Brian Stone (who was 44 at the time of the raid).[4] Stone worked operating a forklift vehicle for a wiring company. He is a devout Christian, the son of a Pentecostal minister. At the time of the raid, he had recently married Tina Mae Stone, also raised in the Pentecostal church. The couple lived in a trailer in Clayton, Michigan, and David Stone regularly attended the Pentecostal church with his three sons and new wife. David

---

practicing paramilitary drills. "We would throw them all in jail or execute them if they tried that stuff here," they said.

[3] This research began as a study of the raid on the Hutaree, as part of the project, "Exploring Government Raids on Unconventional Religious Communities," funded by the Social Science and the Humanities Research Council of Canada. I made three trips to Michigan, where I interviewed five Hutaree members, who were acquitted of sedition charges, and conversed with others. I attended the Hutaree September 8, 2012, hog roast fundraiser party, "Too Late to Apologize," and a dog show (pit bull conformation competition), and the March 27, 2013, celebration one year after their "Victory Over the FBI." I also interviewed three federal attorneys, William Swor (2012), Richard Helfrick (2012) and Michael Rataj (2013) in their Detroit offices or over the phone. I had flown to Detroit on March 26, 2012, to attend the trial and hear the arguments of the defense—but at that point the judge intervened and dismissed the charges. I was disappointed to miss the trial, but found the lawyers willing to share their legal analysis of this fascinating case. William Swor gave me access to the court records of the 2012 trial, and Michael Rataj supplied me with the FBI's 302s.

In my account of the raid and the subsequent trial, I rely heavily on journalist Lee Higgins's excellent articles in www.annarbor.com. For a general understanding of Michigan's militia subculture, I am indebted to Wendy Lineweaver, Michael Meeks and Thomas Piatek for sharing with me their experiences in Hutaree training, and their knowledge of pit bulls, guns, and the Libertarian "Preparedness" political philosophy.

[4] The group may be older, for David Stone claims his sons invented the nonsense word and concept of "Hutaree" (Christian Warrior) while playing in the woods as children. (Interview with David Stone in a restaurant in Adrian, MI, September 9, 2012).

Stone's Christian beliefs turned out to be an important issue in his 2012 trial. According to William Swor, Stone's defence attorney, David Stone had lived in Adrian, Michigan, almost his whole life. His father was a Pentecostal preacher who homeschooled David and raised him on the book of Revelations (*United States of America v. David Brian Stone*).

According to Robert H. Churchill's study of militia groups (Churchill 2008), there are two types: "Constitutional" (political extremist groups who defend the earlier versions of the American Constitution) and "Millenarian" groups (which have a religious agenda, and are preparing for Jesus's return and the final battle between God and Satan). The Hutaree belong to the second type, as may be seen by studying their website which quotes from apocalyptic Bible passages: "We believe that one day, as prophecy says, there will be an Anti-Christ.... Jesus wanted us to be ready to defend ourselves using the sword and stay alive using equipment."

The Origins of the Raid

The origins of the Hutaree investigation can be traced back to 2008, when the Department of Homeland Security produced a report about the rising threat of right-wing terrorism, citing factors like economic troubles, the election of an African-American president, and other perceived threats to U.S. security (Bunkley and Savage 2010). Around the time of Obama's election, the FBI was involved in a background check on militia groups in Michigan. There appear to be three reasons why the government chose the Hutaree as the target of their investigation.

First, David Stone's association with Mark Koernke raised alarm. Koernke has been described in the media as "a notorious anti-government conspiracy theorist with prior convictions for assault of a police officer, resisting arrest and fleeing police, for which he served just over seven years in prison" (Higgins 2010e). The 2008 FBI report claims Koernke had "a long history with law enforcement and was released from prison on 3/15/2007 from his most recent felony conviction" (FBI Report 2008). In fact, Koernke was neither a member nor a leader in the Hutaree. It was later established that he was a close friend and mentor of David Stone, but that he had never attended any of the Hutaree's meetings or training drills. Koernke was an ideologue in libertarian circles, an orator with his own radio station (Lineweaver 2012). According to a court filing by Todd Shanker of the Federal Defender Office, it appears that erroneous information on Koernke derived from an FBI agent's conversations with a member of the South Michigan Volunteer Association, who had identified Mark Koernke as one of the two leaders of Hutaree (Higgins, 2010e).

Second, the FBI investigated the Hutaree as the result of an ATF records check. On December 8, 2008, when ATF agents visited Walter Priest, a federal firearms licensee in Adrian, Michigan, who conducted his business, *Gun Outfitters, LLC*, out of his home, they discovered he had sold components of AR-15s to David Stone. On hearing about the records check, Stone sent out an email encouraging militia members to resist the ATF. On February 5, 2009, the ATF executed a search warrant at Priest's home, looking for materials used to make explosives. Priest's 25-year-old son, Walter Jason Priest, had recently been convicted of using explosive materials and on January 22, 2009, was sentenced to federal prison for possessing a firearm after his first conviction (Higgins 2010c). The government argued at David Stone's March 2010 bond hearing that he had been plotting to break Jason Priest out of jail. Stone and the Hutaree members all denied this allegation.

Third, the Hutaree investigation was one result of the Homeland Security's imperative to root out potential terrorists. In 2008, FBI agent Leslie Larsen had sought out leaders of the Southeast Michigan Volunteer Militia (SMVM) as part of her investigation into the possibility of domestic terrorism among Michigan's "white" militia groups. Two SMVM leaders had provided her with information about Hutaree, according to two emails obtained by journalist Lee Higgins from the online newspaper, AnnArbor.com (Higgins 2010d). These emails were sent eight months before the ATF record check.

In an interview with Lee Higgins, SMVM Coordinator Lee Miracle and SMVM spokesman Michael Lackomar said they had discussed Hutaree with FBI agents the day before the 2008 presidential election. "The decision was made to cooperate with the authorities fully because we do value good relations with local and federal law enforcement," Lackomar said. "In addition, we knew that one of the groups they were talking about, the Hutaree, struck us as potentially unstable and possibly dangerous" (Higgins 2010d).

It appears that the SMVM leaders may have deflected an FBI investigation into their own militia by pointing the finger at the Hutaree, whom they appeared to regard askance, as a fanatical Christian "cult." In her article ("America's New Kinder, Gentler Militia") journalist Temple-Raston contrasts the "old-style militias bent on violence" with the "new, more helpful militia—the kind ... no one needs to be scared of." She quotes SMVM spokesman, Mike Lackomar, who comments on his experience of training with Hutaree in the woods:

> I thought they were a little reckless ... they focused on ambushes, concealment,
> fire team movements ... skills that might be needed in a firefight. They trained at

> Level 10 all the time…. They focused more on the military aspect than on the civil
> aspect, which we try to balance out. (Temple-Raston 2010)

A fourth reason for the investigation emerged during the March-April 2010 bond hearing. FBI agent Leslie Larsen claimed that when she began monitoring the activities of militia groups in Michigan, back in August 2008, she was alarmed by the Hutaree website. It featured the members outfitted in military clothing and backpacks, stalking an invisible enemy, crawling on their bellies through woodlands, and firing rifle and handguns at unseen targets. But what alarmed her, she testified, were the explosions in one of the videos (*United States of America v. David Brian Stone*). But the veracity of her statement was challenged by David Stone's lawyer, William Swor (2012), who pointed to the YouTube records that prove that the alarming Hutaree videos were not posted until June 2009—almost a year after Leslie Larsen sent the FBI's undercover informant in to spy on the Hutaree.[5]

The FBI Investigation

There were three phases to the FBI investigation. First, a paid undercover informer was sent in (Baldas 2012a). Second, an FBI agent who was an expert in making bombs was inserted into the Hutaree undercover. Third, the FBI faked the death of the first infiltrator and staged a memorial service in order to lure the Hutaree to a warehouse in the woods where they could be rounded up, unarmed.

The Paid Informer

In February 2009, the FBI inserted Dan Murray into the Hutaree. Murray, 57, was a martial arts instructor who worked in security. He was first approached by agent Larson while he was minding a security system for the Ford automobile show in Detroit. It was established at the 2012 trial that the FBI had paid Murray $30,677 in cash from August 2008 to January 2010, for 300-odd hours of undercover services and expenses (White 2012). According to William Swor, "Murray did not disclose the payments he received on his income tax. Nor did the FBI report the payments to the IRS. Both were violations of federal law."

---

5   I found out when I attended the Hutaree fundraiser, "Too Late to Apologize" on September 8, 2012, that these videos were filmed by David Stone's youngest son, David Jr., with his friend Joshua Clough, as an entertaining and instructive project.

Murray attended Hutaree meetings and paramilitary drills in Lenawee and Washtenaw counties. Hutaree members welcomed him, and gave him the code name of "Keebilik." Murray was wired with devices to make audio and video recordings of their conversations. He taped David Stone's speeches about the Return of Christ, and of how the government was planting computer chips under the skin of its citizens through flu shots in order to control them, referring to "666 the Mark of the Beast" in Revelation.[6]

According to his own testimony in the trial, Murray tried to bait Stone into expressing seditious sentiments. During a (recorded) late-night phone call, he said to Stone, "God, I hate the government!" But when asked by a defence lawyer if Stone had replied, "Me too," Murray responded, "I don't believe so." While Murray admitted in court that he had never felt personally threatened by the Hutaree, he insisted they stockpiled rifles and submachine guns, grenades and other weapons as well as food and fuel, in order to be prepared for the Tribulation, or hard times ahead when the government would turn against its own people (Higgins 2011b).

The Agent Provocateur

In January 2010 the FBI sent in one of their own agents, Steven Haug, whom Murray had already introduced to David Stone at a fast food restaurant as his "best friend." The FBI established a cover identity for Haug as "Steven Clark," a truck driver living in New Jersey who worked for a transport company that dealt in antique furniture at flea markets in Michigan, and they rented a warehouse in Ann Arbor to add legitimacy to his cover. Haug's code name in the Hutaree was "Jersey Steve," and he proceeded to ingratiate himself with their leader, treating him to restaurant meals and paying for travel expenses to attend militia rallies (Baldas 2012a). He even bought diapers for David Stone's grandson.[7] Stone liked and trusted him, and even chose him as best man at his wedding to Tina. A wedding photograph shows "Jersey Steve" posing beside the happy couple. In his capacity as best man, Steven Haug signed their marriage certificate, using his fake name. In the 2012 trial the defense lawyers raised the point that this faked signature was illegal and may have invalidated the Stones's marriage certificate. Attorney Michael Rataj commented on FBI ethics in this situation, as follows: "[Haug] claimed he had been given permission, but the government never

---

[6]   Stone's most controversial statement (later played in court) was his outline of a scenario in which the Hutaree would kill policemen and their families.

[7]   One SMVM member noted, "That should have been a red flag right there. Everyone knows that militiamen are cheap f-ers!" (Personal communication).

produced any document to support that claim.... I don't understand how the FBI thinks it can authorize an agent to commit a crime!" (Rataj 2013).

The Staged Memorial Service

The Hutaree members were arrested in a dramatic raid on Steven Haug's rented warehouse in Ann Arbor on March 27, 2010 (Reiter 2012). The FBI had arranged for their arrest by staging a phony memorial service. Detroit's FBI Special Agent in Charge, Andrew Arena, declined to provide details about the memorial scenario, but told the Detroit Free Press, "We used the ruse to get them to a location where they didn't have access to their weapons, and everything worked out. We got most of them there" (Schmidt 2010). Steven Haug ("Jersey Steve") phoned David Stone to invite his family and Hutaree friends to the wake he was holding for his late friend Dan Murray (code name "Keebilik") at his warehouse. The FBI waited until all the guests arrived, then secured the perimeter and posted snipers in the woods. David Stone was invited to step outside for a smoke by Jersey Steve, who slammed the warehouse door as they left, as a prearranged signal. The SWAT team then swarmed in, backed up by helicopters and armoured trucks. Hutaree members were overpowered, handcuffed, and all the guests were interrogated. Most of the guests were friends or relatives, so they let them go home.

Wendy Lineweaver, Hutaree member (code name Lady Pit Bull) who attended the memorial service but escaped arrest, offers a detailed account of the raid at the warehouse (Higgins 2010e; Lineweaver 2012). She describes how she drove to the warehouse with her husband, stepson, and other Hutaree members, including David Stone and his family. They arrived at 6:10 p.m., and she immediately noticed several "red flags" as she approached the warehouse.

First, she observed a large sticker of the Hutaree green patch plastered on the warehouse door, which she thought "tacky," since their militia unit didn't actually own the warehouse. Jersey Steve appeared nervous ("his voice was shaking when I spoke to him"). She wondered how he had got there because she hadn't seen his "nice truck with New Jersey license plates" parked outside. Also, it also seemed strange that no members of Keebilik's family were there.

Next, Lineweaver remarked on the lack of effort put into organizing the service. The food consisted of sandwiches, bags of chips and soft drinks. When Lineweaver looked up at the warehouse's loft where boxes were stacked, she noticed that the steps leading up to the loft had been cut off and removed. The first step began five feet above the floor. ("All the stairs were freshly sawed off except the top two.")

Keebelik's "battle dress uniform" and helmet was draped over a chair that was perched on a table, with a white candle lit beside it, his rifles at the foot. Folding chairs were arranged around a brand new television hooked up to a DVD player. Lineweaver noticed mistakes in the program, including a mispelling of "Keebelik," and a reference to Hutaree as "The Hutaree."[8]

"There must have been about fifteen red flags that I totally ignored. Every instinct was telling me to get out," Lineweaver said. "But I liked Dan ... or thought I did."

Jersey Steve announced that his wife had put together a slideshow, but that she was sick so couldn't attend. The guests then helped themselves to the refreshments and sat down to share their memories of Keebilik. Jersey Steve turned on the DVD player and started the program. There were photographs of Keebelik with a soundtrack of the Hutaree's favorite band, Poker Face. The music was turned up to full volume. Fifteen minutes into the service, Jersey Steve tapped David Stone on the shoulder and motioned for him to follow him outside. The door slammed loudly behind them.

Everyone perked up. We all looked at each other like (Lineweaver, 2012), "What in the hell was that?" The music was still blaring. Twenty seconds ticked by. Suddenly, more than twenty men in "riot gear" stormed in with M-4 assault rifles, yelling, "Don't move! Don't move!" "Everybody sat there and just stared at them. We all had this glazed look in our eyes like it was a joke. I thought, 'What? Is Dave testing us?'"

The men wore olive drab uniforms, Kevlar helmets and bulletproof vests. ("Then I saw the FBI patches.") The agents ordered everyone to put their hands on the back of their heads and lock their fingers together. Hutaree members were told to stand up against the wall with their backs to the agents, their hands were placed in zip ties, their shoes removed, and they were directed to lie face down and were searched.

David Stone, Tina Stone, David Stone Jr., Joshua Clough and Michael Meeks were arrested on the spot. The Lineweavers were questioned in separate rooms. Agents asked questions about whether Hutaree members built explosives or possessed automatic weapons. In his interview with journalist Lee Higgins from the *Ann Arbor News*, Ken Lineweaver said he had attended around ten Hutaree trainings, but "Nobody talked about making bombs. We never had any bomb-making classes and if somebody was, I never heard about it" (Higgins 2010d).

Wendy Lineweaver was asked if she hated the government. "We, the People are the government," she responded. When asked whether she hated cops, she

---

[8]   It is a Hutaree convention to omit the article before "Hutaree."

explained how she had worked with Washtenaw County sheriff's deputies to assist in a search for missing Bridgewater Township residents. "I have no issues with local cops or federal law enforcement agents."

FBI agents were simultaneously executing eight other search warrants in Michigan, Ohio and Indiana, for over four-and-a-half hours. Kris Sickles and Thomas Piatek were arrested in Ohio, and Joshua Stone was arrested in northeast Illinois on Monday, April 2. Joshua Stone, David Stone's second son, was not present while the raids were in progress, and he turned to another militia group, the Lenawee County Volunteer Militia (known as the "Wolverines") for help. Matt Savino, one of their leaders, phoned SMVM leader, Michael Lackomar, to tell him he had met with Joshua Stone, three other Hutaree men, two women and a young child around 11 p.m. Saturday, outside an Adrian convenience store. Joshua had told Savino that federal agents (whom he assumed were the ATF) had just raided his home, and was asking him for refuge. Savino encouraged Joshua to turn himself in to the feds, but Joshua Stone replied, "That's not an option" (Higgins 2010a). But two days later, he turned himself in, on Monday night, 48 hours after the raid.

The raid was executed with tremendous force; what Hutaree leader David Stone termed "shock and awe" (Stone 2010). It was comparable to the 1993 Waco raid in its militarized scale. Lineweaver noted, "The INS, the immigration was there, the state police, the local sheriff, the Feds set up a huge command center at the sheriff's place, there were satellites, and multiple homes in three states were raided.... It was mind boggling!" (Lineweaver 2012).

The Indictment

The federal grand jury indictment was unsealed two days later, on March 29, 2010. The accused were David Stone Sr.; his two sons, Joshua and David Jr.; Tina Mae Stone; Michael Meeks, 40, of Manchester, Michigan; Thomas Piatek, 46, of Whiting, Indiana; Joshua Clough, 20, of Blissfield; Jacob Ward, 33, of Huron, Ohio; and Kristopher Sickles, 27, of Sandusky, Ohio. All nine were accused of "conspiring to levy war against the United States." Among the allegations were conspiracy to commit sedition, firearms offenses, and attempted use of IEDs and weapons of mass destruction.[9] More specifically they were accused of plotting

---

[9]   The concept of "weapons of mass destruction" (WMD) originated in the 1940s, and refers to nuclear, biological, chemical, and radioactive weaponry, or combinations thereof. In 1994 Congress redefined the term to include "destructive devices"—weapons such as bombs, grenades, mines, and large-bore guns. Senator Joseph Biden drafted the bill shortly

to kill policemen and to launch a bomb attack on a police funeral procession (Bunkley and Savage 2010).

Two defendants were later dropped from the case. Jason Ward was found mentally incompetent to stand trial. Joshua Clough pleaded guilty in December 2012 to illegal use of a firearm, but still faced a mandatory five-year prison sentence. He agreed to appear as a witness to testify for the government.

The Pretrial Legal Process

Two months after the arrests, in April to May 2010, there was a detention hearing in federal court in Detroit. Assistant U.S. Attorney Ronald Waterstreet argued for the detention of the Hutaree.

On April 7, 2010, FBI agent Leslie Larsen was put on the stand for the detention hearings. Prosecutors fought to keep her off the witness stand, but the judge said the burden was on the defence to show their clients would not be a threat to the public if released. When questioned, Larsen said she couldn't recall many details of the two-year probe; that she had not listened to all the recordings made by the infiltrator and an undercover agent. She did not know if the weapons seized by investigators last month were illegal.

Defence lawyer William Swor asked her if David Stone had ever instructed anyone to make a bomb. She replied, "I can't fully answer that question," since she did not have her notes with her. Judge Victoria Roberts exhibited some impatience with the prosecutors, saying: "I share the frustration of the defence ... with all of the responses that are coming from this witness that she doesn't know anything" (Cary 2010).

On March 31, 2010, FBI agent Steven Haug appeared on the witness stand and described how he had infiltrated the Hutaree. He claimed he had built explosives under the direction of David Stone. He described how he had driven David Stone and other Hutaree members in a van to attend a February 6 rally of militias in Kentucky, and how they were forced to turn back because of bad weather. Haug nevertheless managed to record the speech Stone was rehearsing for the rally. In Haug's recording Stone says, "Now it's time to strike and take our nation back so we will be free of tyranny" (Annarbor.com 2010).

Assistant U.S. Attorney Ronald Waterstreet sought to demonstrate the danger posed by the Hutaree by playing a recording of one of their conversations. In this

---

after the 1993 World Trade Center bombing, in which IEDs killed or wounded over 1,000 people. After 9/11, President Bush spoke frequently of "weapons of mass destruction" and it became a household phrase (See Palmer 2010).

the members were interrupting each other, laughing and making goofy noises as they made disparaging remarks about law enforcement (Annarbor.com 2010).

Within a few days, Judge Victoria Roberts ordered the release on bond of the nine Hutaree, over the objections of federal prosecutors. In her 36-page ruling, Roberts wrote:

> The United States is correct that it need not wait until people are killed before it arrests conspirators. But, the Defendants are also correct: their right to engage in hate-filled, venomous speech is a right that deserves First Amendment protection. (Ashenfelter 2010)

The government prosecutors appealed the judge's decision, and won. However, the government agreed to the release of three members: David Stone Jr, Tina Mae Stone, and Jacob Ward. They were instructed to wear electronic monitors and follow strict conditions set by a judge. The remaining five Hutaree were to remain in prison for the next two years (Annarbor.com 2010).

The Search Warrant

In February 2011 the defense attorneys filed a motion claiming that FBI agent Sandra Larsen of the FBI Joint Terrorism Task Force had made several misrepresentations and omissions in the affidavits she used to obtain search warrants for the 27 March 2010 raid against the Hutaree (Higgins 2012b). The motion requested that evidence seized during two searches targeting Stone Jr. be suppressed, since the searches were "unconstitutional." The lawyers who represented 20-year-old David Stone Jr., challenged an affidavit because, over a twenty-month investigation, it "only recounts three occasions where even a hint of the alleged plot against police officers was arguably mentioned,"—yet Stone Jr. wasn't present, therefore didn't participate in any of those conversations. Moreover, in hundreds of hours of secret audio recordings, David Stone Jr. had never said "anything remotely hostile regarding police or government."

The defense team also raised a concern about omissions in the affidavits. For instance, there was no mention of Stone Jr.'s delight about his newborn son, of his decision to move out of his father's house, and of how he told the undercover agent he was no longer keeping militia "stuff" at his home because of the child.

As part of the pretrial "discovery" process, the lawyers submitted a motion to dismiss seven of the eight charges against David Stone Jr.[10] Todd Shanker argued

---

[10]   The charges were seditious conspiracy, conspiracy to use weapons of mass destruction, teaching and demonstrating the use of explosives, two counts each of carrying a firearm during a crime of violence and possessing a firearm in furtherance of a crime of violence.

in his filing that his client "never said an unkind word about anyone" and that the only "military action" the government could possibly attribute to Stone Jr. was his "setting off fireworks at the command of his father during a training session to avoid trip-wires in June of 2009" (Higgins 2012b).

David Stone Jr.'s attorneys also filed a motion requesting a pretrial hearing in which the government must prove by a preponderance of the evidence that a conspiracy existed, and that the defendants were part of it. The motion claims that the government's evidence shows David Stone Jr.'s presence at militia training was "sporadic at best," had attended only some meetings because he didn't want to "break his father's heart" and "in the rare circumstances Stone Jr. is heard on tape, he either talks glowingly about his newborn son or about providing for his young family—by working long hours in a brake-parts factory."[11] The lawyers also called the charge of conspiracy to use a weapon of mass destruction "curious," because, they claimed, there was no allegation in the indictment that any of the defendants ever "accepted, received, or possessed a real, or fake WMD, IED, or EFP" (Higgins 2012b).[12]

In December 2011, a "motion for disclosure and production of confidential informants" was filed by the defense attorneys, seeking information about "Keebilik" and "Jersey Steve."

The trial of the seven Hutaree members was held from February 13 to March 27, 2012, in the federal court house in Detroit before U.S. District Judge Victoria Roberts. It was covered by the media as a high-profile criminal case. The jury was composed of nine women and seven men. David Stone and the other defendants sat in court wearing respectable black suits that Wendy Lineweaver, had found at the Salvation Army, after obtaining the men's measurements.

In the opening statements of the prosecution, Assistant U.S. Attorney Christopher Graveline told the jurors that the Hutaree militia had an arsenal of machine guns and short-barrel rifles and were preparing for war with the government. "These individuals ... wanted a war," he asserted. One of the surveillance videos filmed in Haug's van was played for the jury. David Stone

---

[11]   Stone Jr., was at the time of the motion out on bond, living with his mother, his wife and son. He was studying to obtain his GED and working at a nearby farm three days a week, taking care of sheep.

[12]   An explosively formed projectile or penetrator (EFP) is a simple device composed of a case, a liner and filled with explosive material. It requires a detonator and a firing chain to set it off. Improvised EFPs are usually constructed from a section of well-casing pipe with a plate welded to one end. A small hole is drilled in the pipe to allow a blasting cap to be inserted. The pipe is then filled with high explosive and sealed with a metal liner. EFPs are based on the same principle as a shaped charge munition, like a warhead, that focuses the power of an explosive device (Burton 2007).

Sr. was saying: "We need to quit playing and get serious. This war will come whether we're ready or not. Now is the time to strike and take the nation back." (Bunkely and Savage 2010). Next, the jury was shown a video clip of David Stone Sr. declaring, "Welcome to the revolution" (*United States of America v. David Brian Stone*).

Stacked right in front of the jury box was an impressive display of weapons seized during the raids, with around 148,000 rounds of ammunition. Federal prosecutors claimed that a search of Michael Meeks's residence alone had turned up a cache of bullets and weapons, an extensive food supply and a small plaque with barbed wire with the caption "Remember Waco."

Graveline told the jury that the Hutaree were looking for some type of conflict to trigger an attack, maybe a traffic stop, a search warrant or a dispute between authorities and another militia. "They wanted to start an armed confrontation. The war to them meant patriots rising up against the government," he said, pointing to their weapons. He claimed the defendants were conspiring to ambush and kill a police officer, then attack the funeral procession with explosives, and their purpose was to trigger a broader revolt against the U.S. government (*United States of America v. David Brian Stone*).

On February 16, the fourth day of the trial, Dan Murray's audio recordings were played in court—and there were some damning moments. David Stone spoke of killing police officers, and then going to their homes to burn them down: "And if I kill their wives and their children inside, then so be it, because I'm sending a message to the rest of them" (Bunkley and Savage 2010).

But, according to William Swor, when the government's witnesses were cross examined, they admitted that Stone's statements were based upon the premise that the police had become part of the Army of Satan, and had accepted the Mark of the Beast, along with their families. The witnesses also admitted that the conflict would have to be initiated by the authorities, not by the Hutaree. Indeed, on several occasions government witnesses admitted David Stone had said he would never be the one to fire the first shot.[13]

The government's lawyers told the jury, "They had the weapons, they had the means, we have evidence they were intending, plotting a lethal attack on the police force. They were preparing bombs—weapons of mass destruction and were planning to use them." The jury was instructed that for a conspiracy charge to stick, there doesn't need to be a violent act, just enough to convince them that violence was intended. But the defense lawyers denied that the Hutaree had

---

[13]   William Swor made this statement in his critique of a preliminary draft of my paper (email message of August 22. 2012).

the means. Swor described Hutaree members as living "hand-to-mouth." They couldn't even afford transportation to a regional militia meeting in Kentucky, he said. Steven Haug, the undercover FBI agent, had supplied the gas and a van equipped with a secret video camera in order to record Stone's statements.

The defense lawyers, in their opening statements, framed the case as a First Amendment issue. They downplayed the Hutaree militia's intent and sophistication. They argued that Stone and his associates were all talk and no action, pointing out that no violence had as yet been perpetrated by any of the seven defendants. They argued that the government had manipulated facts to build their case, and misinterpreted the speculative fantasies in the conversations between Hutaree members as a serious plot to overthrow the government. While Hutaree conversation may have been offensive, they argued, it was not illegal. Stone did indeed threaten to kill police officers and their families someday, but there was no mention of a specific plan.

"There was no plan to launch a war," claimed William Swor (2012). "David Stone was exercising his God-given right to shoot his mouth off, talk tough, and say silly things. He criticized the government, as any American citizen has the right to do. There were no concrete plans to 'wage war' or assassinate anybody—just talk."

Swor described his client as a firm believer in the book of Revelation and the rise of the Antichrist. "The anti-Christ as David Stone understands it will come from overseas, and the troops of the anti-Christ will take over America. That is the resistance that David Stone was preparing for." Swor emphasized the religious purpose of Hutaree training, as "contingency training for the Day of Apocalypse, when the forces if the Antichrist literally—not figuratively, not symbolically, not allegorically—but literally invaded the U.S. and took over the U.S. government and proceeded to impose the will of the Antichrist on the people." The Hutaree saw themselves as training for that day, Swor noted—but they would never give a date.

Steve Haug and Dan Murray both tried to get David Stone to tell them when that day would come. But Mr. Stone consistently said, "We don't know." The Hutaree were consistently defensive in their preparation. Their sole purpose was to defend Christ and Christ's nation against the Antichrist in what they believed was to be a literal physical battle. Swor managed to get Dan Murray to admit that on the stand.

Swor emphasized the ludic, speculative quality of Hutaree battle plans:

> They liked to sit around and fantasize about their battles in the Endtime. Someone suggested that they hire strippers to act as decoys in the future battle with the

Devil (that shows you how realistic they were). Mr. Stone was constantly talking about the Endtime. All you have to do with Mr. Stone is say 'Hello'—and he's off! The government played that section where Mr. Stone talks about Hutaree bicycle corps with 18-speed motors and mufflers—for forward reconnaissance. So then Steve Haug says, "Wouldn't it be easier to steal cars? So, Mr. Stone turns the conversation 90 degrees and talks about stealing cars and providing master keys for the cars, not hard to come by, then getting master keys for homes, so they wouldn't have to sleep in the woods. One of Dave's comments, when he was talking about how to survive was, "there's one hundred and one scenarios here!" This shows it was all speculative, just an entertaining fantasy.

Todd Shanker, attorney for David Stone Jr., acknowledged the "offensive statements" on the recordings were "almost fantasy, between friends who were comfortable with each other." Shanker described the Hutaree as more of a "social club" than any organized militia. Defence attorney Satawa quoted Dan Murray's 302 report to the FBI, in which he had said that the Hutaree engaged in much talk without resources to back up their claims. "Let's just leave them alone, a bunch of people playing army in the woods," Murray had pleaded.

On the second day of the trial, FBI agent Leslie Larsen appeared as the first witness for the prosecution (Reiter 2012). Responding to questions from Assistant U.S. Attorney Sheldon Light, Larsen said she learned about the Hutaree members from their website in August, 2008, and explained why she became concerned after watching one of their videos: "In the shooting in and around the vehicles, the firing appeared to be automatic in nature. It appeared to be a large amount of bullets coming out of the weapons."

Agent Larsen also testified about hiring Dan Murray, who she said had been previously used by the FBI to collect information about militia groups in Michigan. In August, 2008, Murray had met David Stone and his son Joshua at an Ann Arbor restaurant. Murray then infiltrated the group, and over the next 17 months he trained and camped with Hutaree members in Lenawee County, as well as attended other training sessions and meetings at remote locations. Over the course of the investigation, the FBI obtained between 200 to 250 hours of audio or video recordings of discussions, agent Larsen claimed.

Under cross-examination Larsen admitted to writing an email during the investigation that suggested she wouldn't be satisfied with just a few charges. Leslie Larsen had written:

> We haven't worked a year and a half on this investigation and risked an Undercover's life to walk away with three arrests. We are in a position to send a

strong signal to other like-minded groups out there that we take them seriously.
(*United States of America v. David Brian Stone*)

Defense lawyers claimed this message proved that justice was not the focus of the FBI's Hutaree probe (White 2012).

Tina Stone's lawyer, Michael Rataj, criticized Larsen's handling of the case, claiming that "Ms. Larsen ... was inexperienced, it was her first case ... and she claims she wants to defuse the situation, but instead she's ramping it up." She had ignored the profilers' report and their recommendations.

The defense team worked to discredit Dan Murray, the chief witness for the prosecution, to portray him as an unstable character. They produced police reports to prove that, in February 2010, Murray had fired a gun at his wife. Murray explained to the court that the shooting had occurred during a domestic argument. "I did not shoot at my wife. I shot my gun at a door," he testified. He had pleaded guilty to discharging a weapon at a building and had received three years' probation (Higgins 2012a).

On another occasion Murray had attempted suicide by stabbing himself, and then accusing his wife of stabbing him when the police arrived. Under cross examination, Murray admitted he had lied to the police about the stabbing incident. The defence lawyers then suggested that Murray's personal psychological problems may have distorted his perceptions of the Hutaree while he was working as an informant.

Attorney Michael Rataj later used this argument in his concluding statement: "And the irony in this case, Your Honor, is that the only person that committed any act of violence was the Government's own confidential informant, Mr. Murray, who shot a nine-millimeter [gun] at his wife, and then stabbed her" (*United States of America v. David Brian Stone*).

Steven Haug appeared as a witness on March 12, 2012. He testified that he had participated in military-style training with the Hutaree in 2009, and often met with leader David Stone at his home and at a fast-food restaurant in Adrian (Reiter 2012). He showed the jury the Hutaree's alleged "kill list" that featured the names of targets he claimed he heard mentioned in Hutaree conversations. These included judges, senators, members of Congress, journalists, bank executives and presidential candidates in 2008. Under cross examination, however, Haug admitted the alleged "kill list" included people who had been dead for years (Reiter 2012).

Haug claimed that guns were an everyday item in Hutaree households. Wedding photographs were shown to the jury in which David Stone Sr., his bride Tina, and four members of the wedding party (including the best man,

Steven Haug) are all holding rifles. In Joshua Stone's wedding photo, several rifles are on display behind the happy couple. Haug claimed that Joshua Stone had once shown him two AR15 rifles stashed in his bedroom and boasted that he was working on one to make it fully automatic, once he received a missing piece. Then Joshua Stone had complained to him about U.S. health care policies, saying, "I look forward to us shootin' this fall ... cause if they push that health care, we're goin' in." Haug had recorded this statement, and it was played for the jury (Baldas 2012c).

David Stone Sr. often spoke of targeting officers, Haug claimed. The jury listened to a recording in which Stone said in case of a domestic war, they could drive around in a minivan, open the sliding door and shoot at officers on the side of the road: "Then you roll to the next one. They start splintering off. Once you divide, you can conquer.... They're going to be screaming on the radio, 'We're under attack!'" (AnnArbor.com 2010).

Haug claimed that Stone Sr. had extensive knowledge about explosives. He often invited Stone to his warehouse to discuss weapons, and they had frequently spoken about building pipe bombs and obtaining other, more sophisticated explosives (Baldas 2012c). Haug claimed he was "shocked" by Stone's work with explosives, noting it matched some of his own instruction as a federal agent: "It was clear to me that (Stone) had a working knowledge of explosives ... IEDs, things of that nature" (Fox News 2012).

William Swor objected that Steven Haug was the only person in the whole case who had ever set off an explosive device. After reporting to agent Larsen that David Stone was afraid of large explosives and determining that David Stone would never build one himself, Haug had built and detonated plastic explosives and a shaped charge. Then, "he tried to get David Stone to order more of them, but Mr. Stone never did" (Swor 2012).

Attorney Michael Rataj summed up the IED situation in his concluding statement at the trial:

> About the IUDs, Stephen Haug was the one who brought the bombs to the party. Twice he brought bombs and exploded them. Mr. Stone said, "Oh! Wow! That's real cool!" That was it—that was the extent of Mr. Stone's "sophisticated knowledge of explosives." (Rataj 2013)

On Thursday, March 15, 2010, the defense lawyers presented a new argument. They argued that, while the government had decided to "nail" the Hutaree as terrorists, they, in fact, never took this backwoods militia seriously. The lawyers then disclosed to the jurors some jocular internal emails written by FBI agents in which they portray the Hutaree as incompetent fools. Agent Larsen refers to Tina Mae Stone as "toothless Tina" in one message, and calls David Stone "scatterbrained." Agent Steven Haug joked about David Stone's infamous hate speech that he had recorded during their trip to Kentucky. When he emailed this speech to various FBI agents, he wrote, "Please hum the Star Spangled Banner and the Battle Hymn of the Republic while reading this. It'll give you goose bumps." In the cross examination William Swor asked, "You were mocking Mr. Stone, weren't you?" Haug replied, "No. I thought it was funny. We joke in law enforcement, sir" (Baldas 2012c).

The jury also listened to a taped telephone conversation in which Haug reports back to the FBI about Stone Sr.'s ranting against police officers. "He really hates the sheriff.... Yeah, it's pretty funny." Swor pointed out that the FBI's internal emails showed a discrepancy between the portrait of a dangerous terrorist group they were trying to construct and the behind-the-scenes expressions of humour and contempt for the Hutaree as a bunch of silly, incompetent backwoods bozos. "The government never took the Hutaree seriously," Swor told the jury (Baldas 2012c).

On March 21, 2012, just before the prosecution finished resting its case, the defense lawyers asked for a mistrial, claiming the government had withheld information that should have been provided under federal law (Baldas 2012b). The information in question concerned a previous relationship between Steven Haug, the government's star witness, and a New Jersey informant on white supremacists and hate groups in 2003. Stephen Haug had been the FBI's handler for the New Jersey informant, Hal Turner, who was a right-wing radio host and blogger who made threats against critics and public officials while on the FBI payroll.

Attorney Michael Rataj noted, "As a defense team, it was just one more example of the government not turning over stuff it should have been turning over."[14] According to Rataj, the prosecution had consistently tried to hide embarrassing information, which amounted to eight violations in the course of the trial (Rataj 2013). William Swor also noted, "This was the eighth time the defense sought a mistrial based on the failure of the government to turn over material that it was legally obligated to disclose" (Swor 2012, email Interview).

Another argument in favor of dismissal of the case was made by William Swor on 26 March 2012. He noted that in April 2010, Leslie Larsen and Mr. Waterstreet swore to the Court that the FBI were expecting an imminent attack by the Hutaree, scheduled to occur in the second week of April. Innocent bystanders were at risk of being injured, and that was the compelling reason for

---

[14] The informant, Turner, had no role in the Michigan militia investigation.

the March 27 raid and arrests. At the time of the Hutaree arrests, U.S. Attorney Barbara McQuade had been quoted in the media saying the time had come to "take them down" (Higgins 2011b). McQuade had defended the timing of the arrests, claiming that the government had vital information that an attack was planned for April 7, 2010.

"Imagine if they had been successful and we had waited," McQuade told the Press. "I think most people would agree that you stop them when you can to protect the public safety. And I think that's what happened here" (Baldas and Swickard 2012). However, it became clear in the course of cross examinations of the government's witnesses that there had never been any emergency, because there had never been any specific date on which an attack was planned (*United States of America v. David Brian Stone*).

The Acquittal

After hearing out the prosecution's case, which started on February 13 and ended on March 26, U.S. District Judge Victoria Roberts called one day of recess to consider motions filed by the defence. At the end of the day, on March 27, Judge Roberts suddenly acquitted all seven of the Hutaree of the seditious conspiracy charges of plotting to overthrow the U.S. government with weapons of mass destruction, and she ordered their immediate release (Baldas and Ashenfelter 2012).

Judge Roberts stated in her 28-page decision that, after five weeks of trial, the federal prosecutors had failed to prove that the Hutaree had any specific plan to kill a police officer and attack law enforcement personnel at the subsequent funeral. She wrote:

> What the government has shown, instead of a concrete agreement and plan to forcibly oppose the authority of the government, is that most—if not all—of these defendants held strong anti-government sentiments. But the court must not guess about what defendants intended to do with their animosity. [While David Stone] may have wanted to engage in a war with the federal government [the evidence] is totally devoid of any agreement to do so between Stone and the other defendants. (Baldas 2012c)

"This plan is utterly short on specifics," she concluded. "It is a stretch to infer that other members of the Hutaree knew of this plan, and agreed to further it." The judge described the prosecution's evidence "minuscule" and "woefully lacking." David Stone's diatribes, she stated, "evince nothing more than his own hatred for—perhaps even desire to fight or kill—law enforcement; this is not the same as seditious conspiracy." Judge Roberts then proceeded to give the prosecution a lesson on law: "The court is aware that protected speech and mere words can be sufficient to show a conspiracy. In this case, however, they do not rise to that level."

As journalist William Grigg pointed out, in the midst of the trial "the Feds shifted their focus" (Grigg 2012). The original indictment accused the Hutaree members of making material preparations to carry out specific criminal acts. Judge Roberts, however, was presented with no evidence to support that charge, and eviscerated their case in a preliminary ruling. At that point the feds shifted their focus and focused on the vague charge of "seditious conspiracy."

Judge Roberts rebuked the prosecution for this shift, citing a Supreme Court precedent (*United States v. Russell*). She noted that the prosecution isn't "free to roam at large—to shift its theory of criminality so as to take advantage of each passing vicissitude of the trial." Roberts observed that the Feds were not free to say that the alleged plan set forth [in the original indictment] was irrelevant. "Yet that is precisely what they attempted to do" (Grigg 2012).

Judge Roberts pointed out the absurdity of some of the allegations. Tina Mae Stone, for example, was described by the prosecution as an "active, engaged and vocal member" of the purported conspiracy—just because she happened to overhear two conversations—one regarding her husband's planned trip to a militia rally in Kentucky with "Jersey Steve"; and the other when she accompanied her husband to the warehouse where he "discussed explosives" with the Stephen Haug. This latter conversation had touched on using coffee cans and wine bottles to make improvised explosively formed projectiles (EFPs). Judge Roberts notes, "Ms. Stone had joked that she would take one for the team and drink more wine, presumably so that the bottles could be used to make explosives." And yet the government took that "wisecrack" as "evidence" that Tina Mae had "played an active, unhesitant, and continuing role in obtaining materials to use in building EFPs" (Grigg 2012).

Judge Roberts acquitted all of the defendants of the two most serious charges: seditious conspiracy and conspiring to use weapons of mass destruction. Because the federal prosecutors had failed to prove their case on those charges, Judge Roberts noted, she also was required to acquit the defendants on five other counts: demonstrating the use of explosives and carrying and possessing a firearm in relation to a crime of violence (Grigg 2012).

As legal experts explained, the prosecutors could not appeal Roberts' decision, which is, in effect, the same as a jury acquittal. The judge's decision left federal prosecutors with what legal experts described as a "run of the mill illegal firearms case." David Stone Sr. and his son, Joshua, were still charged with possession of a machine gun,[15] but they had already pleaded guilty to illegal weapons possession and, in fact, received no further punishment. At their August 2012 trial, Judge Roberts noted that the two years they had already spent in prison were sufficient punishment. Federal prosecutors had asked for additional months in prison, but that, the judge had said, "would not make much sense" (Higgins 2012c).

Significance of the Hutaree Story

The Hutaree was a militia group with a Christian and millenarian worldview. A combination of factors led to the FBI investigation of the "Christian Warrior" Hutaree, as opposed to one of the more secular, politically oriented militia groups in Michigan. The Hutaree story is significant because it addresses important issues; political, legal, religious and human and civil rights. From a political perspective, the Hutaree ordeal is an example of a FBI "sting operation" in the post-9/11 era in which a non-Muslim group was targeted.

Three weeks after the Hutaree's acquittal, an article exposing FBI sting operations appeared in the *Washington Post* (Finn 2012). Author Peter Finn analyzes the March 2012 Pittsburgh arrest of Khalifa Ali al-Akili as an attempted "sting operation" by agent provocateur, Shahed Hussain. Finn describes Hussain as "one of the FBI's most prolific and controversial informants for terrorism cases." Hussain had approached Akili, preaching the ideology of jihad and trying to sell him a gun—but Akili suspected a setup. He wrote on his Facebook page: "I had a feeling [I was in] some Hollywood movie where I had just been introduced to the leader of a 'terrorist' sleeper cell." Akili saw through Shahed Hussain's cover, so the sting failed, although Akili was subsequently arrested on relatively minor gun charges.

Finn notes that "voluminous court records" since the September 11, 2001 attacks have exposed a tactic used increasingly by the FBI, in which "suspects are monitored almost from the beginning of plots and provided with means to help them carry them out." Quoting statistics supplied by the Center on National Security at Fordham Law School, Finn claims there have been 138 terrorism or national security cases involving informants, and the U.S. government has secured convictions in 91% of these cases. Law enforcement officials have

---

[15]   The charges of possession of an unregistered firearm carry maximum penalties of 10 years in prison.

claimed that "sting operations" are a necessary and vital tactic for heading off terrorism. But, according to Michael German (a former FBI undercover agent) they are a "theatrical event that produces more fear in the community."[16] U.S. District Judge, Colleen McMahon, who presided over the trial of four men from Newburgh, New York, who were convicted on terrorism charges, was quoted saying, "I believe beyond a shadow of a doubt that there would have been no crime here except the government instigated it, planned it, and brought it to fruition." Finn quotes civil activists who "say the FBI has been targeting individuals with radical views who, despite brash talk, might have little ability to launch attacks without the government's help." Certainly the Hutaree fit this description.

In a more recent (2013) study, journalist Trevor Aaronson in his book *The Terror Factory* examines over 500 documented cases of men who went to trial as accused terrorists since 9/11 (Aaronson 2013). Aaronson claims his data demonstrates that only five were real, undisputed "terrorists," connected to terrorist cells and had the means to carry out acts of terrorism. Aaronson points out that since 9/11, the FBI have received three billion dollars a year as part of the war on terror initiative, so they are under heavy pressure to come up with results.

From a legal perspective, the Hutaree case should interest historians as one of the rare applications of a law historically rooted in the War of Independence when, in 1798, President John Adams signed into law the Alien and Sedition Acts. Only five cases of seditious conspiracy have gone to trial since the 1967 unsuccessful prosecution of Vietnam War protesters. In the trials of each of these cases, the First Amendment has been a major issue, and the onus has been on the lawyers to redefine the boundaries between Free Speech and Sedition. The Hutaree trial provided a new testing ground for the rarely applied law of sedition and its outcome hinged on this distinction.

U.S. Attorney Mcquade denied that the case was about the First Amendment, as the defense lawyers had claimed. "It wasn't just free speech," McQuade said. "It involved substantial steps in furtherance of a plot to kill police officers. They were stockpiling weapons and machine guns and rounds and rounds of ammunition. And they were building bombs. To me, that is well beyond protected First Amendment speech."

But the defense lawyers argued that Free Speech was the main issue, as Attorney Michael Rataj eloquently explained:

---

[16] He is a counsel at the American Civil Liberties Union and former undercover FBI agent, according to Finn (2012).

The FBI took a few sentences out of 200 hours of surveillance audios and videos, took them out of context, and didn't show what was said before and after. Big talkers can say some nasty things. But anyone can sit on their back doorstep and drink beer and tell their friends. "I hate cops! I would like to put a bullet in their heads!" But that's not illegal, that's protected speech. It's like the rapper, Ice Tea [sic]. After the Rodney King incident, he came out with a rap song, "Cop Killer." Yet no-one arrested him for seditious conspiracy! But if you say, 'I want to kill this specific cop, and here is where we meet to do this—then the government would have a case (Rataj 2012).

Free speech was the issue, as far as Hutaree member, Michael Meeks, was concerned. He told the Press the day he was released from prison that, for him, the salient lesson was to "watch what you say: Even the most innocent of statements can be used against you." Journalist William Grigg goes a step further: "The lesson is that anything said in your presence can be used against you—and if a sufficiently incriminating remark isn't forthcoming from you or your friends, the Feds can always pay somebody to perform on cue, and on camera."

The Religious Dimension

Finally, the question remains, "Were the Hutaree more vulnerable to being framed as terrorists because they were a *religious* militia? Were they portrayed as dangerous because they were devout Christians?" One concern discussed in the media was the double standard in the government's treatment of Muslims and Christians. As Grigg notes, "During the past decade, false flag operations targeting disaffected Muslims have become the FBI's métier" (Grigg 2012). Yasmin Mogahed, writing in the *Huffington Post*, complains, "If there's news of a Muslim terrorist, Islam becomes complicit in the crime.... Hutaree means 'Christian Warrior'—yet the American public is not likely to blame Christianity" (Mogahed 2012). But the leader of the Hutaree claims he was persecuted because of his Christian beliefs.

In my interview with David Stone that took place in a restaurant in Adrian, Michigan, he told several stories to illustrate this point. Leslie Larsen, he claimed, had hired Dan Murray to investigate the Hutaree partly because she considered their radical Christian orientation to be threatening: "It was all about our Christian faith badge which features a cross," he explained, and he noted that Larsen had referred to Hutaree in a conversation with Murray as "the Jesus Taliban." Stone claimed when he was arrested and taken in for questioning by Sandra Larsen, a Michigan State Trooper, she had opened the interrogation by saying:

> "So, I understand you consider yourself a Christian?"
> "Yes."
> "Well, let's see if your God saves you now."

David Stone also mentioned that the FBI classified the Bible as "antigovernment literature." When his apartment was raided, the FBI found three King James Bibles, and these were shown in court as part of the government's evidence, along with the guns and ammunition. When Judge Roberts queried their presence, she was told the search warrant had instructed agents to seize any "antigovernment literature." The FBI then provided her with their list, which included "the Bible."

From a sociological perspective, the Hutaree story contains new lessons in the complex relationship between religion, violence and state control. Sociological analysis has focused on the dynamic relationship between apocalyptic expectations and the violence and volatility of certain new religions. Post-mortem discussions of tragic events have focused on ideological factors that have propelled several infamous new religious movements into violent homicidal or suicidal directions (for example, the Solar Temple, Aum Shinrikyo, Jonestown, Nation of Islam, Heaven's Gate).

Scholars have explored the influence of millenarian expectations on the decision-making processes of charismatic leaders (Wessinger 2000; Melton and Bromley 2002; Hall et al. 2000). Lorne Dawson notes, "In each of the instances of mass religious violence involving NRMs, apocalyptic beliefs ... have played a crucial role ... in fostering extreme behaviour" (Dawson 2006). Scholars such as Wessinger (2000), Hall (2000), Mullins (1998), and Mayer (1999) have all argued that, while apocalyptic beliefs do not always or necessarily lead to violent behaviour, that certain prophets of new religions have been known to pre-emptively attack at the onset of Armageddon and to view non-members as demonic or subhuman, hence morally justifiable targets for guns, bombs or sarin gas. For prophets expecting the imminent destruction of the world, they argue, violent or self-destructive resolutions to conflicts or to obstacles may be rationalized in religious terms.

In the case of the Hutaree, one finds an exception to this model. David Stone, his family and core group certainly espoused a religious, millenarian worldview. The purpose of militia training was to prepare to resist the New World Order and the rise of the Antichrist government. This was the gist of his lawyer, William

Swor's arguments in court, which he summarized as follows in our meeting in his office:

> When David was talking about a future war with the government, it was always in the context of his apocalyptic vision. He believed that there would be a real physical battle between the forces of Satan and the forces of Christ. The Christians were called upon to be prepared to defend themselves and their families from Satan's forces. He based it all on the Book of Revelation. There were various signs, like the Mark of the Beast, but these signs were constantly changing. We don't know when this is going to happen, he'd say, but we have to be prepared. The police would become part of the Devil's army, they would turn into extensions of the Antichrist, and so we would have to take them on. (Swor 2012)

David Stone, himself, makes this important distinction between the present (secular) government and the future (Antichrist) government which he believes in, as a devout Pentecostal Christian. In our conversation in a restaurant in Adrian, he made this very clear. He told the story of his interrogation by the FBI, when they kept asking him, "So, you hate the government, don't you?" He kept telling them, he had nothing against the *current* government but was trying to prepare for the *future* government of the New World Order." He concluded, "They seemed confused. Were they trying to tell me that they think *they're* the Antichrist government?" (Stone 2012).

The Human Dimension

For the five Hutaree who spent two years in prison, they were vindicated of the charges but faced daunting economic and personal challenges as they took up their lives again. As Michael Rataj pointed out, "they have to eat their loss. There is no vehicle for compensation. One of the things that makes this whole situation so despicable is there is no recourse for these people, those five who spent two years in jail for no reason" (Rataj 2013, personal interview).

In the months following their arrests in 2010, the Hutaree members had weathered stigmatizing portraits in the media, in which they were portrayed as "Christian terrorists" (Housley 2010). But two years later, after their acquittal, they suddenly found themselves lionized by journalists, and they became a legend among Patriot groups and left-wing radicals in America. While the Hutaree story has confirmed the right-wing Patriot groups' mistrust of the government and law enforcement, it has also demonstrated the independence and reliability of the U.S. judicial system. Archy Cary sums up this paradox:

> Was this flamboyant raid primarily driven by political rather than law enforcement motives? This whole Hutaree ordeal, is looking more like a government ruse to demonize militias, Christians and the "right-wing," than it does a legitimate threat.... It's lucky the nine working-class folks charged in this "conspiracy" have an honest judge. U.S. District Judge Victoria Roberts doesn't seem to be letting the government agents get away with any shenanigans. (Cary 2010)

For Michael Meeks, an ex-marine who spent two years in prison, something valuable resulted from his ordeal: "Our story gives other people who are being harassed ammunition with which to defend themselves."

References

Aaronson, T. 2013. *The Terror Factory: Inside the FBI's Manufactured War on Terrorism*. New York: If Publishing.

AnnArbor.com. 2010. "Hutaree militia leader advocated killing cops, transcript shows." April 8. Available at http://www.mlive.com/ann-arbor/.

Ashenfelter, D. 2010. "Judge orders release of 9 Hutaree militia members." *Detroit Free Press*.

Associated Press Detroit. 2012. "Militia leader on Fed recordings fantasizes about shooting cops." *Associated Press*, March 10.

Associated Press Detroit. 2010. "FBI agent short on details on militia inquiry." *Toledo Blade*, April 28.

Baldas, T. 2012a. "Jersey Steve was really FBI informant in Hutaree case." *Detroit Free Press*, March 14.

Baldas, T. 2012b. "Hutaree defense seeks mistrial, accuses U.S. of withholding information." *Detroit Free Press*, March 22.

Baldas, T. 2012c. "Judge acquits Hutaree militia members of conspiracy charges." *Detroit Free Press*, March 28.

Baldas, T. and D. Ashenfelter. 2012. "Judge acquits 5 Hutaree militia members of all charges; 2 face only weapons counts." *Detroit Free Press,* March 27.

Baldas, T. and J. Swickard. 2012. "Last 2 Hutaree go free." *Detroit Free Press* March 30.

Bunkley, N. and Charlie Savage. 2010. "Militia charged with plotting to murder officers." *New York Times*, March 29.

Burton, F. 2007. "The imminent spread of EFPs." *Stratford Global Intelligence*, April 11. www.stratfor.com/imminent_spread_efps.

Cary, A. May 5, 2010. "The 'Hutaree Militia' case starts to unravel—on first amendment grounds." www.liveleak.com/view?i=4b0_1273038967.

Churchill, R.H. 2008. *To Shake Their Guns in the Tyrant's Face: Libertarian Political Violence and the Origins of the Militia Movement*. Detroit: University of Michigan Press.

Dawson, L. 2006. *Comprehending Cults: The Sociology of New Religious Movements*. New York: Oxford University Press.

FBI Report. 2008. "Document 479-2." Washington, D.C.: Federal Bureau of Investigation, September 30.

Fox News. 2012. "Militia leader talked of foreign troops in US." *Fox News*, March 9. www.foxnews.com/us/2012/.../militia-leader-talked-foreign-troops-in-us/.

Fraser, T. 2012. "Trinidad islamic group leader faces sedition trial." *The Guardian*, June 13.

Grigg, W.N. 2012. "The Hutaree case: Next, time, they'll send in the drones." *Pro Libertate*, April 1. axisoflogic.com/artman/publish/printer_64412.shtml.

Helfrick, Richard. 2012. Interview with Richard Helfrick, Deputy Federal Defender, who represented David B. Stone Jr. over the telephone, April 10, 2012

Hall, J. with P. Schuyler and S. Trinh. 2000. *Apocalypse Observed*. New York: Routledge.

Higgins, L. 2010a. "FBI raids in Washtenaw, Lenawee counties tied to Michigan militia group." *Ann Arbor News*, March 28. http://www.annarbor.com/news/fbi-conducts-raids-in-washtenaw-lenawee-counties/.

Higgins, L. 2010b. "Hutaree members describe FBI raid at phony memorial service in Ann Arbor." *Ann Arbor News*, April 18. http://www.annarbor.com/news/witnesses-describe-fbi-raid-at-phony-hutaree-memorial-service/.

Higgins, L. 2010c. "Bomb manuals, suspected steroids seized during Hutaree raids, search warrant records show." *Ann Arbor News*, April 12. http://www.annarbor.com/news/bomb-manuals-suspected-steroids-seized-during-hutaree-raids-records-show/.

Higgins, L. 2010d. "Militia group gave FBI information on Hutaree two years ago, e-mails show." *Ann Arbor News*, April 15. http://www.annarbor.com/news/militia-group-provided-fbi-information-on-hutaree-two-years-ago-emails-show/.

Higgins, L. 2010e. "Tip about militia member Mark Koernke led to Hutaree investigation, court filing says." *Ann Arbor News*, December 6. http://www.annarbor.com/news/crime/fbi-launched-hutaree-probe-after-tip-about-mark-koernke-court-filing-says/.

Higgins, L. 2011a. "Defense attorneys for Hutaree member challenge search warrant affidavits, want evidence suppressed." *Ann Arbor News*, February 2. http://www.annarbor.com/news/crime/defense-attorneys-in-hutaree-case-challenge-search-warrant-affidavits-want-evidence-suppressed/.

Higgins, L. 2011b. "Defense attorneys seek information on FBI informants in Hutaree case." *Ann Arbor News*, December 6. http://www.annarbor.com/news/crime/defense-attorneys-in-hutaree-case-seeking-information-about-fbi-informants/.

Higgins, L. 2012a. "FBI informant in Hutaree case was arrested for firing gun during argument." *Ann Arbor News*, January 19. http://www.annarbor.com/news/crime/fbi-informant-in-hutaree-case-was-arrested-for-firing-gun-at-wife/.

Higgins, L. 2012b. "Judge: Hutaree head, son, held long enough." August 8. www.annarbor.com.

Higgins, L. 2012c. "Lawyers for Hutaree member file motion to dismiss 7 charges." *Ann Arbor News*, September 22. http://www.annarbor.com/news/crime/lawyers-for-hutaree-militia-member-file-motion-to-dismiss/.

Housley, M. 2010. "Violent underbelly of arrested Hutaree militia members revealed." *National Post*, March 20. www.news.nationalpost.com/.../violent-underbelly-of-arrested-hutaree-militia-me.

Lineweaver, Wendy. 2012. Personal Interview, June.

Mayer, J-F. 1999. "'Our terrestrial voyage is coming to an end': The last voyage of the Solar Temple." *Nova Religio* 2: 172–96.

Melton, J.G. and David G. Bromley. 2002. *Cults, Religion and Violence.* Cambridge: Cambridge University Press.

Mogahed, Y. 2010. "Does the Hutaree militia represent Christianity? A Muslim knows better." *Huffington Post*, March 31.

Palmer, B. 2010. "When did IEDs become WMDs?" *Slate*, March 31. www.slate.com/articles/news_and.../when_did_ieds_become_wmd.html.

Rataj, Michael. 2013. "Personal Interview with Michael Rataj, Federal Attorney for Tina Stone." April 1. (Also interviewed by phone several times in 2012.) Reiter, M. 2012. "FBI agent testifies in Hutaree trial about findings by paid confidential informant." *Toledo Blade*, February 14.

Schmidt, B. 2010. "FBI used ruse to flush out Hutaree militia." *Detroit Free Press*, April 1.

SPLC Hatewatch. 2010. "Nine members of the Hutaree Militia indicted in plans for 'armed conflict.'" March 29. www.splcenter.org/blog/2010/03/.../nine-members-of-the-hutaree-militia.

Stone, David. 2012. "Personal Interview." Adrian, MI, September 8.

Swor 2012. Interview with William Swor, federal attorney assigned to defend David Stone Sr. Detroit, April 1, 2013.

United States District Court for the Eastern District of Michigan, Southern Division. 2012. *United States of America v. David Brian Stone* (Case No. 10-20123), February 13.

Temple-Raston, D. 2010. "America's new kinder, gentler militia." NPR News Investigations, *NPR*, April 13.

Wessinger, C. 2000. *How the Millennium Comes Violently*. New York: Seven Bridges Press.

White, E. 2012a. "Hutaree informant ends testimony in Michigan militia trial." Associated Press, March 2.

White, Ed. 2012b. "Judge: Hutaree head, son, held long enough". Associated Press. August 8.

Zeskind, L. 2009. *Blood and Politics: The History of the White Nationalist Movement from the Margins to the Mainstream*. New York: Farrar, Straus and Giroux.

Chapter 7

The Dang Case:
When *Chakras* Opening Leads to a Belgian Criminal Court

Henri de Cordes

Introduction

In January 1999, a luxury hotel located in Genval, some 20 kilometers southeast of Brussels, was the venue of a conference by the founder of Spiritual Human Yoga, Luong Minh Dang, known to his followers as 'Master Dang'. Luong Minh Dang, a South-Vietnamese born in 1942 who had emigrated to the U.S in 1987, had developed a therapy based on the Vedic concept of *chakras*, a form of esoteric anatomy.[1] The seven main *chakras* correspond to seven parts of the human body: base, sacrum, solar plexus, heart, throat, brow (or third eye) and fontanelle (top of the head). Dang claimed that a spiritual master of Sri Lanka, Desira Narada II,[2] had transmitted to him the knowledge of controlling a 'Universal Energy' that can enter human bodies via the *chakras*. Through his teachings, the followers of 'Master Dang' learned the technique of opening the *chakras* to this 'Universal Energy'. Dang began exercising his technique through a movement presently known as Spiritual Human Yoga (SHY).[3]

In its report of May 1997, the Select Committee of the Belgian House of Representatives on the dangers of cults had described Spiritual Human Yoga as a movement whose founder presents himself as a 'prophet, healer and spiritual guide'. The spiritual references of Dang are numerous: starting with the Vedic

---

[1]   In his teachings (Therapy by Universal Energy, course level 2), Dang had defined his practice as follows: 'Universal energy therapy is a holistic method which allows self-healing and spiritual healing.... It works through seven specific points called the chakras'.

[2]   The existence of Desira Narada II being not documented except in Dang's writings, one can infer that Dang is a self-proclaimed 'Master'.

[3]   Dang's organisation is also active under the following denominations : Mankind-Enlightenment-Love (MEL), Institute for Human and Universal Energy Research.

tradition of *chakras* he also refers to ancient Egypt mythology, to Abd-ru-shin[4] and to the messages of Fatima. Dang affirms that he communicates with many of the 'Divine Beings' such a Jesus or Buddha. According to this report, the main criticisms against Dang were 'illegal exercise of medicine' and 'high financial demands'. The report also mentioned the announcement by the 'guru' of catastrophic events. 'The followers gather in the St. Louis (USA) centre where teachings are provided. They pray and after a while, the guru announces that the catastrophe has been avoided thanks to their prayers'.[5]

During a seminar in Brussels in July 1996, Dang had presented cataclysmic scenarios to which his devotees could survive if they would be using their 'sixth sense' in the way he was going to teach them. His apocalyptic discourse attracted the attention of Belgian police services who feared that it could be used to exploit gullible persons. Thus, the presence of police officers during the conference of Luong Minh Dang in January 1999 was no surprise. They had interrogated the 'Master' a few days before the Genval conference. At the end of the conference, attended by some 800 persons, Luong Minh Dang was arrested and placed in custody where he remained for two months before being released on bail. The 1,240,000 euros of bail were collected among his Belgian and Dutch followers within 48 hours.

The year before (November 1998), the grandfather of a child suffering from an incurable disease and whose parents had turned their back to traditional medicine – in the sense of evidence based medicine – on the advice of a follower of Dang, the grandfather had filed a complaint because he feared his grandchild was in danger. The policemen, who belonged to a specialised team dedicated to cult activities, had found in the plaintiff's account some 'warning lights' which convinced the prosecutor to issue an arrest warrant against Luong Minh Dang. The teachings of Dang were quite explicit in terms of healing benefits of his techniques: the second of the seven levels of teachings allegedly enables the student to treat a wide array of diseases such as Alzheimer's, cancer, gangrene, and even AIDS. At level three, the student is supposed to diagnose AIDS or mental diseases and to determine a treatment. Although Dang pretends that his healing method is a complementary medicine and that the patient should continue to consult his doctor, the fear of the grandfather that his granddaughter could be deprived of appropriate medical care was real.

---

[4]   Abd-ru-shin is the pen name of Oskar Ernst Bernhardt, the German author of *In the Light of Truth: The Grail Message*, published in 1926.

[5]   Belgian House of Representatives, Parliamentary document 313/7– 95/96: 323–4.

The criminal investigation led to a trial in 2005 in a criminal section of the Brussels First instance court. The case concerned facts committed between 1 November 1990 and 14 January 1999. The only defendants were Luong Minh Dang and the president of Spiritual Human Yoga Belgium, Mrs. Vo Thi Minh Hiep. The association itself – Spiritual Human Yoga Belgium – could not be sued because, at the time when the facts being brought to court happened, the criminal responsibility of associations or corporations had not yet been introduced into the criminal code. The trial opened in October 2005 with an incident: Dang, who respected the conditions of his bail, appeared at the tribunal but was immediately arrested on the request of Swiss judicial authorities who had issued an international arrest warrant in 1996. Consequently, the trial was postponed by two months. Meanwhile, the Centre for Information and Advice on Harmful Cultic Organisations (CIAHCO) had been requested by the prosecutor to present to the court an expert opinion on Spiritual Human Yoga and its founder, Luong Minh Dang. The report of the Centre was based not only on the information available at the Centre but also on documents seized as evidences during police raids. The advice of the Centre being an official document of the proceedings, it could not be published.[6]

Charges in the Case

The charges against Master Dang were: forgery, use of false academic titles, fraud, illegal practice of medicine and criminal conspiracy as a leader. The same charges were filed against Mrs Vo Thi Minh Hiep, except the last one, which was replaced by criminal conspiracy as a member.

Forgery

The first count of the indictment, forgery, relied mainly on the illegal money transfers from the Belgian SHY association bank accounts to Dang's own bank account in the United States. Several documents showed that different SHY centres appear to be beneficiaries of money transfers while the money was destined to and pocketed by Dang. He explained that these payments came from donations received by the centres and forwarded to him. But her Belgian representative told the court that 'Master Dang' expected that 50% of the income

---

[6]   According to the Belgian law on public archives, this document will be accessible to the public 30 years after the end of its judicial use.

of courses in different countries – where he, sometimes, only appeared on the phone for some minutes to open *chakras* – were sent to him. Dang eventually admitted that he gave her instructions to collect the money from these countries and then send it to him. The court concluded that these pseudo-invoices had no real backing but were used to distract the tax services from the profits of the various seminars and conferences.

Use of False Academic Titles

The second count, use of false academic titles, referred to the title of Doctor in Philosophy and Doctor *honoris causa* in Sciences delivered by the Open International University for Complementary Medicines in Colombo, Sri Lanka, titles he used to reinforce his credibility among his followers. Luong Minh Dang allegedly received these diplomas after writing memoirs based on his research but did not produce these documents to the court. The court noticed that the reference in one of the diplomas to a Peace University in Sri Lanka under the auspices of the United Nations did not match the only initiative of the UN with this title which was a discussion forum in Costa Rica rather than a real university. The conclusion of the court was that these diplomas had no value and that they had been made up in order to reinforce Dang's wisdom towards his students.

Fraud

The count of fraud is based on the system of courses and healing techniques provided by the organisation founded by Dang with the final objective of collecting money intended to Dang himself. The court checked that the facts responded to the constitutive elements of fraud, being fraudulent intention, use of false names or false qualities, use of fraudulent manoeuvres, and remittance of goods by the abused person, and it decided that the abuse of trust or gullibility of the victim was present in the organisation set up by Dang. The court noted that for the period between 1993 and 1998, 57% of the income was sent to personal bank accounts of Dang for a total of 38 million Belgian francs (some 942,000 euros). This amount is to be compared with the 50,000 to 70,000 U.S. dollars Dang pretended he needed annually for his family and his own subsistence.

The way 'Master Dang' introduces himself as a Knight Commander of the Order of Saint John in attire imitating the ceremonial gown of a Knight of the

Order of Malta[7] is considered by the court as an element of seduction of the participants to his courses. The defence representing Dang tried to explain that the money he had received was destined to the funding of his charity works. But none of the witnesses could testify on any concrete achievement of their 'Master' in this field.

The court rejected the argument of the defence pretending that the case was void because there was no civil claimant considering that the absence of civil claimant did not remove the fraudulent aspect of Dang's enterprise. Thus, the charge of fraud was also considered as being justified.

Illegal Practice of Medicine

With the count of illegal practice of medicine, the criminal investigation aimed at the core business of SHY: the opening of *chakras* in order to receive 'Universal Energy' as a healing technique. Dang is not qualified as a medical doctor (physician) – he used to be a non-commissioned officer in the South-Vietnamese navy – therefore he is not allowed to make diagnostics or determine a medical treatment. When learning to open the *chakras*, Dang claims the student will first be able to cure his own illnesses and those of his next of kin, but, as soon as he reaches level 3, he is supposed to be able to diagnose and to determine a treatment for others. At level 4, the students were taught how to teach the theories and techniques to lower levels. The wide array of diseases and infections that the Universal Energy practitioners are trained to treat, without any medical background as a prerequisite, presents a high level of risk to public health. The defence lawyer tried to compensate the lack of proper medical background of his client by presenting several witnesses, all medical doctors. They all gave a rather similar account of their experience in the use of Universal Energy in their medical practice, so much so that the president of the court interrogated one of the witnesses about this similarity; his answer led to the conclusion that an email of Dang's lawyer could have oriented the testimonies.

Three criteria need to be met when illegal practice of medicine is to be proven: to practice medical acts without the required titles, to practice these acts on a habitual basis and to perform medical acts. The first criterion was met after the demonstration that Dang had not studied medicine and that his diplomas did not establish such training. The criterion of habitual practice is found in

---

[7]   The official website of the Sovereign Military Order of Saint John of Jerusalem of Rhodes and of Malta (http://www.orderofmalta.int/) cautions against 'mimic orders' claiming to be the 'Order of Saint John'.

the publicity made for the courses and seminars as well as by the publication of manuals for each course level. Diagnostic and indication of a treatment are the medical acts referred to by the third criterion. Consequently, the court decided that the activity of Luong Minh Dang was the illegal practice of medicine.

Criminal Conspiracy

The last count of his indictment, criminal conspiracy, summarises the whole activity of Dang as founder and leader of an organisation involved in fraud and other crimes under the guise of a spiritual quest. As soon as a group of persons is organised with the aim of committing crimes and offences with the deliberate volition of being a member of such a group, the offence of conspiracy exists. The existence of the association was obvious as well as the techniques used to attract people to paying seminars and courses, after free courses for the two first levels; the declarations of Luong Minh Dang admitting he was the leader and mastermind of SHY completed the scrutiny of this charge. 'Master Dang' was therefore recognised as a leader of a criminal conspiracy.

Outcome of the Case

In April 2006, the Brussels trial court, criminal section, found Dang guilty on all charges and convicted him to four years of imprisonment, with a three-year suspension, and a fine of 10,000 euros. The verdict for his accomplice, Mrs Vo Thi Minh Hiep, was the same. The court also pronounced the confiscation of 'objects, documents and printers' and the seizure of large amounts of money.

Dang appealed his sentence but died before the appellate court could review his case. Mrs Vo also appealed her condemnation, and eventually her prison term was reduced to three years, and the fine was halved because of her lesser role in the SHY organisation.[8] Had Dang lived long enough to attend his appeal trial, this last argument could not have been used to reduce the sanctions.

The rather lenient conviction is the result of three elements. Firstly, Dang was granted the benefit of mitigating circumstances, which means that his case had been referred to a first instance court and not to a criminal jury, reducing the maximum sentence for forgery from ten years to five years imprisonment.

---

[8]   The appellate court had taken into account the 'ancientness' of the facts – already taken into account by the court of first instance – and the lesser role she played by comparison to her 'Master's' role.

Secondly, the court concluded that the facts constituting the charges were bound by a 'unity of intention' and therefore were to be considered as a collective offence. Consequently, Dang could only be punishable by the maximum of the highest sentence and not by the addition of the penalty meant for each charge. Finally, Dang had never been condemned before in Belgium, and the facts were considered as 'old' (nine years old) by the court.

Nevertheless, the court stated that both accused deserved an exemplary penalty due to their behavior which consisted in 'the abuse of the fragility of some individuals'.

Discussion and Conclusions

This court case is one of the very few criminal cases in Belgium in recent years where the leader of a 'New Religious Movement'[9] was the defendant. The main reason for the paucity of criminal cases in the field of 'cults' is that there are few complaints,[10] fewer investigations, fewer cases and shorter sentences even if a defendant is found guilty.

The condemnation of Dang is the result of the enforcement of general criminal provisions, and not of any specific legislation targeting controversial religious movements.[11] These movements, whatever doctrine they profess, must comply with the laws and regulations in the same way that every citizen has to; invoking a philosophical or religious justification for a criminally reprehensible practice has no effect on a court of a State governed by the rule of law. This general law decision confirms that spiritual, religious or philosophical arguments cannot justify any special treatment, as far as criminal law is concerned.

The central point of the Dang case was the allegation of the illegal practice of medicine. In its 1997 report[12] the Select Committee of the Belgian House of Representatives on the danger of cults had already described Spiritual Human Yoga as a therapeutic group. Dang knew that, without any medical background and any possibility to prove clinically the effectiveness of his practice, his credibility towards his followers had to rely on the spiritual dimension of the transmission of knowledge – i.e. Universal Energy that would (or should?)

---

[9] 'New Religious Movement' (NRM) is the term commonly accepted by sociologists of religion(s) to refer to what the general public call 'cult' or 'sect'.

[10] The defence barrister argued that the file was empty because there was no civil plaintiff.

[11] 'Controversial religious movement' is used as a synonym of NRM.

[12] Belgian House of Representatives, Parliamentary document 313/7 and 313/8 – 95/96.

enter human bodies via their *chakras* – by a master / *guru*.[13] *Chakras* theory which is well-known in Asia for ages is rather suitable for this kind of master-to-follower transmission. Furthermore, the attractiveness of *chakras* theory in the western world – especially among those who contest the so-called 'monopoly' of evidence-based medicine – makes it a profitable resource in a commercial scheme[14] purporting to be spiritual or religious. The credibility of Dang is even reinforced by the fact that the followers to whom his knowledge is passed on consider themselves as being 'chosen' by the 'Master' even if they can benefit from his 'science' by paying for the courses.

The success of Dang was the combination of his own charisma, his convincing power and the expectancy of recovery by people in need of physical or psychological comfort.

The defence lawyer oriented his pleading on the medical practice of Dang; the defence witnesses[15] were all presented as medical doctors who considered Dang as their master in their medical field. This tactic of the defence was not successful because Dang's writings were centered on a spiritual and religious discourse based on the *chakras* theory and not on evidence-based medicine. This argument, which could strengthen Dang's position towards his followers – who knew he was not a doctor – fell short in the criminal case. It's doubtful that a defence based on a 'spiritual healing power' of Dang would have been more successful because the investigation had collected evidence on each and every element of the illegal practice of medicine. Had Dang been a 'licensed' physician, he could have argued that he used 'Universal Energy' within the framework of his 'therapeutic freedom'; in this case, the College of Physicians would have been the first level body to which a complaint should have been filed. This institution, whose members are elected by and among physicians, would have checked if the therapeutic practices of Dang were in compliance with the deontological obligations of the profession, notably the physician's commitment 'to provide attentive care to the patient, conscientious and consistent with current and science-based data'.[16]

---

[13]   In Sanskrit, *guru* means a spiritual master. In its 'westernised' sense, it is often used as a synonym of 'cult leader'.

[14]   The commercial aspect of Spiritual Human Yoga is confirmed by the transfer of SHY from Dang to his son, more as a business-like succession than as a Master to follower transmission making it difficult or impossible for Dang's son to rely on the 'spiritual legitimacy' his father used successfully.

[15]   The hearing of the defence witnesses has been perceived as 'too well organised', all witnesses having received from the defence barrister an email explaining what was expected from them.

[16]   Belgian Medical Deontological Code, article 34, § 1.

Money had been pivotal in Dang's organisation of Spiritual Human Yoga. The case proved that the sums paid by Dang's followers to participate to an event where the master was appearing – sometimes only on screen – to 'transmit Universal Energy' were the fee of the speaker. This practice had already been noted by the Select Committee of the French National Assembly on 'cults and money'[17] (June 1999). In a reply to a questionnaire of the Committee, the French association Spiritual Human Yoga admitted having paid to Dang the equivalent of some 488,000 euros between 1995 and 1998. The level of Dang's fees was so high that it made it difficult to support that SHY members' contributions were meant for the benefit of the organisation as a whole. Money: means or end? Dang's case clearly demonstrated that SHY was primarily conceived as a source of profit for its founder, whatever the spiritual, religious or philosophical doctrine it was offering – or selling? – to its followers.

References

Belgian House of Representatives, Parliamentary document 313/7– 95/96, pp. 323–4.

Belgian Medical Deontological Code, article 34, § 1.

Bernhardt, Oskar. 1926. *Im Lichte der Wahrheit – Gralsbotschaft* (In the Light of Truth: The Grail Message), Stuttgart : Verlag der Stiftung Gralsbotschaft.

French Assemblée nationale, report no. 1687, p. 186, http://www.assemblee-nationale.fr/11/dossiers/sectes/r1687.pdf.

Sovereign Military Order of Saint John of Jerusalem of Rhodes and of Malta, http://www.orderofmalta.int/.

---

[17] French Assemblée nationale, report n 1687: 186, http://www.assemblee-nationale.fr/11/dossiers/sectes/r1687.pdf.

PART III
Legal Issues Raised by Cases Involving Minority Faiths

Chapter 8

How to Know the Truth: Accommodating Religious Belief in the Law of Libel

Alastair Mullis and Andrew Scott[1]

Introduction

Religion unites, and divides, billions of people around the world. In the United Kingdom, some 45 million citizens profess adherence to one of the major world religions or other devotions.[2] Of these, many are committed to minority creeds and faiths.[3] While religious pluralism, liberty and equality are now general cultural and legal expectations, the history of interplay between religious identities in the UK is one of intellectually – and sometimes physically – violent discord.[4] Today, religious frictions – albeit an inevitable

---

[1]   School of Law, University of Leeds and Department of Law, London School of Economics and Political Science, respectively. We owe a debt to John Charney for research assistance undertaken on the themes of this paper.

[2]   The 2001 Census included a question on religion for the first time (outside of Northern Ireland). The question used a measure based upon identity rather than practice, and so may overstate the extent of actual religious commitment. The 2001 Census showed that 71.6% of people self-identify as Christian (circa 42.1 million), 2.7% (circa 1.59 million) as Muslim, 1.0% (circa 0.56 million) as Hindu, 0.6% (circa 0.34 million) as Sikh, 0.5% (circa 0.27 million) as Jewish, 0.3% (circa 0.15 million) as Buddhist. Around 0.3% (circa 0.18 million) self-designated as being of some other religion, while 15.5% (circa 9.1 million) professed themselves to have no religion, and 7.3% (circa 4.3 million) did not answer.

[3]   The Census data does not allow differentiation between various denominations of the major faiths. Around 0.3% (circa 0.18 million) respondents to the 2001 Census were counted as being of some other religion. Very many self-designations as 'other', however, were reallocated to the Christian religion grouping. Famously, a further 390,000 people 'humorously' professed commitment to the inter-galactic 'Jedi' tradition, notionally making this the fourth largest religion in the UK. These designations were counted in the 'no religion' category.

[4]   For an overview of the legal framing of religion in British modern history that traces four phases of development, see Sandberg (2011), *Law and Religion*, ch. 2.

facet of a plural society – persist. Both low-level antipathies and serious religious disputes are driven by any number of factors: long-standing and incipient factionalism within religious groupings, more or less aggressive secularist critique, fears of indoctrination by charismatic leaders of new-fangled faiths, discordance with the prevailing culture of materialism, the perceived frustration of the reasonable desire for some to manifest their faith, and the resentment among some faiths of the proselytising zeal of others. Occasionally, perhaps surprisingly infrequently, the general law is called upon to regulate or to resolve disputes engendered by religious difference. From time to time, it is the law of libel – that aspect of legal doctrine that exists to provide protection for reputation against unfounded and damaging criticism – that is invoked.[5]

A basic concern regarding the application of libel law to the context of religious disputes is that the primary concern of that area of law is with the truth or otherwise of allegations made. The task of understanding the truth, however, is also a core disputed theme both within and between religions. It is inherently difficult for any purportedly neutral, secular law properly to adjudicate between competing conceptions of the righteous and the good. It may be foolhardy even to make the attempt. This chapter proceeds in four parts. First, we outline briefly the basic features of English libel law in order to underpin the subsequent discussion. Secondly, we suggest a typology of criticisms or allegations that might be made regarding religious faiths and their adherents, and we indicate in general terms how each type of allegation would be countenanced by the law of libel. Thirdly, we offer a more developed critique of the approach adopted by the English courts to one of these types of allegation, specifically that seen in *Blake v. Associated Newspapers Ltd* (2003), *His Holiness Sant Baba Jeet Singh Ji Maharaj v. Eastern Media Group* (2010 – hereinafter *Hardeep Singh's Case*), and *Shergill v. Purewal* (2010). That approach involved the abjuring on the part of the court of any role on grounds of non-justiciability and deference to religious modes of dispute resolution. Finally, we suggest a conceptually and jurisprudentially preferable manner for the resolution of legal disputes in such cases, one that

---

[5]   This may be genuinely to right a false and defamatory slight, or because this aspect of the law is considered a useful means of curtailing – or 'chilling' – even legitimate criticism. Certainly, the latter was thought by some to be the more accurate explanation of the motivation of the claimant in one recent case – see *Shergill v. Purewal* (2010) EWHC 3610 (QB): '[The claimant has] no genuine interest in bringing these proceedings to protect or preserve his reputation, but rather is seeking to gag the defendants from criticising the claimant's active campaign to establish control and ownership for the benefit of a "holy man" in India of three Gurduwaras in the UK' (at 10).

would properly ensure the neutrality of libel law as between disparate views on questions of religious faith.

The Basic Features of English Libel Law

English libel law is largely derived from the common law.[6] Its ostensible purpose is to allow individuals to defend their reputations against false and defamatory imputations published by others. In doing so, it must recognise the individual and social importance of reputation,[7] while also limiting the extent to which the law curtails the freedom of expression that is core to any democratic society. The starting point in every case is that, in law, it is presumed that the statement complained of is false and that it has caused harm to reputation.[8] To pursue a claim, a claimant must then show three things. The first is that publication to some third party has occurred (Doley and Mullis 2010: ch. 5). It is not important quite how this communication occurs, so that an email, a letter, a spoken statement, or a waxwork sculpting can amount to publication as much as the writing of an article in a newspaper, in a magazine or in some online platform, or the broadcasting of a piece on radio or television. The second element of the

---

[6] The law of libel has been the subject of much policy debate. At the time of writing, the UK Parliament has passed the Defamation Act 2013 with the expectation that the Act will come into force late in 2013. The Act will affect a number of amendments to the scheme of law outlined in this section and places much of the law onto a statutory footing. The basic features of the substantive law, however, will remain essentially the same. For a discussion of the historical development of the common law in this regard, see Mitchell (2005).

[7] This importance has been reflected increasingly in the jurisprudence of the European Court of Human Rights, which now considers an individual's reputation to fall within his or her Article 8 right to respect for private life – see Alastair Mullis and Andrew Scott, 'The Swing of the Pendulum: Reputation, Expression and the Recentering of English Libel Law' (2012) *Northern Ireland Legal Quarterly*, 63, no. 1: 27–58; Dean Spielmann and Leto Cariolou, 'The Right to Protection of Reputation Under the European Convention on Human Rights', in Dean Spielmann, Marialena Tsirli and Panayotis Voyatzis (eds) *The European Convention on Human Rights: A living instrument* (Brussells: Bruylant, 2011), 401–25.

[8] This differs from the position in U.S. law, where claimants bear the burden of demonstrating falsity. Moreover, following *New York Times v. Sullivan* 376 US 254 (1964), U.S. law operates under an actual malice standard applicable in respect of commentary regarding 'public figures'. This standard requires that the plaintiff in a defamation case proves that the publisher of the statement in question knew that the statement was false or acted in reckless disregard of its truth or falsity. Within the bounds set by the constitution, defamation is state-level law (with the result that, for example, precisely whom is considered to be a public figure differs depending on jurisdiction).

claim is that the publication must somehow have identified the claimant as the subject of the imputation (Doley and Mullis, 2010).[9] Identification by name will obviously be the most common method, but a photograph, a cartoon, a description or identification of a group to which the person belongs can all be enough. The key question is whether the audience for the publication would reasonably have understood it to refer to the claimant.

The third requirement of the claimant is that he or she must show that the publication – or some imputation contained within it – has a defamatory meaning (Doley and Mullis 2010: ch. 4). In turn, this has two component parts: the determination of meaning and the assessment of whether the meaning was defamatory. The meaning of the imputation is determined by reference to how the words would have been understood by the ordinary, reasonable recipient of the publication in question.[10] Disputes about meaning are often central to libel actions: 'Very often if not always the most important issue is meaning.'[11] In general, there is no attempt to divine the *actual* inferences drawn by recipients of the publication at issue. Determination of meaning is not an empirical question. Neither is the publisher's *intended* meaning directly relevant. Counterfactually, in accordance with the 'single meaning rule', the court is usually required to pretend that only one interpretation of an imputation will have been inferred by all such ordinary, reasonable people. Should a claimant wish to contend that a publication also holds a 'hidden' meaning beyond that apparent on its face and accessible only to some group of persons who have particular extraneous knowledge, he or she must adduce evidence to that effect.[12]

---

[9]   An important case in this regard was *Orme v. Associated Newspapers Group Limited*, unreported, High Court, 1 January 1981. The case concerned newspaper criticism and parody of the Unification Church (the 'Moonies'). A preliminary legal point at issue was how far general reference to the grouping could be understood to identify Mr Orme – the Director of the Church in England – so as to allow him personally to sue for libel. The High Court determined that he was identified. In the event of the substantive hearing of the case, following protracted preliminaries which involved extended discussion of the utility of psychiatric evidence, the court found in favour of the defendant.

[10]   An 'impeccable synthesis of the authorities' on this theme offered by Eady J was reiterated by the Court of Appeal in *Gillick v. Brooke Advisory Centre* [2001] EWCA Civ 1263, at [7] (*per* Lord Phillips MR).

[11]   Uncorrected evidence given by Mr Justice Tugendhat to the Joint Committee on the Draft Defamation Bill, 7 July 2011, at Q40. For an illuminating discussion of, *inter alia*, the law and practice regarding the determination of meaning in English and Australian defamation law, see Andrew T. Kenyon, *Defamation Law: Comparative Law and Practice* (London: UCL Press, 2006).

[12]   This is known as a 'legal' innuendo meaning, in contrast to 'popular' or 'false' innuendo which comprises the deliberate inclusion of ambiguous terms that could be

Different tests have been used to determine when a statement is defamatory. The standard test is that of whether the words have a tendency to lower the claimant in the estimation of right-thinking people generally.[13] This has recently been restated by Mr. Justice Tugendhat following a review of numerous previous definitions: 'A publication is defamatory of a claimant if it substantially affects in an adverse manner the attitude of other people towards him, or has a tendency so to do' (*Thornton v. Telegraph Media Group Ltd*, 2010).[14] The question is assessed from the perspective of the public generally, although again there is no attempt to ascertain whether the publication might in fact have affected the perception of the claimant in the estimation of the audience. One caveat arises where the audience for the publication concerned is itself somehow specialised or particular in nature, in which the assessment is made from the perspective of the average member of that particular audience. Hence, given the differing underpinning knowledge of the average recipient of reader of the statement, the impact of the same statement may be understood differently in law when published in *The Times* newspaper as opposed to when published in the Jehovah's Witnesses' *Watchtower*, the Scientologists' *Freedom Magazine*, or the *Sikh Times*.

A defendant publisher may contest any of the three elements of the claim or seek to rely on one of several available defences. The two key defences relate to meaning. Which is to be deployed will depend on whether the contested imputation is properly understood to be a statement of fact or an expression of opinion. In the former case, the defendant may rely on the defence of justification should he or she be able to demonstrate that what was published is substantially true (Doley and Mullis 2010: ch. 9). If the contested imputation

---

interpreted in alternative ways by any reader. A classic example is that of a literal reference in a publication to the claimant's frequenting of a particular address, which might be seen as defamatory only when coupled with the extrinsic knowledge that the address in question is that of a house of ill-repute. Notably, in the *Hardeep Singh* case, Mr. Justice Eady emphasised that the claimant relied on natural, ordinary or inferential meanings and did not seek to rely on any legal innuendo – see *Hardeep Singh's* case, at 8.

[13]   This test is drawn from *Sim v. Stretch* [1936] 2 All ER 1237, at p. 1250 (*per* Lord Atkin). For a recent discussion of the concept of defamatory meaning, see Lawrence McNamara, *Reputation and Defamation* (Oxford University Press, 2007), esp. pt. 3.

[14]   *Thornton v. Telegraph Media Group Ltd* [2010] EWHC 1414 (QB). Alternative, older formulations of the test that may sometimes be brought to bear in the context of religious disputes are that a statement causes a person to be hated, held in contempt or subjected to ridicule (*Parmiter v. Coupland* (1840) 6 M & W 105, at p. 108 (*per* Parke B); *Villiers v. Monsley* (1769) 2 Wils 403, at p. 404 (*per* Gould J)), or that it causes others to shun or avoid a person (*Youssoupoff v. Metro-Goldwyn-Mayer Pictures Ltd* (1934) 50 TLR 581, at p. 587 (*per* Slesser LJ)).

is better characterised as an expression of opinion, then the defendant might seek to rely on the defence of 'fair comment' (now relabelled as 'honest comment').[15] This absolves the defendant of liability if he or she can show that the opinion was one that could be honestly held given the background facts (Doley and Mullis 2010: ch. 10). Other defences focus on whether the occasion on which the statement was made was in some way privileged[16] or on whether the publication was made in a responsible manner on a matter of public interest.[17]

A Typology of Damaging Claims Involving Religion

When considering the application of the law of libel to disputes that include a religious dimension, it is important to distinguish between a number of conceivable scenarios. We outline four such, although we do not suggest that there are necessarily stark divisions between the categories listed.[18] In each context, criticisms may emanate from within the ranks of the given religion, from adherents to other religious faiths, or from persons with no religious commitment. In principle, the origin of the potentially libellous criticism is unimportant, but it may have a bearing in fact on both the type of criticism made and on the question of whether there may be some extra-legal forum internal to

---

[15]   The defence was relabeled 'honest opinion' by the Court of Appeal in *British Chiropractic Association v. Singh* [2010] EWCA Civ 350, at [36], while in *Spiller v. Joseph* [2010] UKSC 53 the Supreme Court echoed Lord Nicholls in *Reynolds* [2001] 2 AC 127, at 165 when preferring 'honest comment' (at [117]). Perhaps confusingly, the Defamation Act 2013 refers to this defence in section 3 as 'honest opinion'.

[16]   An 'absolute privilege' is available where public policy dictates that a person should be able to speak freely without fear of possible legal consequences. Examples include statements made in the course of parliamentary proceedings, and statements made in the course of judicial proceedings in the UK – see, generally, Doley and Mullis 2010: ch. 11. Qualified privilege, which can be defeated by proof of malice on the part of the publisher, is available on the basis of statute or in circumstances where the publisher falls under some duty to communicate and the recipient of the publication has a corresponding interest in receiving it. Examples of such circumstances include replies to an attack made by the claimant, and references written at a third party's request. See, generally, Doley and Mullis 2010: ch. 12. Clauses 6 and 7 of the current Defamation Bill seek to extend the range of statutory privilege to include statements published in peer-reviewed scientific or academic journals.

[17]   The so-called *Reynolds*-privilege – see, generally, Doley and Mullis 2010: 336–73. Clause 4 of the current Defamation Bill seeks to abolish the existing common law defence and replace it with a new statutory formulation.

[18]   We exclude from this typology 'criticism' that manifests in physical assault or incitement to public disorder.

a particular religion or denomination to which the disputants may be willing to submit for resolution of the argument. Criticisms of the types outlined may be made against the proponents of major world religions, of schismatic groups, or of emergent minority religions, 'sects' or 'cults'. Less prevalent, but now recognised in English law, such criticism may also be levelled against active secularists and more passive non-believers.[19]

General Criticism of Religious Doctrine or Practice

The first scenario arises where some criticism is offered of a religion in general, or of some particular aspect of religious practice or doctrine. Such criticism may be expressed in a pejorative fashion or more neutrally. Signal examples might include the reflections on founding ideas of the Islamic faith in Salman Rushdie's *The Satanic Verses*,[20] the critiques of Christianity and other religions offered by Richard Dawkins (2006) and Christopher Hitchens (2007), 'blood libels' against adherents to the Jewish faith,[21] and the critique of Islam offered in some of the cartoons published by the newspaper *Jyllands-Posten*.[22] An earlier instance of this type of dispute can be seen in the heresy 'libel' raised in 1878 against Professor William Robertson Smith on account of his publication of a number of articles based on historical criticism of the Bible in the *Encyclopædia Britannica*.[23] This type of criticism may extend to include some consequential critique of representative figures of the faith concerned. An infamous example can be seen in the derision offered of the Roman Catholic faith by Ian Paisley Snr – a Free Presbyterian Moderator and a Northern Irish Member of the

---

[19] See the Racial and Religious Hatred Act 2006 and commentary in Ivan Hare and James Weinstein (eds), *Extreme Speech and Democracy* (Oxford University Press, 2009).

[20] See, generally, Daniel Pipes, *The Rushdie Affair: the Novel, the Ayatollah and the West* (New York: Birch Lane Press, 1994); Kenan Malik, *From Fatwa to Jihad: The Rushdie Affair and Its Legacy* (London: Atlantic, 2009); Paul Weller, *A Mirror for Our Times: The Rushdie Affair and the Future of Multiculturalism* (London: Continuum, 2009).

[21] See, generally, Alan Dundes (ed.), *The Blood Libel Legend: Casebook in Anti-Semitic Folklore* (Madison: University of Wisconsin Press, 1992). Of course, on occasion, blood libels may have been levelled with particular individuals as targets, and more generally were issued in order to generate hatred of and disquiet regarding the presence of Jews as members of communities.

[22] Perhaps the definitive explication of the Danish cartoons affair is that offered in Jytte Klausen, *The Cartoons That Shook the World* (New Haven: Yale University Press, 2009).

[23] In that case, the 'libel' in question was merely the name of the writ under which the scholar-preacher was brought to the Assembly of the Free Church of Scotland. The case was left undetermined with Robertson Smith being instead stripped of his academic chair.

European Parliament – on the occasion of the 1988 visit of Pope John Paul II to the Strasbourg institution.[24]

Such criticisms are likely to be deemed offensive to adherents of the impugned religion, striking as they do at the articles of faith on which individual and collective convictions and conceptions of identity are premised. It must be questionable, however, whether – even when expressed in virulent, abusive or scurrilous form – they should provide a basis for legal complaint.[25] In terms of libel law, such statements will not usually identify particular adherents as the subjects of criticism, or will do so only in an institutional as opposed to personal manner.[26] This fact has been one motivation behind calls for the introduction of 'group defamation' laws oriented towards criminalising the abuse of religious faiths and ethnic or racial minorities. Moreover, such criticism would generally involve highly contestable imputations of nothing more than metaphysical error or turpitude. Hence, given that the average recipient of such commentary would be understood by the court to be versed in the fact and desirability of religious pluralism, it would be considered unlikely to affect the estimation of adherents of

---

[24]   On that occasion, Paisley's critique took the form of a banner emblazoned with the words 'John Paul II Anti-Christ' and a characteristically robust vocalisation: 'I denounce you as the Antichrist' – see Susan MacDonald, 'Paisley Ejected for Insulting Pope', *The Times*, 12 October 1988; John Palmer, 'Paisley Thrown Out of Euro Assembly After Pope Attack', *Guardian*, 12 October 1988. Paisley has elaborated on his thesis in the text, *The Pope is the Antichrist: A Demonstration from Scripture, History and His Own Lips*. Available at www.ianpaisley.org/antichrist.asp.

[25]   Nevertheless, the European Court of Human Rights has been forgiving of restrictions placed on freedom of expression by member states oriented towards the protection of religious sentiment, usually on the basis of the margin of appreciation left when competing Convention rights are at stake or when an assessment is required of the needs of public safety – see, generally, AR Mowbray, *Cases and Materials on the European Convention on Human Rights*, 2nd edn (Oxford: Oxford University Press, 2007), ch. 11; Sandberg, *Law and Religion*, ch. 5.

[26]   While there is no general rule as to when words spoken of a group or class of persons – such as the adherents of a given religion – sufficiently refer to a particular individuals to allow him or her to bring an action for libel, the larger the class or group against whom the imputation is made, and the more general or sweeping the charge, the less likely it is in practice that the claimant will be permitted to proceed. Vulgar generalisations are not actionable. In the United States, it is a very rare action in which a member of a group of more than 25 persons will be allowed to sue as a person individually identified by comments relating to the group as a whole: 'It is far better for the public welfare that some occasional consequential injury to an individual, arising from general censure of his profession, his party, or his sect, should go without remedy, than that free discussion on the great questions of politics, or morals, or faith, should be checked by the dread of embittered and boundless litigation' (*Ryckman v. Delavan* 25 Wend 186: at 199 (NY 1840)).

the given religion in the minds of people generally. General criticism is unlikely to be deemed defamatory. Indeed, the stronger the tone of any attendant abuse, the greater the likelihood that the criticism would rebound to the detriment of the speaker.

General Criticism Coupled with Specific Allegations

The second type of dispute involving a religious dimension arises where general criticism is made of a religious doctrine or practice, and this is coupled with some specific, associated critique of a particular adherent. Often the complaint is that particular actions of the person who ultimately sues for libel are not warranted by religious doctrine. One might envisage also criticism that seeks to challenge a general rule of doctrine (for example, bars on homosexual practice), but which does so through the vehicle of coupling an allegation of 'wrongdoing' against the religious benchmark by an eminent cleric with one of hypocrisy for prescription of standards for others that are not maintained personally.

It is this type of dispute that has arisen in a number of cases decided by the English courts in recent times. At the root of both the *Hardeep Singh* case and *Shergill v. Purewal* was a schism in the Sikh faith that arose following the death intestate of an acknowledged religious leader, and which involved acrimonious dispute over the legitimacy of the purported succession.[27] The concomitant allegations included complaints over blasphemous and heretical divergence from accepted teachings, the status of the purported Baba and his followers, the causing of violent disorder, and the fraudulent claim to and misappropriation of a range of valuable properties in the UK. The case of *Blake v. Associated Newspapers* involved questions surrounding the legitimacy of the consecration of a purported bishop, and concomitant allegations that he was an imposter intent on deceiving his congregation and the wider public (See paragraphs[11]–[18]) The approach adopted by the judges in those cases, predicated on a dual concept of non-justiciability and deference to religious modes of dispute resolution, is discussed further in the following section.

Specific Allegations of Failure to Meet Prescribed Standards of Behaviour

A third type of dispute sees the specific critique of particular individuals for failure to meet standards or expectations of behaviour prescribed by

---

[27] The details of this schism are set out at length by reference to the case pleadings in the judgment of Mr Justice Eady in the *Hardeep Singh* case, at paragraphs 7–27.

religious doctrine. Here, the force of the allegations in question concern the interpretation of matters of fact. Such allegations will tend to be levelled between members of the same faith, although this will not be universally the case. It may be that the standards themselves are contested and that the behaviour in question is acceptable from one perspective but not the other. In such circumstances, such disputes are akin to those outlined in the second category above. The typical case falling within this category is distinguishable, however, in that the doctrinal benchmarks for acceptable behaviour are agreed and instead an individual's standard of behaviour is impugned. Obvious examples may include allegations of 'sinful' conduct, such as homosexual practice, adultery, apostasy, or witchcraft.[28]

In such cases, there will seldom be any difficulty with the question of identification or publication. The alleged perpetrator of the 'sin' will likely have been publicly identified for exemplary purposes. There may sometimes be greater difficulty, however, on the question of whether imputations were defamatory. On one hand, allegations that would not be considered defamatory from a broader societal perspective – for example, that a person was a homosexual – may be judged harmful to reputation when made to a more cloistered or specific audience. On the other hand, it might reasonably be argued that the impact of the allegation among the specific audience was not such as to adversely affect reputation or to evoke hatred, ridicule or contempt, but rather to engender pity or to solicit aid. Insofar as an impugned individual wishes to remain within the religious grouping, it is conceivable that such cases would never come to the secular court. Rather, they would likely be resolved, if at all, by internal dispute resolution mechanisms. Interestingly, when such cases have come to court in the United States, there has been a tendency to forego adjudication by reference to the 'free exercise of religion' First Amendment rights.[29] Given the qualified

---

[28]   An interesting, historic example can be seen in the complicated case of *R v. Newman* (1853) 1 Ellis and Blackburn 558; 118 E.R. 544. The case involved allegations of sexual and religious misconduct made by Cardinal Newman against a former Dominican friar and demagogue who had converted to Protestantism and lectured against Roman Catholicism in the febrile atmosphere of mid-nineteenth Century England. The trial became a political referendum on Roman Catholicism in England – see, generally, Matthew Mirow, 'Roman Catholicism on Trial in Victorian England: The Libel Case of John Henry Newman and Dr Achilli' (1996) *Catholic Lawyer*, 36: 401–53.

[29]   See, for example, *Purdum v. Purdum*, 2011 WL 1430279 (Kan. Dist. Ct. Apr. 11, 2011); *Cimijotti v. Paulsen*, 230 F. Supp. 39 (N.D. Iowa 1964). For a recent discussion of the First Amendment jurisprudence in this regard, reflecting on the case of *Snyder v. Phelps* 131 S. Ct 1207, US 2011, see Joseph Russomanno, '"Freedom for the Thought That We Hate": Why Westboro Had to Win' (2012) *Communication Law and Policy*, 17: 133–73.

nature of the right to manifest one's religion under Article 9 of the European Convention, the same argument is not easily applied in the UK or Europe more broadly.

Specific Allegations Without Basis in Religious Doctrine

A final type of dispute that includes a religious dimension arises where criticism of religious adherents is offered without any basis in religious doctrine. A key question in such cases will be that of whether or not the imputations at issue rest upon a doctrinal dispute. That is, whether they are better understood to fall within the second category outlined above. This assessment may not always be straightforward. In the *Hardeep Singh* case, Mr Justice Eady explained that 'a specific inquiry ... [must] be made on the facts. It is not simply a question of general impression' (6). In cases where the judge determines that there are stand-alone questions of 'pure fact', in principle these will be actionable. As Mr Justice Eady noted in the *Hardeep Singh* case, 'if an allegation were made of someone, who happened to be a religious leader, that he had his hand in the till, or assaulted a follower, this could be determined separately and without reference to religious doctrine or status' (41). In those circumstances, however, the judge must still decide whether in the circumstances of the given case the court should proceed in the usual way. He or she must recognise that after the exclusion of primary doctrinal or other religious issues, the 'residue or rump of purely factual questions' may be 'incidental or peripheral to the primary conflict' such that to go ahead may be disproportionate or distorting (see paragraph 6). Conversely, in some cases any non-justiciable aspects will be so marginal to the overall nature of the case that there is no problem with proceeding to trial. A useful illustration can be seen in the *Hardeep Singh* case.[30] There, the claimant contended that an allegation that an individual had sexually exploited a number of women did not rely on any religious underpinning. Mr Justice Eady agreed that had such an allegation been made, there would have been no obstacle to considering it in the normal way (see paragraphs 37–9). The problem for the defendant was that no such imputation had been included in the published story.

---

[30]   A further example can be seen in the ECtHR case of *Klein v. Slovakia* (2010) 50 EHRR 15, in which a journalist successfully contested his conviction for offending religious feelings following personal criticism he had made of the Archbishop. See also, *Giniewski v. France* (2007) 45 EHRR 23.

The Approach of the English Courts in Recent Cases

In three relatively recent cases – *Blake v. Associated Newspapers*, the *Hardeep Singh* case, and *Shergill v. Purewal* – the English High Court was asked to determine libel claims arising from allegations that fell within the second category outlined above. These were claims involving purportedly false and defamatory imputations that rested upon some question of religious doctrine. Accepting some differences of emphasis, the approach adopted in each of these cases has been consistent. The first question addressed by the judges involved has been that of whether the imputations do in fact rest upon doctrinal or religious questions. Where this has been deemed to be the case, the courts have pursued a policy of judicial abstention. For instance, in the *Hardeep Singh* case, notwithstanding the attempt by the claimant to eliminate doctrinal assertions from the particulars of claim, Mr Justice Eady found that 'issues of a religious or doctrinal nature permeate the pleadings' (28).[31] In the earlier case of *Blake* (2003), even the claimant's pleadings were 'redolent with doctrinal, procedural, jurisdictional and historical arguments' (17). Justice Gray's unsurprising conclusion was that 'many of the issues raised ... fall within the territory which the courts, by self-denying ordinance, will not enter' (24).

The abstentionist approach has been the chosen response to an obvious, but bipartite problem that the courts have faced. This is, in short, that those using legal methods in legal forums are 'hardly in a position to regulate what is essentially a religious function' (*R v. Chief Rabbi* 1992: 1042, per Simon Brown J). On one hand, it is arguably not the place of the legal regime to seek to answer questions that should be determined, if at all, in religious forums. As it has been expressed in the High Court, 'the court must inevitably be wary of entering so self-evidently sensitive an area, straying across the well-recognised divide between church and state' (*R v. Chief Rabbi* 1992: 1042, per Simon Brown J).[32] Similarly, in *Sulaiman v. Juffali*, Mr Justice Munby explained:

---

[31]   In particular, Mr Justice Eady was called on to address the inferred imputation that the claimant was an 'imposter', which was considered by the claimant to be 'the sting of the article'. Counsel for the claimant had argued that whether the second defendant was right or wrong in his doctrinal assertions was neither here nor there, and that the concept of an impostor involves an allegation of fraud irrespective of doctrinal differences. The judge rejected those submissions, on the basis that 'it seems ... plain that the allegation of 'impostor' cannot be divorced from questions of Sikh doctrine and practice.... Whether this claimant is or is not fairly described as an 'impostor' cannot be isolated and resolved without reference to Sikh doctrines and traditions' (at paragraphs 40–41).

[32]   The court continued, 'One way or another th[e] secular court must inevitably be drawn into adjudicating upon matters intimate to a religious community.'

> Religion ... is not the business of government or of the secular courts ... the
> starting point of the law is an essentially agnostic view of religious beliefs and a
> tolerant indulgence to religious and cultural diversity. A secular judge must be
> wary of straying across the well-recognised divide between church and state. It
> is not for a judge to weigh one religion against another. All are entitled to equal
> respect. (2002: 47)[33]

On the other hand, aside from this policy of deference, there is often the more
basic problem that the religious dispute at the core of the matter may be simply
non-justiciable. This idea was encapsulated by Mr Justice Eady in the *Hardeep
Singh* case:

> Such disputes as arise between the followers of any given religious faith are often
> likely to involve doctrines or beliefs which do not readily lend themselves to
> the sort of resolution which is the normal function of a judicial tribunal. They
> may involve questions of faith or doctrinal opinion which cannot be finally
> determined by the methodology regularly brought to bear on conflicts of factual
> and expert evidence. [5]

In *Blake* (2003), it was agreed by both parties that the core uncertainty –
over the question of whether a person could be seen as a properly consecrated
bishop – could not be determined by a court of law (paragraphs 19–20). Indeed,
any resolution of the issue would require

> a detailed and painstaking examination of questions of doctrine, theology and
> ecclesiology combining an assessment of history and a full understanding of
> contemporary and emergent theology and ecumenism ... [matters on which]
> legitimate yet differing views may be held with integrity (20).

Hence, the abstentionist approach is 'partly a matter of a self-denying ordinance,
applied as a matter of public policy, and partly a question of simply recognising
the natural and inevitable limitations upon the judicial function' (*Hardeep
Singh's case*: 5).[34]

---

[33] *Sulaiman v. Juffali* (2002) 1 FLR 479, at [47].

[34] The scope of the non-justiciability is open to debate. It may extend beyond questions
of doctrine to matters such as the procedures adopted by religious bodies or the customs
and practices of a particular religious community or questions as to the moral and religious
fitness of a person to carry out the spiritual and pastoral duties of his office – see *Blake*,
at 21. Arguably, however, some such themes fall within the area of self-denial and not of non-
justiciability per se.

Although in at least one of the three cases discussed the judge demonstrated a certain pained reluctance (*Blake*: 25), the natural upshot of the approach is that proceedings must then be stayed. Should such actions be permitted to proceed, justification would be impossible. This would create obvious injustice against the defendant. Moreover, there would be a real danger that commentators would henceforth be forced to abstain from arguably truthful, and at the very least important, criticism of religious practices. This would amount to a profound and troubling inroad into the freedom of expression protected by Article 10 of the European Convention.

A Preferable Means of Accommodating Religion in the Law of Libel?

The abstentionist approach is not without cost. As Justice Gray recognised from the outset of his judgment in *Blake* (2003), it results in a measure of unfairness to the claimant. As he explained, the claimant is 'denied the opportunity to vindicate his reputation' (see paragraphs 1, 25 and 38) and defend his 'integrity' (30). Today, one might add that he or she is left unable to seek protection for his Convention right to reputation (Mullis and Scott 2012). Moreover, to the extent that other religious practitioners were dissuaded from engaging with the claimant following the publication of the libel, there may be a prima facie restriction of the freedom to manifest one's religious belief in association with others that is protected by an amalgam of Articles 9 and 11 of the European Convention.[35] This may be particularly problematic if, as would seem likely to be the case, the victim of the libel is drawn from a minority or subordinated grouping. In contrast to representatives of mainstream religions, those of minority religions may have few other avenues by which they might respond to criticism other than by recourse to law. They may experience an antagonistic, contemptuous, or at least sceptical hearing from the Press. Frustrating their attempt to pursue libel claims by electing the defendant publisher to be always the beneficiary of the legal indeterminacy of questions of religious doctrine may be to systematise disadvantage.

There remains a question over whether there was any realistic alternative approach open to the court. In considering this, it is noteworthy that in each of the recent cases, defences of both justification and fair comment were postulated

---

[35]   That Article 9 may be at issue was accepted by counsel for the defendant in *Blake* at paragraph 31. She – and the judge – would appear to have conceived of the case, however, as involving a straightforward balancing exercise between Articles 9 and 10. Compare the view of the European Commission of Human Rights in *Church of Scientology v. Sweden* app. no 8282/78, 14 July 1980.

by the respective defendants. In some instances this was with regard to one and the same imputation. This suggests a certain lack of clarity as to whether the imputations were themselves statements of fact or opinion, albeit that the abstentionist approach appeared to leave the question moot. This could, however, be an important question. It may be that the defence of fair or honest comment might be developed so as to offer a more balanced means of reflecting the indeterminacy of underpinning questions of religious doctrine.

It would seem to be axiomatic that if imputations are based upon premises to be found in interpretations of religious doctrine, then they are best understood as comments that rely upon those interpretations. They are not straightforward imputations of fact, and consideration of the defence of justification is not the appropriate course. Instead, where such published imputations are shown to be defamatory and to have identified the claimant, then only the defence of fair comment should be available. The assertion that, for example, a bishop is an imposter intent on deceiving the public or a Baba is a fraud aiming at embezzling wealth, is best seen not as a statement of fact, but rather as an inference of fact based on an interpretation of religious doctrine or practice. Giving the judgment of the Court in *British Chiropractic Association v. Singh*, Lord Chief Justice Judge rejected the position that had been adopted by Mr Justice Eady at first instance to the effect that 'comment' was to be understood as antithetical to statements of 'verifiable fact' (2010: 17).[36] This is surely correct: it must be possible to draw inferences of fact from other primary facts, and for the law to protect communication of such inferences under the defence of fair comment as it would the expression of value judgments based on the primary facts. If the inference is plain to readers so that its content can be identified as an opinion, then it should not matter whether the statement is factual or value-based in character.

The issue in the context of libels involving religious indeterminacy, then, is whether and how this might be accommodated within the defence of fair comment. In *Spiller v. Joseph* (2011), the Supreme Court offered a review of the historical development of the defence before restating the five elements that must be proven if a defendant is to rely upon it. In addition to the understanding that the defence is defeated by malice, the five requirements are now that the comment must be on a matter of public interest; the comment must be recognizable as comment, as distinct from an imputation of fact; the comment must be based on facts which are true or protected by privilege; the comment must explicitly or implicitly indicated, at least in general terms, the

---

[36] This position perhaps owes something to the jurisprudence of the Strasbourg court where a distinction is drawn between statements of fact and value judgments.

facts on which it is based;[37] and the comment must be one which could have been made by an honest person, however prejudiced he might be, and however exaggerated or obstinate his views. For the honest comment defence to be available, notwithstanding the indeterminacy of the underpinning facts, the court would have to bracket the indeterminacy that would otherwise see the fourth requirement of the defence lost and assess whether the remaining facets of the defence were met. Crucially, the publisher would have to show that the allegation was recognizable as a comment and that he or she had indicated, at least in general terms, the indeterminate question of religious doctrine, upon which the comment was based.

On this approach, then, a libel claim would be defensible whenever the publisher had alluded to or represented the underpinning question of religious doctrine before stating a view on the more tangible, immediate or corporeal issue.[38] Applying this approach to the three cases discussed above, it seems clear that the *Hardeep Singh* case would have been decided in favour of the defence. The original newspaper article went to some lengths to explain the origins of the immediate dispute. In *Blake v. Associated Newspapers Ltd*, there was little or no such allusion. In his pleadings, the claimant explicitly noted that the readers of the *Daily Mail* had been left in ignorance of important 'facts' regarding his appointment as a bishop (30). On the basis of the information set out in the judgment, it is not possible to determine whether enough was done to satisfy the

---

[37]   Delivering the judgment of the court, Lord Phillips revised somewhat the fourth element of the test that had been stated by Lord Nicholls in *Tse Wai Chun Paul v.Albert Cheng* (2001) EMLR 777 (105). The fourth element had been that 'the comment must explicitly or implicitly indicated, at least in general terms, what are the facts on which the comment is being made.... The reader or hearer should be in a position to judge for himself how far the comment was well founded' (at 19). It had earlier been questioned by Mr Justice Eady in *Lowe v. Associated Newspapers Ltd* (2006) EWHC 320 (QB), at 21–60. The revision of the fourth proposition reflected a different understanding of why the comment must include some allusion to the underpinning facts. Lord Phillips considered that identification of the facts with sufficient particularity is required not in the first instance to enable the reader to judge for himself whether the comment was well founded, but rather just to allow the reader to understand what the comment is about (at 104). The idea was that, armed with a general knowledge of the facts as alluded to by the person who made the comment, the reader would subsequently be able to seek out an expanded understanding and thereafter to take a view on the appropriateness of the comment.

[38]   Under section 3 (4) of the Defamation Act 2013, it will become possible to rely not just on true facts when using the honest comment defence, but also on any statement that was privileged under the section 4 defences of responsible publication and reportage. This will mean that any representation of a pre-existing dispute would suffice for the section 3 defence insofar as the speaker did not then adopt a position on one side or the other of the dispute.

test in the three articles complained of in *Shergill v. Purewal*. From the discussion offered by the judge, it would seem that this was certainly the case with regard to the last of the three articles, but less so in respect of the first two (35). The cases evidence that even if the suggested approach to these cases is adopted, much will be left to be determined on the facts of individual cases.

References

Blake v. Associated Newspapers Ltd (2003) EWHC 1960 (QB).
British Chiropractic Association v. Singh (2010) EWCA Civ 350.
Dawkins, Richard. 2006. *The God Delusion*. London: Bantam Books.
Doley, Cameron, and Alastair Mullis eds., 2010. *Carter-Ruck on Libel and Privacy*. 6th Ed. London: LexisNexis.
His Holiness Sant Baba Jeet Singh Ji Maharaj v. Eastern Media Group (2010) EWHC 1294 (QB).
Hitchens, Christopher. 2007. *God is Not Great: How Religion Poisons Everything*. London: Atlantic Books.
Mitchell, Paul. 2005. *The Making of the Modern Law of Defamation*. Oxford: Hart Publishing.
Mullis, Alastair and Andrew Scott. 2012. "The Swing of the Pendulum: Reputation, Expression and the Recentering of English Libel Law." *Northern Ireland Legal Quarterly* 63, no. 1: 27–58.
R v. Chief Rabbi of the United Hebrew Congregations of Great Britain and the Commonwealth, ex parte Wachmann (1992) 1 WLR 1036.
Sandberg, Russell. 2011. *Law and Religion*. Cambridge: Cambridge University Press.
Shergill v. Purewal (2010) EWHC 3610 (QB).
Spiller v. Joseph (2010) UKSC 53.
Sulaiman v. Juffali (2002) 1 FLR 479.
Thornton v. Telegraph Media Group Ltd (2010) EWHC 1414 (QB).

Chapter 9

Religious Libel: Are the Courts the Right Place for Faith Disputes?

Hardeep Singh

Introduction: Libel in England & Wales

The purpose of this chapter is to examine the place of religion within the backdrop of the tort of defamation. In simple terms defamation is subdivided into libel, when the defamatory words are in writing, or slander when they are spoken. The Courts generally tend to treat a statement as defamatory when it 'lowers a person in the estimation of right thinking members of society in general'. This chapter will look at some key questions, examining cases in which religious adherents resort to legal action. Can we bring God into court? Can the Judiciary adjudicate doctrinal differences and disputes? Are there occasions when the Courts will make a ruling on religion? In order for us to come to any sound conclusions on the subject matter, we shall refer to a number of legal cases, some of which have set precedents in the field of ecclesiastical law.

It is clear that right of reputation needs to be fairly balanced with freedom of speech, both cornerstones of western democratic values. The ability to be able to criticize without malice is fundamental to our freedoms, so matters of public interest can be discussed unfettered. This allows ordinary citizens, journalists, bloggers, tweeters, and broadcasters the right to hold people in power to account, be it MP's fiddling their expenses, footballers having extramarital affairs, highlighting offshore tax avoidance in the corporate world, or genuine concerns around the activities of New Religious Movements (NRMs). There is no doubt that those defamed also need remedy. If someone is falsely accused of being a child abuser, murderer or a rapist, protection of reputation is paramount.

In England and Wales the burden of proof is on the defendant in a libel action, this is opposite to other jurisdictions like the United States, where protection afforded by the first amendment. Here the law is designed to discourage capricious libel suits by putting the burden on the claimant to prove that the defendant's speech has caused damage before the suit can go forward. In England, libel actions are notoriously expensive; an Oxford University report illustrated that funding an action in England is 140 times as expensive as in other European countries (Programme in Comparative Media Law and Policy Centre for Socio-Legal Studies 2008). An average case going to trial may cost one million pounds, which means most people, including large publishers, often back down rather than risk the cost of ruin. This is even if what they have written is absolutely true.

This can make libel law attractive to wealthy religious groups, NRMs or 'faith' leaders, a few of whom may have deep pockets. Cases where there is a marked disparity in wealth between claimants and defendants leads to an 'inequality of arms'. Picture a potential scenario: Claimant A is the founder of a group which claims it can use spiritual healing techniques to cure cancer, rectify digestive tract problems, and has the antidote to mental illness. Defendant B, a village blogger, publishes a comment on his view of the claims made by Claimant A. Even if defendant B were entirely justified in their assertion, he or she would risk home and livelihood to defend any claim. This type of scenario has a stifling effect on matters of public interest.

The Libel Reform Campaign, a coalition of Non-governmental Organisations (NGOs) has been instrumental in lobbying the government for fairer laws. Under the heading 'English Law is becoming a global disgrace' (Libel Reform Campaign n.d.). On the Libel Reforms Campaigning website, John Kampfner the former Chief Executive Officer (CEO) of Index on Censorship, Britain's leading free speech organisation says:

> If we don't act we're at risk of becoming a global pariah. There are US States who view English libel law as so damaging to free speech they have passed laws to effectively block the decisions of English judges. Our report is an important milestone in modernizing our antiquated and chilling approach to free expression. (Libel Reform Campaign n.d.)

In the run up to the General election in 2010 all three main political parties made a manifesto commitment to reform libel laws. This commitment was driven in part by the Libel Reform Campaign, which managed to get 50,000 signatories to an online petition for free speech. In 2011, The Joint Committee on the Draft Defamation Bill welcomed many of the reforms proposed in the draft defamation bill.

Chairman of the Committee, The Right Honorable Lord Mawhinney has gone on record to say:

> Defamation proceedings are far too expensive, which is a barrier to all but the richest. Our recommendations should help minimise the reliance on expensive lawyers and the courts, bringing defamation action into the reach of ordinary people who find themselves needing to protect their reputation or defend their right to freedom of speech. They are based upon firm principles, which I am sure the Government will support.[1]

Religion and Libel Law

In the sixteenth to nineteenth century, scoffing at the holy scriptures or reproaching Christ would get you in a lot of hot water, jail, or worse still the death sentence. The case of *Whitehouse v Lemon* (1978) was the only prosecution for blasphemy since 1922. It was not that long ago that the Criminal Justice & Immigration Act abolished the common law offense of blasphemy and blasphemous libel in England and Wales, with effect from 8 July 2008. This was following a campaign instigated by the then Member of Parliament Dr. Evan Harris of the National Secular Society, who is incidentally now a key protagonist in both the Libel Reform Campaign and more recently the Hacked Off campaign, which followed developments in The Leveson inquiry into culture, practice, and ethics of the press. The judicial public inquiry was set up following the News International phone hacking scandal, chaired by Lord Justice Leveson, who was appointed in 2011 (Leveson Inquiry 2012).

Disputes amongst the faithful in Christianity, Islam, Judaism, Hinduism, and Sikhism have all been before the courts in England and Wales. Cases range from employment disputes to the place of religious symbols in schools and the workplace to family law, but also matters of reputation and free speech. The clash of secular courts and religious values is an area where libel judges have been asked to intervene. Newspapers articles in which adherents of faith groups have been accused of 'brainwashing', the uncovering of inimical activities of an 'accused cult leader', a bus driver accused of fanaticism, a think tank publishing a report entitled 'The hijacking of British Islam' are all examples of instances the libel courts have been asked to rule on issues related to religious ideology.

---

[1]   http://www.parliament.uk/business/committees/committees-a-z/joint-select/ draft-defamation-bill1/news/publication-report/, accessed May, 2013, but no longer available.

In the post-9/11 era there have been a number of libel threats issued where individuals, trustees or charitable organisations have been accused of supporting, funding or being directly affiliated to Al Qaeda inspired terrorism or radical clerics. Certain law firms, like London's Carter Ruck (Carter-Ruck n.d.) have a specialty for bringing such claims on behalf of individuals and charities which have been falsely accused of supporting or being affiliated to Al Qaeda, in funding or supporting terrorism. Herein we will briefly examine this development in media law.

The chapter will first examine the case brought by the Unification Church against the publishers of the *Daily Mail* and the Associated Press between 1980 and 1981. This was a watershed moment in NRM cases in the British libel courts.

Unification Church v Associated Press

The movement today known as the Unification Church was originally called the Holy Spirit Association for the Unification of World Christianity, and then in the 1990s it became the Family Federation for World Peace and Unification.

The Unification Church is also referred to as the 'Moonies', albeit members of the Church assert this term is disparaging. It is one of the most controversial NRMs of our times. It was founded by the Korean religious leader, Rev Moon, in the 1950s, and it has a significant number of adherents worldwide. They are known for conducting mass marriages. Reports indicate nuptials by 20,000 brides and grooms at one time (BBC News 2000).

In 1978 the publishers of the *Daily Mail* and Associated Press published an article about the Unification Church headed: 'They took away my son and then raped his mind'. The article involved an interview with two former members of the Church and described them as 'the Church that breaks up families'. As a consequence the then British leader of the Church, Dennis Orme, issued libel proceedings, and the case went to the High Court in 1980.

Extracts from the article:

> Daphne told us that David had been subjected to sophisticated mind-control techniques pioneered by the people who trained the Kami Kaze, and used effectively during the Korean War and by the Chinese communists during World War II.

They included love bombing (constant affection and touching between groups of people), sleep deprivation, protein withdrawal, sugar buzzing (increasing in blood-sugar level so that the brain becomes muddled), repetitive lectures, familiar music with 'restored' lyrics, and other seemingly innocent but insidious devices.

David had been terrorized into believing that Moon was the second coming of Christ ....

The Moonies we had met at the camp were robots, glassy-eyed and mindless, programmed as soldiers in this vast fund raising army with no goals or ideals, except as followers of the half-baked ravings of Moon, who lived in splendor while his followers lived in forced penury. (Barker 1986)

The case continued for five months, eventually leading to a jury trial (involving over 100 witnesses) that resulted in a verdict that the article was not libelous. The Unification Church appealed the decision, which was upheld in the Court of Appeal. They were eventually ordered to pay one million pounds in costs and the Inland Revenue was advised to investigate their tax-free status. The case is a rare example of an NRM taking a publisher to full trial and subsequently through to the appeal courts. At the time, it was the longest such case in English legal history.

Although they were not vindicated for their 'right of reputation', the litigious leaning of certain NRMs like the Unification Church predisposes many publishers to avoid publishing any such stories in the first instance. However, the ruling was thought of as a landmark decision favorable to the publisher, reinforcing the view that there is still a place for campaigning journalism on matters of significant public interest. In this instance an investigative story with a message that may well have resonated with many families in Britain and abroad was found acceptable by the courts. The case especially illustrates how the enormous wealth of a NRM can put them in a unique position to challenge criticism through libel courts; otherwise, this kind of legal action is cost-prohibitive.

Newspapers are not alone, when it comes to the threat of libel. In 2009 Gary Beesley withdrew his book on the New Kadampa Tradition (Wikipedia 2013b) fearing legal action (McBretney 2010). In January 2013 British publishers Transworld cancelled their publication of Lawrence Wright's book on Scientology, *Going Clear: Scientology, Hollywood and the Prison of Belief* (Wikipedia 2013a), after seeking legal advice. It was however published in other countries including the U.S. In the same month, John Sweeney's publisher, Silvertail Books, published his book *The Church of Fear, Inside the Weird World of Scientology*, every other publisher had rejected his proposal due to the fear of libel action (*Independent* 2013). Publication online has also been the subject of libel threats when it comes to NRMs. In December 2011, David Gamble, a UK-based blogger was personally sued by a Canadian based group, not for something he had personally written, but for a comment posted on his blog in response to one of his articles. He removed the comment in order to avoid financial ruin (Gamble 2012).

The question then arises, are some NRMs using the libel courts to effectively 'gag' their opponents or critics? Is it a pernicious use of our libel laws? There is no doubt that many cases involve an inequality of arms; therefore the vast majority of individuals, organisations and publishers who are threatened with libel are simply forced to back down.

Post-9/11 Libel Cases

It is by no means unsurprising that in the era following the 9/11 terrorist attacks in New York, the London 7/7 terror attacks and the Madrid Bombings in 2004, there has been a significant increase in stories in the media which aim to highlight matters relating to Al Qaeda inspired terrorism, these being invariably linked with matters of national security. Religion has been propelled to the forefront of the government's agenda. The news generated is often a reflection of the times we live in. After the London bombings in 2005 the British government became aware of 'home grown terror' or the 'enemy within'.

There have since been many stories which delve into Muslim communities in Britain, sometimes bringing into question their apparent affiliation with 'radical clerics' who espouse hate filled ideologies. There have been regular reports in the print media on terror raids, terrorist trials and foiled terror attacks. The press has an important role to play in this instance, and such coverage is intrinsic to the essential key workings of democracy. Clearly the issue of radicalisation, terrorism and counterterrorism is in the public interest. In recent years there has been a trend in the tabloid press, focusing more on the religious or cultural differences between Islam and British Culture. This was heightened by the former Archbishop of Canterbury's speech in 2008, in which he called for an accommodation between English law and Sharia law. In reaction to the fear from further terror attacks on mainland Britain, the government in 2007 launched the Prevent Strategy, with the aim of stopping people from becoming radicalized and thus preventing them supporting or carrying out acts of terrorism.

The government asserts: 'The current threat level to the UK from international terrorism is severe. The most significant international terrorism threat to the UK remains violent extremism associated with and influenced by Al Qaeda' (gov.uk 2013).

There have been many occasions where the press, academics and authors have legitimate reasons for bringing the activities of certain individuals and organisations into question. The press has had an important part to play in highlighting problematic 'radical clerics', the likes of Abu Hamza, Abu Qatada, and Omar Bakri Mohammed. There are examples where the publication has been well researched and consistent with responsible journalism. There also are a few examples where publishers have paid damages for unfounded allegations against individuals or organisations in the Muslim community. Some of these cases have gone to trial before libel judges. These include the case of *Islam Expo v Spectator Ltd (1828) & Pollard* (2010) and *North London Central Mosque Trust v Policy Exchange & Anor* (2010). Many cases however are settled before they go to trial.

One such case involves allegations leveled by a tabloid against a Muslim doctor working for the NHS. In a front-page article 'Terror case doc works in casualty' dated 10 August 2009, *The Sun* alleged that Dr. Mohammed Asha was linked to violent extremism and that there were strong grounds to believe he would be a threat to national security. The claimant issued proceedings, and the defendant made an offer of amends, accepting that the allegations it had made were entirely false. The claimant won significant damages from the publishers of the Sun Newsgroup Newspapers Ltd (*Mohammed jamil Abdelqader Asha v News Group Newspapers Limited* 2010).

Similarly in another case, the trustees of a charitable organisation sued the publishers of *Express Newspapers* for an article in which it was alleged that the charity Interpal was linked with Hamas, an organisation classified as a terrorist organisation under UK antiterrorist legislation. The article published online headed 'Jet Bomb Ordered by 9/11 spiritual leader' concerned a terror plot to blow up an aeroplane over the U.S. on Christmas day. The article also linked the charity with a Yemeni cleric and alleged Al Qaeda commander. The publishers of the *Express* admitted that the allegations linking Interpal with Hamas were completely false, published an apology online, whilst paying £60,000 damages to the trustees (*Ibrahim Hewitt, Essam Mustafa, Shahan Husain, Ghassan Faour, Ismail Ginwalla, Mohammed Rafiq Vindhani v Express Newspapers* 2010).

In *Islam Expo v Spectator Ltd (1828) & Pollard* (2010), a company which organised exhibitions issued libel proceedings after an article on *The Spectator* website. The article made suggestions that the company was a 'fascist Party' and it was 'dedicated to genocide'. The determination of meaning was heard by Mr. Justice Tugendhat with the defendants relying on hyperlinks to the article, submitting that the article could not bear the meaning alleged by the claimants. The court ruled in favour of the claimants, who then issued an apology online (*Spectator* 2010).

In *North London Central Mosque Trust v Policy Exchange & Anor* a charity took legal action against a right-wing think tank for the publication of a pamphlet *Hijacking of British Islam* which made allegations of extremist activity in some British mosques. Mr. Justice Eady struck out the claim on a technicality, that an unincorporated trust could not have a reputation, so could not bring defamation proceedings, as it didn't exist as a legal entity (*The North London Mosque Trust v The Policy Exchange and Another* 2010).

In another case which settled pre-trial *Akhtar v News Group Ltd* 2009 Edward Yell a solicitor from Carter-Ruck negotiated an Offer of Amends and damages of £100,000 plus costs for his client, Mr Shakil Akhtar: Mr Akhtar sued *News Group Newspapers Limited* for the publication of an article 'Evil on Benefits' along with an editorial entitled 'Sick Parasites Spawn Terror' in the now defunct *News of the World* on 3 February 2008. The articles had described Mr Akhtar as the central figure in a dangerous militant Islamist group, where he was responsible for channeling funds to banned terrorist organisations, including Jaish-e-Mohammed (*Shakil Akhtar v News Group Newspapers Limited* 2009).

The most notable of the post-9/11 libel cases is that of Dr Rachel Ehrenfeld. In 2005 the American academic, writer, terrorism expert, and researcher was ordered to pay £30,000 in damages plus costs after being sued in the High Court in London by the Saudi Arabian billionaire Sheikh Khalid Bin Mahfouz and his sons. They sued over the publication of Ehrenfeld's book *Funding Evil*, in which it was alleged that the billionaire had financed Al Qaeda through his bank and a charitable organisation. Although the book was published in the U.S., 23 copies were sold in England via Amazon. Ehrenfeld refused to respond to the writ, receiving a default judgment. The New York legislature enacted the Libel Terrorism Protection Act or 'Rachel's law' (named after Dr Rachel Ehrenfeld) (Wikipedia 2013c), making its legislature retrospective. The act stated that courts could not hold U.S. citizens liable for the enforcement of judgements of foreign libel courts. As a result U.S. citizens have been granted impunity from judgements coming from foreign courts. As of July 2010, six other states have passed analogs to 'Rachel's Law'. A federal bill based on Rachel's Law was passed unanimously out of the Judiciary Committee and has since then been approved by both Houses of Congress. President Obama signed the bill into law on 10 August 2010.

In an age post-9/11 where the state is at a constant threat from violent extremism, the courts will inevitably be dealing with further defamation cases involving members of the Muslim community. The threat from terrorism will continue to be a matter of significant public interest; therefore, newspapers, authors, academics and the like will continue to highlight concerns to national security.

Doctrinal Disputes and Differences

On the question of the courts role in adjudication of doctrinal disputes and differences, there have been three cases, two in the last few years. The recent legal authorities here stem from disputes within Sikhism, the fifth largest religious group in the world, whose adherents have a sizeable population in the United Kingdom. Sikhism was recorded in the 2001 census as having 336,179 adherents, the largest population outside of India, although according to the census there were more members of the quasi-religious movement knows as the Jedi Knights. The first Sikh settlers came to the United Kingdom in the 1950s mainly from Punjab, to come and work in industries such as foundries and textiles. A later wave of migration came from East Africa. The 2011 census reported a Sikh population of 423,000, an increase of 0.2 of a percentage from 2001 (Office for National Statistics 2012). Today, Sikhs, with their rich heritage with the British, having served in both great wars for Britain and been awarded 14 Victoria Crosses, form a visibly distinct and prominent group in the United Kingdom. Notably in 2011, the first turbaned Sikh representative, Lord Singh of Wimbledon, joined the House of Lords.[2] In 2012 a Sikh solider, Jatendarpal Singh Bullar, made headlines parading outside Buckingham Palace wearing a turban instead of a bearskin (English 2012).

The first of the doctrinal libel cases is *Blake v Associated Newspapers (The Right Reverend Jonathan Clive Blake v Associated Newspapers Limited* 2003*)*. It was a Valentine's Day transmission in 2001, which resulted in a religious libel action against the publishers of the *Daily Mail* and the Associated Press. The claimant, Bishop Jonathan Blake was seen on daytime television officiating what was described to be a homosexual marriage. The bishop was dressed in robes similar to those worn by bishops in the Church of England or the Roman Catholic Church. Bishop Jonathan Blake was referred to by the darlings of daytime television, Richard and Judy, as a 'real bishop'; reference was made in an interview that he had been ordained as a priest and had 'traditionally worked in the Church of England for 12 years'.

---

[2] 'Indarjit Singh', Parliament.UK, http://www.parliament.uk/biographies/indarjit-singh/94240, accessed May 2013, no longer available.

Subsequently, two articles appeared in the *Daily Mail*. Both articles were complaints. The first was headed 'A gay "wedding" conducted by a self-styled bishop, with Richard & Judy as witnesses. How daytime TV celebrated Valentine's Day'. The second article, published a few days later was a comment piece with the headline 'Rites and Wrongs'. I quote from the article:

> This week's most repulsive stunt shown on TV when elderly ladies and small children were almost certainly watching was the Valentines day 'marriage' of two particularly cheesy homosexuals on the Richard and Judy show. Officiating was an imitation bishop who was a once divorced former clergyman. The only thing that surprised me about this disgusting event was that the producers could not find a real bishop to do it. Given the appalling moral confusion of the Church of England these days, I'd of thought its Bishops would have been queuing up. It's at times like this I wish I was an atheist.

Proceedings were commenced, and the claimant set out the defamatory meanings based on the two articles complained of, which in summary equated to the inferential meaning that he was nothing but an imitation Bishop who dishonestly masqueraded himself publicly as such. In 2003, during an interlocutory hearing, Sir Charles Gray ruled the case was non-justiciable. The reason being that the courts could not adjudicate the validity of the appointment of Bishop Jonathan Blake. Furthermore *Blake* highlights the reluctance of secular courts to regulate procedures adopted by religious communities or questions the moral or spiritual fitness of someone to carry out religious, pastoral, and spiritual duties associates with their appointment. This was an exceptional case where the court's decision indicated that justice required the case to be stayed.

I was on the sharp end of one of these 'religious' libel actions involving a schism within Sikhism. It was dubbed *His Holiness v Singh* or the *Singh2* case after Simon Singh's victory for free speech in his defence against a claim brought by the British Chiropractic Association (BCA). I stood accused of libeling a self-appointed Indian 'Holy man' from Punjab, India. We will touch on the significance of the case, adjudicated by Mr. Justice Eady. The second action, *Shergill v Purewal,* is a related case involved a 'Sikh activist' Daljit Singh Shergill who claimed he had been libeled by Rajinder Singh Purewal, the first defendant and Derby based, *Punjab Times International Limited* (PTI), the second defendant.

Sikhism and New Religious Movements

Before discussing *His Holiness v Singh* and *Shergill v Purewal*, it's important to provide a snapshot into Sikhism.

- Sikhism is a little over 500 years old and started with teachings of Guru Nanak in 1469.
- He was born at a time of considerable conflict between the majority of the Hindu faithful who were largely sunk in ritual and superstition and the Muslim invaders from the North who were often bent on forced conversion.
- The Guru taught that there is one God who is not aligned to any particular faith. Our different religions were compared to paths up a mountain leading to an understanding of God.
- He taught that all these paths should be equally respected and our different religions should not get in the way of our understanding that we are equal members of the same one human family; this equality extended to women from day one.
- Sikhism had ten living Gurus; in order to uphold the ecumenical principles of Guru Nanak, two were brutally martyred by the Muslim rulers.
- The ninth Guru, Guru Tegh Bahadur was beheaded in 1675 for standing up for the freedom of expression of Hindus.
- The last and final Guru, Gobind Singh created a military fraternity called the Khalsa, or brotherhood of the pure, which evolved into the sword arm of India.
- He collected the writings of the Gurus and compiled the Guru Granth Sahib, promulgating that Sikhs should only follow these teachings after his departure.
- This is a fundamental part of the Sikh code of conduct or Reht Maryada, in particular, paragraph 9.4 the definition of a Sikh. Section 9.4.1 states:

A Sikh is any person who faithfully believes in (1) one immortal Being; (2) ten Gurus, from Guru Nanak Dev to Guru Gobind Singh; (3) the Guru Granth Sahib; (4) the utterances and teachings of the ten Gurus; (5) the baptism bequeathed by the tenth Guru, and who does not owe allegiance to any other religion.

Over the last few decades there has been a mushrooming of hermitages across many parts of India as well as Punjab, the only Sikh majority state.

In some instances the *Mahant* or caretaker of the hermitage or *Dera* declares himself as a living Guru. Many of the larger Dera's have growing political sway, and it's not unusual for astute politicians to make a beeline for the 'holy men' nearer to election time: swathes of sycophantic devotees equates to significant voting power at the ballot boxes. The ability to swing an election with the help of your followers grants special privileges for the *Mahant,* which include fleets of Mercedes cars and perhaps even armed bodyguards.

New religious schisms impacting on mainstream Sikhism have hit the headlines, both nationally and internationally:

> Darshan Das the founder of a group called Sachkhandnanakdham was shot dead in Southall, West London in 1987.[3]

> In 2007 the Independent reported on riots in response to Dera Sacha Sauda whose leader allegedly dressed up as Guru Gobind Singh. One person was killed and more than 50 were injured during the tumult. India's Prime Minister Manmohan Singh called for calm and put the army of standby as the central government sent thousands of police to Punjab & Haryana.[4]

> In 2009 The Guardian reported on the murder of a 'Sikh sect leader' of Dera Sach Khand in Vienna, which resulted in rioting in several North Indian states. Again the Prime Minister called for calm and was 'deeply distressed' by the tumult (*Guardian* 2009).

In 2007, I wrote a piece expressing concern over a group calling itself the 'Nirmal Sikh faith'. The article was headed 'Cult divides Sikh congregation in High Wycombe' (Jack of Kent 2010). What was unique about the investigation was that a dispute in India had essentially spread to the British Sikh community. This led to a breach of peace in Gurdwaras in Britain as well as intervention by the Police. From a doctrinal perspective, the 'Nirmal Sikh Faith' was deviating from section 9.4.1 of the *Reht Maryada*. The deviation from mainstream Sikhism resulted in the description of its leader as 'an accused cult leader'.

Proceedings were instigated by His Holiness Sant Baba Jeet Singh Maharaj, which resulted in trial in May 2010 before Mr. Justice Eady. The claimant was an Indian national who had apparently never travelled to the UK, nor apparently

---

[3]   ITN Source, http://www.itnsource.com/shotlist//ITN/1987/11/12/T12118701 /?s=punjab, accessed May, 2013, no longer available.

[4]   http://www.independent.co.uk/news/world/asia/cult-leader-sparks-sikh-riots-with-guru-stunt-449763.html, accessed May, 2013, no longer available.

read, wrote, nor spoke any English. The defamatory meanings the claimant attributed to the article complained of were natural and ordinary meanings, not relying on any innuendo. The claimant alleged that he had been referred to as a leader of a cult and an imposter, that he had disturbed the peace of the Sikh community in High Wycombe, as well as promoting blasphemy and the sexual exploitation of women. There was also an allegation that the article complained of meant that the claimant had dishonestly produced counterfeit trust deeds to remove the trustees and Management Committee of a Gurdwara (Sikh Temple). All three defences available in libel proceedings were used: justification, fair comment and qualified privilege.

The primary issue in the case was the validity or otherwise of the Claimant's purported appointment as the 'Third Holy Saint'. There was reference in the proceedings to the significance of a 'turban tying' ceremony in Punjab, where it was alleged that the claimant was officiated as the next in line to a succession of a lineage of saints. This ceremony, it was submitted, gave the claimant spiritual authority as well as rights over assets, which included three Sikh Temples in the United Kingdom. The defendant submitted that the affront at the expression 'leader of cult' or 'imposter', and each and all of the subsequent specific matters raised by the claimant, were all derived from the primary issue, which it was submitted was non-justiciable. The defendant argued that there were no discrete issues that could be determined without the court entering into the forbidden territory of Sikh doctrine, polity or tradition. The particulars of the claim in the defendants view could not be adjudicated without the courts resolving the primary issue concerning the validity of the claimant's alleged appointment as the 'Third Holy Saint' in the proceedings.

On the first day of what would have been a ten-day trial, as with the *Blake* case, the case was permanently stayed. As Mr. Justice Gray observed when imposing the stay in *Blake*:

> It seems plain to me that there are numerous questions raised on the parties' statements of case, which, according to the authorities already cited, are non-justiciable. Such questions include, by way of example only, substantive doctrinal questions including the canon law of catholic apostolic churches; questions of ecclesiastic procedure such as the authority and entitlement of Richard Palmer to consecrate the Claimant and the validity (in the absence art the time of any denomination or established church) of the consecration of the Claimant; questions whether the consecration of the Claimant was in conformity with the customs and practices of any established Christian denomination or criteria independently of POEM and finally questions as to the moral standing and

fitness of both Richard Palmer and the Claimant for Episcopal office. I emphasise that these are no more than examples of the questions arising on the pleadings, which appear to me to come within the forbidden territory of non-justiciability.

In paragraph 31 of the judgment in *His Holiness v Singh*, Mr. Justice Eady quoted the decision of Mr. Justice Munby in *Sullaiman v Juffali* (2002) (*His Holiness Sant Baba Jeet Singh Ji Haharaj v (1) Eastern Media Group Limited (2) Hardeep Singh* 2010).

> Religion ... is not the business of government or of the secular courts. So the starting point of the law is an essentially agnostic view of religious beliefs and a tolerant indulgence to religious and cultural diversity. A secular judge must be wary of straying across the well-recognised divide between church and state. It is not for a judge to weigh one religion against another. All are entitled to equal respect, whether in times of peace or, as at present, amidst the clash of arms.

In paragraph 41 Mr. Justice Eady clearly stated general occasions when the courts would intervene.

> Of course, I recognise that if an allegation were made of someone, who happened to be a religious leader, that he had his hand in the till, or assaulted a follower, this could be determined separately and without reference to religious doctrine or status, but that is far from this case. The issue whether this Claimant is or is not fairly described as an 'impostor' cannot be isolated and resolved without reference to Sikh doctrines and traditions.

It is clear in the judgment made by Mr. Justice Eady that issues of fact can be determined by a libel court, however they need to be distinct from any doctrinal dispute or difference. The claimant appealed the decision, although not given permission to appeal in writing. He was later given permission to appeal by Lady Justice Smith on limited grounds at an oral hearing (*Free Speech Blog* 2010). These were the ancillary particulars of claim, which the appellant submitted could be adjudicated without reference to Sikh doctrine. The case eventually came to a head in a hearing before Lord Justice Sedley and Lord Justice Pitchford on 1 February 2011 (*His Holiness Sant Baba Jeet Singh Ji Maharaj v Eastern Media Group and Anr* 2011). The respondent applied to the courts for security for costs and was successful in securing an order for £250,000 security, which the appellant failed to lodge in the Court funds office. The case was then finally struck out (*Independent* 2011).

The most recent of the 'religious libel' cases brought before the courts in England and Wales is another case involving His Holiness Sant Baba Jeet Singh Maharaj and journalists. Daljit Singh Shergill, a 'Sikh activist', brought libel proceedings against PTI for three articles published in 2008, again relating to the legitimacy of the Indian preacher residing in the Punjab (*Shergill and Purewal & Another* 2010). The three articles complained of, amongst other things stated, 'not only Jeet Singh, his supporters in the UK are a sham too'. There was also reference made to events involving the claimant which were said to have occurred on 11 and 16 June 2008. The meanings pleaded by the claimant for the articles: In the first of the three articles, it was pleaded that the claimant had 'sought to instigate serious riots and create an atmosphere of terror' by proclaiming that Baba Jeet Singh had won a court case in India and was seeking to misappropriate local Sikh temples.

The defences relied upon by the defendants were justification and fair comment. They requested Sir Charles Gray to stay the proceedings and submitted that the claims related to religious issues and could not be divorced from such, therefore the case could not be adjudicated. As in *His Holiness v Singh,* Sir Charles Gray made the same decision as Mr. Justice Eady: the facts could not be separated from religious matters.

In paragraph 34 of the judgment, Sir Justice Gray asserts:

> It is open to a defendant in a libel action to justify words of which the claimant complains in any meaning which those words are reasonably capable of bearing. In my judgment, it would not be possible to hive off or divorce the issue of the legitimacy or otherwise of the claims that Baba Jeet is the successor to the sainthood. To attempt to do so would be unjust to the defendants. It appears to me to be fundamental to their case on justification that the claims of Baba Jeet to be the true leader and owner of the Gurudwaras are unjustified. (*Shergill v Purewal & Another* 2010)

In paragraph 35 Sir Justice Gray makes reference to the two legal authorities on the point of non-justiciability. (Sir Justice Gray was in fact the presiding judge in *Blake v Associated Newspapers.*)

> That pleaded case inevitably raised the doctrinal issues relating to the Sikh religion and its traditions. This case, like the cases of *Blake* and *Baba Jeet v Hardeep Singh,* is one where, in my view, it is impossible to adapt the issues in such a way as to circumvent the insuperable obstacle placed in the way of a fair trial of the action by the fact that the court is bound to abstain from determining questions which lie at the heart of the case.

The claim was effectively thrown out, and there was no subsequent appeal. Of relevance to these decisions by the libel courts are the amendments made by the House of Lords in 2006 to the Public Order Act of 1986 against inciting religious hatred (hatred against persons on religious grounds). There is now a free speech defence, which was inserted after the controversial case of *Jerry Springer the Opera* (2005) and protects preachers, politicians, polemicists, and satirists so long as their attacks focus on beliefs and practices.

Section 29 (j) on protection of freedom of expression reads as follows:

> Nothing in this Part shall be read or given effect in a way which prohibits or restricts discussion, criticism or expressions of antipathy, dislike, ridicule, insult or abuse of particular religions or the beliefs or practices of their adherents, or of any other belief system or the beliefs or practices of its adherents, or proselytising or urging adherents of a different religion or belief system to cease practicing their religion or belief system.

Some academic lawyers and commentators have argued that the decision in *Shergill v Purewal* may have gone too far. The argument is that not all of the articles were simply about issues of doctrinal disputes; there were also allegations that the claimant was a party to 'conspiracies to provoke violence'. Some argue that the decision breaches the claimant's rights to access to a court under article 6 of the European Convention on Human Rights.

It is clear that secular courts should not make decisions giving credence to one religious belief over another. This includes those with no belief. It is also well accepted that the courts should give all religious observances equal respect. The question arises, are the courts doing enough or perhaps even too much to exclude matters of religious doctrine, polity, and tradition? It has been observed in cases involving both religion and human rights or discrimination that the courts will give credence to the rights in secular society over religious beliefs. There are a number of examples in which this has occurred, albeit outside of the libel courts. An example is the Cornish hotel gay discrimination case, in which the judge ruled against Christian hotel owners for discriminating against a couple in a civil partnership who wanted to share a room (News Bristol 2011). In the Jewish free school case, the Supreme Court made a ruling that anti-discrimination laws trumped Jewish religious traditions (*R(E) v Governing Body of JFS* [2009] UKSC 15).

In another such case a Christian sex therapist, Gary Macfarlane, challenged his sacking for refusing to give sex therapy to gay couples. His case was taken to the European Court of Human Rights, but the court did not admit the case for adjudication. The balance was struck between religious rights and those of homosexual couples, the rights in secular society given more credence. *Macfarlane* had previously made headlines due to the intervention of the former Archbishop of Canterbury Lord Carey. The Strasbourg Judges ruled on three other Christian cases along with Macfarlane's in January 2013: those of Nadia Eweida, Shirley Chaplin and Lillian Ladele (*Telegraph* 2012).

Nadia Eweida, a customer service staff member for British airways was the only one to win her case. Eweida was sent home for refusing to remove or conceal her cross. A few months later the airline changed their policy allowing her back. Strasbourg's view was the UK courts had given too much weight to corporate image when compared to Eweida's desire to manifest her Christian faith. Furthermore, Muslim or Sikh employees of BA were allowed to wear hijabs and turbans, respectively, without negatively impacting on the airline's image (*Guardian* 2013).

The decisions made in Strasbourg will have far reaching implications in the interface of religious beliefs, both in public service delivery and in the workplace. It is incumbent on Member States to strike a balance between conflicting rights of religion and rights in secular society.

Summary and Update

The prospect of getting caught up in defamation proceedings as either a claimant or defendant is viewed by most as an entirely undesirable place to be. In the words of Sir Stephen Sedley, a former Judge in the Court of Appeal of England and Wales: 'A defamation lawsuit is always an emotional and financial nightmare for one party, and as often as not for both'(English Pen 2012).

In many instances, cases involve those who challenge power, resulting in an immediate 'inequality of arms' between parties. Defamation has historically been known as a tort of the super wealthy. It is considered as the preserve of billionaires, Premier League footballers, A-list celebrities, or oligarchs. We can safely add some NRMs to the list of privileged players on London's libel circuit. The exorbitant costs, drawn out procedures, and uncertainty of litigation mean that many cases settle before they come to court due to factors such as cost rather than merits of the case.

The current system could be viewed as detrimental to matters of public interest and, by implication, to the right of free speech itself. Furthermore in England and Wales the claimant is not required to prove harm when they bring a claim; consequently, many trivial claims come to court. Unlike in the U.S., the burden of proof is entirely on the defendant. Similarly the current system can undermine reputational rights, where ordinary people are unable to bring a claim due to costs associated with taking legal action. With the onset of 'no win, no fee' agreements, also known as conditional fee agreements (CFAs), ordinary members of the public have been able to secure legal representation and get 'access to justice'. The government is reforming costs in civil litigation. The initial drafting of the Legal Aid, Sentencing and Punishment of Offenders Bill (LAPSO) would have removed 'access to justice' for ordinary people who sought to bring a claim or defend it against powerful organisations or wealthy individuals.

Justice Leveson made strong recommendations that cost protection should be provided in defamation and privacy claims to protect those of modest means (Leveson Inquiry 2012). On 12 December 2012 the government announced that provisions relating to sections 44 and 46 of the LAPSO Act, which would remove recoverability of success fees and insurance premiums would not come into effect until cost protection had been introduced for defamation and privacy claims (UK Parliament 2012).

Reform of Britain's libel law is well underway. In March 2012 the Ministry of Justice published a statement in response to the report of the Joint Scrutiny Committee on the Draft Defamation Bill. Here the government demonstrated its commitment to the Bill, in recognition of the serious problems faced by NGOs, bloggers, authors and scientists. The Libel Reform Campaign set out wide-ranging evidence along with hundreds of other individuals and organisations (UK Parliament 2012). Proposals include the introduction of a statutory public interest defence and increased use of alternative dispute resolution (ADR). The government committed to the Defamation Bill in the Queens speech, which heralded the first wholesale libel bill since 1843. The Defamation Bill is now passing through Committee Stage in the Lords; it will then go to Report Stage, Third Reading and Consideration of Amendments, prior to Royal Assent in 2013.

The government has made a commitment that it will make changes by introducing a single publication rule, reduce libel tourism, whilst having proposed some procedural changes. Notably, libel claimants will be required to show 'serious harm' before their case can proceed under government proposals contained in the defamation bill. The test will be applied during the early resolution procedure, which will also be developed further to encourage swift remedies. The government believes this threshold test, combined with procedures allowing key preliminary issues, such as meaning resolved early in any litigation, will remove concerns about corporations suing. This extends to the use of libel by a few NRMs as a tool to silence critics.

References

Barker, Eileen. 1986. *The Making of a Moonie: Choice or Brainwashing?* Oxford: Blackwell Publishing.

BBC News. 2000. 'In Pictures: Moonies' Mass Wedding'. http://news.bbc.co.uk/2/hi/asia-pacific/641588.stm.

Carter-Ruck. n.d. http://www.carter-ruck.com/.

English Pen. 2012. *The Alternative Libel Project.* http://www.englishpen.org/wp-content/uploads/2012/03/Alternative_Libel_Project_FinalMarch2012.pdf.

English, Rebecca. 2012. 'Sikh Soldier Makes History as he Guards Buckingham Palace Wearing Turban Instead of Traditional Bearskin'. *Mail Online.* http://www.dailymail.co.uk/news/article-2246410/Sikh-soldier-makes-history-guards-Buckingham-Palace-wearing-turban-instead-traditional-bearskin.html.

Free Speech Blog. 2010. 'Appeal Granted in Sikh Holy Man Libel Case'. http://blog.indexoncensorship.org/2010/10/22/appeal-granted-in-sikh-holy-man-libel-case/.

Gamble, Dave. 2012. 'I Got Sued for $3 Million by a Religious Cult'. http://www.skeptical-science.com/religion/sued-3-million-religious-cult/.

GOV.UK. 2013. 'Protecting the UK Against Terrorism'. http://www.homeoffice.gov.uk/counter-terrorism/review-of-prevent-strategy/.

The Guardian. 2009. 'Riots Flare in India after Sikh Sect Leader Killed in Austrian Temple'. http://www.theguardian.com/world/2009/may/25/india-sikh-riots-killing-austria.

The Guardian. 2013. 'Balancing Christian and Gay Rights Isn't Easy – Give Strasbourg Some Credit'. http://www.theguardian.com/law/2013/jan/15/christian-gay-rights-strasbourg?intcmp=239.

His Holiness Sant Baba Jeet Singh Ji Haharaj v (1) Eastern Media Group Limited (2) Hardeep Singh. 2010. England and Wales High Court (Queen's Bench Division) Decisions. http://www.bailii.org/ew/cases/EWHC/QB/2010/1294.html.

His Holiness Sant Baba Jeet Singh Ji Maharaj v Eastern Media Group and Anr. 2011. England and Wales Court of Appeal (Civil Division) Decisions. http://www.bailii.org/ew/cases/EWCA/Civ/2011/139.html

Ibrahim Hewitt, Essam Mustafa, Shahan Husain, Ghassan Faour, Ismail Ginwalla, Mohammed Rafiq Vindhani v Express Newspapers. In the High Court of Justice Queen's Bench Divsion. Statement in Open Court. Carter-Ruck. http://www.carter-ruck.com/Documents//Interpal_Statement.pdf

The Independent. 2011. 'Holy Man Looks Set to Drop Libel Case'. http://www.independent.co.uk/news/uk/home-news/holy-man-looks-set-to-drop-libel-case-2201170.html.

The Independent. 2013. 'Scientologists Believe the Holocaust was Planned and Carried Out by Psychiatrists'. http://www.independent.co.uk/news/world/americas/scientologists-believe-the-holocaust-was-planned-and-carried-out-by-psychiatrists-8440369.html.

Islam Expo Ltd v The Spectator (1823) Ltd (2) Stephen Pollard. 2010. England and Wales High Court (Queen's Bench Division) Decisions. http://www.bailii.org/ew/cases/EWHC/QB/2010/2011.html.

Jack of Kent Blog. 'Libel and the Holy Man'. http://jackofkent.blogspot.co.uk/2010/10/libel-and-holy-man.html.

Legislation.gov.uk. 2012. 'Racial and Religious Hatred Act 2006'. http://www.legislation.gov.uk/ukpga/2006/1/schedule/enacted.

Leveson Inquiry: Practice and Ethics of the Press. 2012. 'The Leveson Inquiry'. http://www.levesoninquiry.org.uk/.

Libel Reform Campaign. n.d. http://libelreform.org/.

McBretney, John. 2010. Letter to Mr Gary Beesley. http://thedorjeshugdengroup.files.wordpress.com/2010/07/2010-05-16-nkt-letter-to-gary-beesley1.pdf.

Mohammed jamil Abdelqader Asha v News Group Newspapers Limited. 2010. In the High Court of Justice Queen's Bench Division. Statement in Open Court by the Solicitor for the Claimant. Carter-Ruck. http://www.carter-ruck.com/Documents/ASHA-SIOC-270410.pdf.

News Bristol. 2011. 'Bristol Gay Couple Win Cornwall B&B Bed Ban Case'. http://www.bbc.co.uk/news/uk-england-bristol-12214368.

The North London Mosque Trust v The Policy Exchange and Another. 2010. England and Wales Court of Appeal (Civil Division) Decisions. http://www.bailii.org/ew/cases/EWCA/Civ/2010/526.html.

Office for National Statistics. 2012. *2011 Census: Key Statistics for England and Wales, March 2011*. http://www.ons.gov.uk/ons/dcp171778_290685.pdf.

Programme in Comparative Media Law and Policy Centre for Socio-Legal Studies. 2008. *A Comparative Study of Costs in Defamation Proceedings Across Europe*. Oxford: University of Oxford. http://pcmlp.socleg.ox.ac.uk/sites/pcmlp.socleg.ox.ac.uk/files/defamationreport.pdf.

R (on the Application of E) (Respondent) v Governing Body of JFS and the Admissions Appeal Panel of JFS (Appellants) and others R (on the application of E) (Respondent) v Governing Body of JFS and the Admissions Appeal Panel of JFS and others (United Synagogue) (Appellants). 2009. United Kingdom Supreme Court. Judgement. Before Lord Phillips, President Lord Hope, Deputy President, Lord Rodger, Lord Walker, Lady Hale, Lord Brown, Lord Mance, Lord Kerr, and Lord Clarke. http://www.supremecourt.gov.uk/decided-cases/docs/UKSC_2009_0136_Judgment.pdf.

The Right Reverend Jonathan Clive Blake v. Associated Newspapers Limited. 2003. England and Wales High Court (Queen's Bench Division) Decisions. http://www.bailii.org/ew/cases/EWHC/QB/2003/1960.html.

Shakil Akhtar v. News Group Newspapers Limited. 2009. In the High Court of Justice Queen's Bench Division. Statement in Open Court. Carter-Ruck. http://www.carter-ruck.com/Documents/Akhtar_Statement_in_Open_Court_OCR.pdf.

Shergill v. Purewal & Another. 2010. England and Wales High Court (Queen's Bench Division) Decisions. http://www.bailii.org/ew/cases/EWHC/QB/2010/3610.html.

The Spectator. 2010. 'Islam Expo: Apology'. http://www.spectator.co.uk/features/6232858/islam-expo-apology/.

The Telegraph. 2012. 'The Four Christians Accusing Their Employers of Discrimination'. http://www.telegraph.co.uk/news/religion/9519785/The-four-Christians-accusing-their-employers-of-discrimination.html.

UK Parliament. 2012. *Implementation of Part 2 of the Legal Aid, Sentencing and Punishment of Offenders Act 2012; civil litigation funding and costs.* Written Ministerial Statement, Ministry of Justice. http://www.parliament.uk/documents/commons-vote-office/December_2012/12-12-12/8-Justice-ImplementationofPart2.pdf.

Wikipedia. 2013a. 'Going Clear: Scientology, Hollywood, and the Prison of Belief'. http://en.wikipedia.org/wiki/Going_Clear:_Scientology,_Hollywood,_and_the_Prison_of_Belief.

Wikipedia. 2013b. 'New Kdampa Tradition'. http://en.wikipedia.org/wiki/New_Kadampa_Tradition.

Wikipedia 2013c. 'Rachel Ehrenfeld'. http://en.wikipedia.org/wiki/Rachel_Ehrenfeld.

Chapter 10

The European Court of Human Rights, Minority Religions, and New Versus Original Member States[1]

Valerie A. Lykes and James T. Richardson

Introduction

This chapter will examine how the European Court of Human Rights (ECtHR) has dealt with cases involving minority faiths and will address controversies that have arisen concerning its pattern of jurisprudence in this important area. Cases from two societies within the Council of Europe – France and Russia – will be examined to assist in understanding the ECtHR's developing pattern of jurisprudence. A brief explanation of how the ECtHR is organized and changes in how it processes cases will also be presented.

The ECtHR is perhaps the most important court in the world when issues of religious freedom and other human and civil rights are considered. It serves as the court of last resort for over 800 million citizens in the 47 nations comprising the Council of Europe (COE), including many new members that were formerly part of Soviet-dominated Eastern and Central Europe. Case law from the ECtHR is influential around the world. For instance, a recent review of High Court decisions in Australia reveals that 41 cases from that court had cited ECtHR decisions. Also, the famous *Lawrence v. Texas* decision of the United States Supreme Court (539 U.S. 558 (2003)), which established the right of gay couples to privacy in sexual relations, cited ECtHR case precedents, the first time a majority decision of that Court has done so.

The ECtHR is playing a powerful role in efforts to align values and practices of former Soviet-dominated states with those of Western nations.

---

[1] This chapter is based on a presentation at the annual meeting of the American Academy of Religion, San Francisco, CA, November, 2011, and is a considerable expansion of a section of a chapter by the two authors in Cumper and Lewis (2012).

All these new Member States from Eastern and Central Europe agreed, by their decision to seek membership in the COE, to abide by the European Convention of Human and Civil Rights, the governing document for the COE and the ECtHR. This has led to a dramatic increase in the case load of the court and also to a significant change in the role and purview of the court. Wojciech Sadurski (2005), noted legal scholar, has written concerning the role of constitutional courts in Eastern and Central Europe, and how those courts have been encouraged and assisted by actions of the ECtHR. Sadurski points out that the ECtHR has begun to act more as a Supreme Court in a hierarchical arrangement of courts within the COE, noting that this seems analogous to the role played by the United States Supreme Court. Sadurski has also developed the concept of "pilot judgment" by which he means that the ECtHR is now issuing decisions that are expected to be treated as precedents by COE Member States, thus establishing the primacy of the ECtHR over the member states' own laws (Sadurski 2009).

There has been controversy concerning the role of the ECtHR in its developing jurisprudence concerning religion over the years. James Richardson (1995), among others (also see Evans 2001), has discussed the fact that the court took 40 years to find any violation of Article 9, which guarantees freedom of conscience and religion, even though many such claims were submitted to the court.[2] The court finally ruled in 1993, in a split vote, in *Kokkinakis v. Greece* that the statute criminalizing proselytizing violated Article 9, in what may have been an early "pilot judgment" (see below).[3] Carolyn Evans (2001) has discussed the inconsistencies in court opinions dealing with religious freedom since that initial violation found in 1993. More recently, criticisms have developed about possible biases in the jurisprudence of the court concerning minority faiths. Richardson and Garay (2004) suggested the possibility of a "double standard" operating with the court, with original Member States being granted a considerable "margin

---

[2]   Article 9 states:

    1. Everyone has the right to freedom of thought, conscience, and religion; this right includes freedom to change his religion and belief, and freedom, either alone or in community with others and in public and private, to manifest his religion or belief, teaching, practice, and observance.

    2. Freedom to manifest one's religion or belief shall be subject only to such limitations as are prescribed by law and are necessary in a democratic society in the interests of public safety, for protection of the public order, health or morals, or for the protection of the rights and freedoms of others.

Article 14 also precludes discrimination on a number of grounds, including religion.

[3]   Sadurski (2009) does not refer to this key decision as an example of a "pilot judgment", but it seems to fit his criteria.

of appreciation" that allowed these nations to regulate religious minorities as they saw fit, while former Soviet-dominated countries were dealt with more rigorously in Article 9 cases (also see Richardson and Shoemaker 2008). Carolyn Evans (2010) and Lech Garlicki (2007), however, interpret this same pattern as meaning that the court is protecting religious organizations and communities, but not supporting individual religious freedom rights. Both claim that in former communist countries the basic right of religious organizations to exist is called into question, whereas in original Member States, this is not such an issue. Richardson and Lykes (2012) take issue with this view, citing the overwhelming pattern of deference shown to France in ECtHR cases as indicating that the double standard may still be operating.[4]

Another criticism of the ECtHR's jurisprudence concerning religion posits strong biases in favor of French style neutrality and Christian values and practices. Peter Cumper (1999) and Karen Meerschaut and Serge Gutwirth (2009) suggest that the court favors Christian values in its decision making, and particularly Meerschaut and Gutwirth argue that a major decision in a case involving Turkey indicates a narrow and quite negative view of Islam.[5] Before drawing conclusions concerning what, if any, biases might be operating within the ECtHR's jurisprudence, a brief history of the Council of Europe and the court and its processes for handling submitted cases will offer some background and context for our analysis.

History and Process[6]

The Council of Europe was formed after WWII at the urging of Winston Churchill, who called for the establishment of a "United States of Europe" to rebuild Europe after the devastating war. Also, western political leaders were attempting to establish an organization of democratic states to counter the growth of communism in the post-war era. The COE was officially formed

---

[4]   This pattern of deference toward France and most other original Member States has held for decades, but several recent cases to be discussed below may signal a change of considerable import.

[5]   The case on which they focus is: *Refah Partisi (the Welfare Party) and others v. Turkey* (Apps no 41340/98, 41342/98, 41343/98, and 41344/98) (13 February 2003); (2003) 37 EHRR 1. The case resulted in the ECtHR ruling in favour of the abolishment of a large political party in Turkey based on the court's view of the party being associated with radical Islam, and therefore opposed to democratic values.

[6]   This section draws partially on Richardson (1995) as well as Gomein (1991).

on May 5, 1949, with 10 original members (Belgium, France, Denmark, Italy, Luxembourg, Netherlands, Norway, Sweden, Ireland, and the United Kingdom) signing the Treaty of London. Greece and Turkey joined three months later, followed by Iceland and Germany in 1950. The Convention for the Protection of Human Rights and Fundamental Freedoms was drafted by these original Member States, and came into force on September 3, 1953, after being ratified by the Member States. The COE also established the European Court of Human Rights to enforce the provisions of the Convention, and all Member States, including newer ones from the former Soviet-dominated regions, agreed to be bound by provisions of the Convention by virtue of their application for membership.

The COE also established two other bodies of import, including the Parliamentary Assembly, made up of representatives from all Member States, and the Council of Ministers, which includes all the Foreign Ministers of Member States. The Parliamentary Assembly acts as a quasi-legislature for the COE which can make recommendations to the Council of Ministers and issue reports on various matters deemed important to the COE. For instance, it has generated several reports concerning minority religions (referred to as "sects") over the years.[7] The Assembly also elects judges (one from each Member State) to the ECtHR, which makes it of special importance to enforcement of provisions of the Convention.

The structure and operation of the COE has changed in recent years (see Gomien (1991) and Richardson (1995) for descriptions of the early COE operations and structure), but one major element has not changed: individual citizens continue to have the right to bring cases against their own government to the court for review and possible action. This one crucial procedural element has resulted in the court being inundated with thousands of claims over the years, a pattern that increased dramatically with the inclusion of former communist states in the COE in recent decades (See ECtHR Facts and Figures (2010) for details in case numbers).

When a claim is submitted to the court for review, the current procedures are as follows: The claim must have been filed within six months of a final determination within the legal system of the country against which the claim is filed, and the claimant must demonstrate that they exhausted all internal remedies in the country of origin. If the claim passes this initial review, then

---

[7]   See James Beckford (1985) and Richardson and van Driel (1994) for discussions of the COE and actions of its Parliamentary Assembly; and Richardson (1995) on the processes of the COE concerning implementation of the Convention.

the issue raised is examined in light of the specific provisions of the Convention that are claimed to have been breached. There is also an assessment of whether the complainant has suffered a "significant disadvantage" by the action of the claimant's country's legal system (see COE/ECtHR (2011) for further information on admissibility criteria).

Each application is assigned to a section of the court (the court is divided into five sections for administrative purposes), and the President of that section then designates a rapporteur whose job it is to determine the judicial formation of a case. Until 2011, this screening was primarily done by a "filtering committee" composed of three judges, one of whom was from the country against which the complaint had been lodged. In fewer cases, admissibility and merits were decided by a Chamber composed of seven judges.

In line with the establishment of Protocol No. 14, a major revision of ECtHR procedures, a new filtering section was created in 2011 which requires only a single judge formation rather than a three judge formation for five of the most case-heavy member states: Russia, Turkey, Romania, Ukraine, and Poland. For these countries (comprising over half of all cases received by the ECtHR in a year), one judge (not from the state from which the complaint was filed) with the assistance of a non-judicial rapporteur, determines the admissibility of an application (ECtHR 2011a). The remaining countries are now assessed using one of the judicial formations: Single Judge, Committees, Chambers, or the Grand Chamber.

Additionally, per Protocol No. 14 reforms, a committee may also determine the merits of the case (although the judge from the represented state is not compulsory to the committee) (COE 2010). It is estimated that around 90% of all cases are deemed inadmissible or struck out of the list (ECtHR 2011a). Some cases involve a request for more information, a process that can result in lengthy delays. (A typical case can take up to five years from initial submission to final resolution, if it is deemed admissible and is then adjudicated.) Not all cases are recorded in the HUDOC database maintained by the court, making it very difficult to find out details of the vast majority of cases brought to the court[8] (ECtHR 2012b).

If a case is admitted for adjudication, it is eventually heard by a panel of judges which includes the judge from the country against which a claim is being

---

[8]   All judgments, all admissibility decisions from 1986 to present and some from 1955 to 1986, reports from 1963 onward, resolutions (execution) from 1972 onward, resolutions (merits) from 1959–2004, and communicated cases from December 2011 onward are available for review (ECtHR, 2012b).

brought.[9] The panel can find in favor of the claimant on any of the provisions cited, or deny on any or all as well, based on majority vote. From the date of judgment delivery, either party has three months to request the case be referred to the Grand Chamber, which "includes all the judges in a specific chamber of the court."[10] Requests are reviewed by five Grand Chamber judges, with only about 5% of requests being accepted for full Grand Chamber judgment (ECtHR 2011b). Decisions by the Grand Chamber are final, and the country losing the case is expected to adhere to the decision, which is referred to the Council of Ministers for implementation. However, there is no effective mechanism for enforcement of decisions (other than expulsion of the country from the COE, which has never happened), and thus many decisions, particularly from former Soviet-dominated nations, are ignored, only partially implemented, or there are long delays before the decision is implemented (see Richardson and Shoemaker (2008) for a discussion of such issues with Russian cases).

Early Article 9 Machinations

As indicated above, 40 years of history with the Convention passed before a violation of Article 9 was found with the *Kokkinakis* case from Greece in 1993. Prior to this decision, some rigorous criteria were established for finding a violation in Article 9, and it seemed as if the court was doing everything possible to avoid finding a violation against one of the original COE members. Article 9 was considered a "dead letter" by many, and the "margin of appreciation" doctrine prevailed, allowing Member States to regulate religion and religious groups as they desired. An example of how limited Article 9 jurisprudence was viewed by the court can be found with the 1978 decision in *Arrowsmith v. the United Kingdom*.

Pat Arrowsmith, a devoted pacifist, was arrested for leafleting British soldiers, urging them not to go to Northern Ireland during the "time of troubles" there. She was convicted under British law of violating the 1934 "Incitement to Disaffection Act" and was sentenced to 18 months in prison (later reduced to time served of nine months). Arrowsmith then took her case

---

[9]   Including the judge from the country against which the claim is being lodged in the filtering committee and the panel of judges which initially hears the case would seem to bias decisions against the claimant, and this may in fact occur. The inclusion of that judge is justified by the court on the ground that the judge is familiar with the legal system of the country and therefore has essential information for the court to consider.

[10]   A Grand Chamber consists of 17 judges.

to the European Commission of Human Rights, claiming a violation of articles 9 and 14, among others, and it was deemed admissible and was adjudicated under the older Commission procedures. Her pacifism was accepted as a belief falling under the coverage of Article 9, but the Commission decided that her beliefs did not require the practice of distributing leaflets to soldiers explaining how they could avoid serving in Northern Ireland. Thus was born the *Arrowsmith* "necessity test" that was applied for years, including in several cases involving controversial NRMs, with the usual result being denial of any claim under articles 9 or 14.[11]

Then the *Kokkinakis* case arose, which was adjudicated shortly after the fall of the Soviet Union, just as nations that were no longer under the yoke of communism were turning toward Europe and expressing interest in joining the COE. The timing of *Kokkinakis* seems propitious, and suggests that this may have been one of the first "pilot judgments" designed to send a message to newer members of the COE that the court was going to approach cases involving religion and belief, and religious practices, more rigorously. Kokkinakis, a Jehovah's Witness, had been arrested dozens of times and incarcerated several times after convictions for proselytizing, a criminal offense in Greece since 1938. The law criminalizing proselytizing had never been enforced against any other group, but several thousand Witnesses had been charged under the law.[12] This law (unique among COE original Member States) and its application made the claim by Kokkinakis a good case whereby to send a message concerning Article 9 and other provisions of the Convention, if that was the desire of the COE and judges on the ECtHR.

The message of *Kokkinakis* was a bit qualified but still demonstrated that a new interpretation of Article 9 cases might be adhered to in the future. The qualifications contained within the decision include that it was a split vote (6 to 3), and that some dissenting judges thought the proselytizing methods of the Witnesses were unacceptable, with one judge referring to them as "brainwashing." Also, the court did not state unequivocally that the law criminalizing proselytizing was unacceptable under the Convention, and there were statements in the majority decision suggesting that protection of citizens from being bothered by unwanted proselytizing efforts was a concern of

---

[11]   See Evans (2001) for a full discussion of the *Arrowsmith* case and the aftermath with a number of other cases of applying the "necessity test."

[12]   See a summary of details on the background of this case in Richardson (1995) and a more through presentation of the history of the case at http://www.strasbourgconsortium. org/document.php?DocumentID=4519. Also, see Evans (2001) for a thorough legal analysis of the case.

the court. This piece of dicta became a new basis for decisions on related cases from original COE Member States.

For example, in the 1994 case *Otto-Preminger Institut v. Austria*, the court further developed the concept that the Convention offered some protection for the beliefs of others. The court ruled against the showing of a film that was offensive to some Christians because of "respect for religious feelings as guaranteed in Article 9." As Carolyn Evans (2001) has noted, such a statement does not appear in Article 9. Also, in 1996 the court decided on similar grounds to allow the banning of another film in *Wingrove v. United Kingdom*, claiming the "right of citizens not to be insulted in their religious feelings." It seems clear that Article 9 was being interpreted in a limited manner by the court, particularly as applied to some original Member States.

Article 9 Jurisprudence since Kokkinakis

Since *Kokkinakis*, the court has found a number of violations of Article 9 (sometimes in conjunction with another provision of the Convention). Between 1959 and 2011, 40 violations of Article 9 have been found (ECtHR 2012a). Ten of these cases were from Greece, which has a reputation of having the most government involvement in promoting strong ties with what effectively functions as a state church (the Greek Orthodox Church) compared to other original Member States of the COE. Recall that Greece is the only original Member State to criminalize proselytizing, and 22 of the 40 cases over this time period are from former communist countries that more recently joined the COE. Another interesting aspect of the case law that has developed since *Kokkinakis* is that many of the cases involve Jehovah's Witnesses, although there are a wide variety of other minority religions also involved in this pattern of jurisprudence.

In order to further assess religious freedom cases in the ECtHR, we conducted additional research within the HUDOC database, searching for cases in both English and French, the two official languages of the Court. The ECtHR separates cases by level of jurisprudential importance, with those at the highest level of importance shaping or significantly contributing to case law, those of medium importance holding some legal interest, and those of low importance relying on existing ECtHR case law. Since we were interested in all cases brought to the attention of the Court citing Article 9, all levels of importance were included. The keyword "religion" and all combinations of "Article 9" were included in the search (allowing for combinations with other articles). We then examined all those cases that were found using this search technique for relevancy to issues of our concern, discarding those cases where the keywords turned up incidental uses of the terms. We also reviewed all newsletters of the Human Rights without Frontiers operated out of Brussels by Willy Fautré, adding some cases mentioned therein which we could not locate in HUDOC, and we received personal communications from some NRMs about other cases filed with the court – recall that many cases never appear in HUDOC, thus leaving out the vast majority of cases submitted to the court.

For illustrative purposes, we focus here on a comparison of two major Member States, Russia and France, which developed starkly contrasting records with Article 9 cases in the past two decades, although some very recent decisions involving France are similar to Russian Article 9 jurisprudence developed over the past decade or so. This record should shed light on possible biases of the court's Article 9 jurisprudence, and also speak to the idea that the court is attempting to protect the very existence of religious organizations with its decisions, as proposed by Garlicki (2007) and by Evans (2010), instead of supporting individual religious freedom (although a new ruling in the UK may challenge this theory – see *Eweida and Others v. United Kingdom* 2013). The examination of the Article 9 records of these two major COE nations also should reveal whether the idea of a pro-Christian, pro-neutrality, and anti-Islam (or any other minority faith) pattern of bias in the court's jurisprudence has any credence.

France

France has a unique history concerning the relationship of church and state, in that it has an official policy of *laïcité*, which means that officially it is a secular nation. This stance ignores the fact that French culture is pervasively Catholic and that the Catholic Church has many ties to the institutional structure of France. The ties with Catholicism notwithstanding, the *laïcité* principle with its secular focus is rigorously enforced in a manner that bodes ill for minority faiths, and the "margin of appreciation" doctrine of the ECtHR has allowed France over the years to exert considerable social control over minority religions of all kinds, including both their very right to exist and the right of individual members of such groups to practice their faith. The concern about minority faiths (we include both (NRMs) and older groups that have been present for decades and even centuries in Western Europe; such as the Jehovah's Witnesses and the Church of Jesus Christ of Latter-day Saints) operating in France has resulted in high-level attention from the government, with the establishment of governmental agencies focused on controlling minority religions and several important reports and official acts of the French Parliament that attempt to label minority faiths as "sects" and make some actions of such groups illegal.[13]

One major action involved a Parliamentary report issued in 1995 listing 172 "socially dangerous" groups, leading to another very intrusive review by the French Parliament of the financial records of 60 of the groups selected from that list of 172, a review that in turn contributed to some major ECtHR cases to be discussed below. The Solar Temple episodes of group suicides in 1994, coupled with some court decisions that did not adopt the "party line" concerning sects, also contributed to the passage of a law on 12 June 2001 (with only one dissenting vote) aimed at preventing and suppressing cult groups that allegedly violate human rights and fundamental civil liberties.

The overall record of France in ECtHR Article 9 cases is striking in that until 2012 France lost very few of the many cases filed with the court. Table 10.1 lists all cases from France with Article 9 claims that we have been able to locate, along with the result. Many involve individual expressions of faith, such as wearing head coverings, with others such as the "pig soup" case involving actions disrupting the Islamic community at large by serving food with pork, an insult to Muslims who were attending a religious street festival. Also, note the many cases by the French tax authorities to force the dissolution of multiple NRMs and minority religions by claiming back taxes on hand-to-hand donations using tax laws aided by the parliamentary report on sects mentioned above, resulting in an obvious threat to the very existence of several minority religious groups in France (including the Jehovah's Witnesses, Aumists, and Evangelical Missionary Church).

The situation concerning the treatment of France by the ECtHR may have changed recently, and in a manner that lends support to the Garlicki/Evans view that the court is concerned about allowing religious organizations to exist, even if it appears not so concerned about protecting individual religious freedom related to religious practices. The Jehovah's Witness organization in France was on the list of 172 groups that were considered a threat to society, and afterward they also were part of the group of 60 taken from that list that were forced to submit very detailed information on their finances to the French tax authorities, including the names of contributors and the amounts they had given. After the report was submitted, the tax authorities then submitted a tax bill to the Witnesses in 1999 for the equivalent of $50 million dollars U.S. in claimed past due taxes for contribution from 1993 through 1996.

---

[13]	See Beckford (1985), Richardson (1995), Richardson and van Driel (1994), Beckford (2004), Duvert (2004), Luca (2004), Introvigne (2004), and Palmer (2011) for discussions of the many actions taken by the French government concerning minority faiths.

The tax authorities ignored the fact that the Witnesses had been functioning in France for over 100 years, and decided to define all contributions to the Witness churches as income subject to taxation using a questionable interpretation of inheritance taxes (which are at the 60% rate). The Witnesses appealed the decision to tax their contributions, but were forced to agree to have all their property and funds in France sequestered in order to appeal the decision. They appealed first to the Director of Tax Services (rejected, September 1999), then to the Tribunal de Grand Instance of Nanterre (dismissed, 2 July 2004), followed by the Versailles Court of Appeal (earlier dismissal upheld, 28 February 2002), and finally to the Court of Cassation, which dismissed the case on 5 October 2004.

Having exhausted all possible internal remedies, the case was then filed with the ECtHR on 24 February 2005, claiming a violation of Article 9 and Article 14. Over three years later the case was declared admissible on 17 June 2008, and that decision was affirmed by a Chamber of seven judges on 21 September 2010, although the Article 14 claim was dismissed. On 30 June 2011 the Witnesses won a unanimous judgment against France, with the court stating that France had violated Article 9, and that damages must be paid. Finally, after the obligatory time period for possible appeals to the Grand Chamber, on 30 September 2011 the judgment was declared final, and France was ordered to pay reparation for taxes taken and to remove its legal hold on all Witness property in France. Thus, the case took over six years to resolve with the ECtHR.[14]

Three other similar tax cases were also accepted for adjudication by the ECtHR, including two by the Aumist group which has its headquarters at an enclave called Mandarom in rural southeast France.[15] The Aumist group has been a target for French media, governmental officials, and the French anti-sect movement for some time (Introvigne 2004). Thus it was no surprise to see them on the list of 172 groups in the Parliamentary report, and also that they were targeted for a review of their finances. The Aumists also received large tax bills (for two separate organizations they had established) from tax authorities that would have effectively forced their dissolution. The two organizations appealed

---

[14]　It should be noted that a similar case was filed earlier and dismissed (Application # 53430/99) on nearly the same facts. Why the court decided to accept a new filing and then take the case seriously, leading to the eventually decision in June of 2010 is an open question, but it does indicate some shifting of approach to such cases. See Richardson and Shoemaker (2008: 114) for a discussion of this earlier case.

[15]　Note that Scientology was also targeted by French authorities and dealt with similarly to what happened with the Witnesses and with the Aumist group. However, Scientology decided to pay the fine imposed, but then encountered considerable difficulty in doing so because French authorities refused for a time to allow the fine to be paid by funds received from outside of France.

through the legal system in France, but to no avail. The result of the appeals followed the pattern experienced by the Witnesses as they unsuccessfully sought resolution within the judicial system in France. The group has other legal issues with French authorities (see Table 10.1), including battles over a proper burial place for the group's founder, libel and slander actions against the government and media outlets, action for failure to register the group, and disagreements over the building of large statues of various religious figures, one of which has been destroyed by French authorities even though they were built following adherence to procedures for doing so.[16]

As shown in Table 10.1, the Aumists had filed a total of 15 cases with the ECtHR, with all but two summarily rejected as inadmissible with no explanation given. The two cases that remained active concerned the tax bill presented to the Aumists (Richardson and Lykes 2011). The ECtHR recently rendered unanimous judgments on these cases, as well as one regarding the Evangelical Missionary Church, finding in favor of the defendants with Violations of Article 9, in line with the precedent set by the Jehovah's Witness case just discussed. Large damages were awarded in the three cases, totaling €3,696,005 (including €59,568 in court costs) for the Aumist group and 432,722 Euros (including €55,000 in court costs) for the Evangelical Missionary Church. These very recent decisions provide support for the idea that the ECtHR is more concerned with the rights of religious organizations to exist than for the religious freedom of individuals.

Russia

Russia is one of the new and very important members of the COE. The decision to join the COE represented a monumental shift from the 70 years of communist history during which thousands of Russian Orthodox Churches (ROC) were destroyed and many ROC priests were killed. When the Soviet Union collapsed this afforded an opening for many religious groups to come to Russia, including some controversial NRMs from the West. In 1990 the Russian government passed statutes recognizing religious freedom, and in 1993 religious freedom was enshrined in the new Russian Constitution. This new legal structure, modeled after such ideas enshrined in legal documents of Western nations and organizations such as the United Nations Universal Declaration on Human Rights and the European Convention, was controversial from the start.

---

[16] See http://www.leparisien.fr/faits-divers/la-statue-du-mandarom-detruite-aujourd-hui-06-09-2001-2002418234.php; http://www.batiactu.com/edito/destruction-de-la-statue-du-mandarom-10631.php; http://www.guardian.co.uk/world/2000/aug/27/jonhenley.theobserver.

After initially supporting religious freedom for all immediately after the fall of communism, the ROC began to reassert itself in the early 1990s and argued against allowing other religions, particularly foreign ones from the West, a free rein in Russia. Also, more nationalistic politicians within Russia opposed allowing Western religious groups to promote themselves in Russia. A strong effort to exert social control over newer religions developed in Russia, promoted by ROC leadership, Russian politicians, and assisted by anti-cult leaders from Western Europe, particularly Germany and Denmark (Shterin and Richardson 2000). This effort culminated in development of a new, much more restrictive law regulating religious groups in Russia that was eventually signed by Yeltsin in 1997 (Shterin and Richardson 1998).

One key element of the 1997 law was the requirement that all religious groups registered after the passage of the 1990 statute must re-register following much more stringent procedures that were laid out in the law. This element of the new law was apparently designed to allow the Russian bureaucracy to weed out unwanted religious groups that had come into Russia immediately after the fall of the Soviet Union when registration was much easier. And the Russian bureaucracy did its part by refusing, on sometimes very flimsy grounds, to allow reregistration of new and minority religious groups such as the Society of Jesus, the Church of Scientology (COS), and the Salvation Army. This in turn led to a series of court cases, some of which eventually ended up filed with the ECtHR (Richardson, Krylova, and Shterin 2004, Richardson and Shoemaker 2008).

The legal cases of the groups named above have generally followed a pattern that involves efforts to obtain re-registration which are repeatedly rebuffed by authorities, the filing of a court case that goes through the Russian judicial system on appeal after having been lost at the trial court level, and eventual filing of the case with the Russian Constitutional Court. Some victories at the Constitutional Court level have been won, but the government has refused to enforce some of these rulings, which then leads to filing a claim with the ECtHR (Richardson 2006). There are a few other Article 9 ECtHR cases from Russia which will be briefly discussed as well, and a full listing of cases is available in Table 10.2, but first some discussion of cases following the pattern outlined about the re-registration issue will be covered.

Re-registration cases involving the Salvation Army and the Church of Scientology (COS) have been taken to the ECtHR and won with unanimous and strongly worded decisions quite critical of the actions (or inactions) of the Russian government. The Salvation Army had won at the level of the Russian Constitutional Court, but the ruling was not enforced by the government so the case was filed with the ECtHR and won in 2006. The COS, which had ten efforts to reregister rebuffed, had lost at the Constitutional Court but took the case to the ECtHR and won there in 2007 (Richardson and Shoemaker 2008).

Another common pattern concerning Russian treatment of minority religions involves efforts to dissolve them on what appear to be questionable grounds (Richardson, Krylova, and Shterin 2004). One such case did eventually go to the ECtHR for the Jehovah's Witnesses of Moscow. The Jehovah's Witnesses had fought a continual battle with Russian authorities (still ongoing). This particular case involved years of efforts by authorities to dissolve the Witness organization and fine them for all sorts of allegations. The Witnesses won a dismissal of the case several times but Russian authorities re-filed the case repeatedly with different courts and were ultimately successful in officially dissolving the organization. The Moscow Witness organization eventually filed an Article 9 claim with the ECtHR which issued a unanimous decision on 10 June 2010, in favor of the Witnesses' claims that their rights under Article 9 had been violated.

Another case against Russia in the ECtHR was also won by a Jehovah's Witness group. This case involved a congregation of 100 deaf Witnesses who were meeting in Chelyabinsk. The group had experienced many problems in trying to properly register, being rebuffed 12 times. They were also being harassed with criminal investigations and in other ways. The group had negotiated a lease for use of a meeting facility, but the facility was raided by the police and prosecutor and their lease was canceled. The group took legal action, but to no avail, and eventually filed a complaint with the ECtHR, alleging a violation of their Article 9 rights as well as other claims. The court issued a unanimous ruling on 11 January 2007 that the Article 9 rights of the group had been violated, and damages were awarded.

The Unification Church (UC) has also won a recent case against Russia before the ECtHR. A UC member, Patrick Nolan, was refused reentry into Russia after having lived there for 10 years and being the parent of a young child who was in Russia. Nolan had a valid visa to allow his return but was not allowed to reenter. His efforts to regain entry into Russia were refused and he eventually filed a legal action with the ECtHR in 2004, alleging violation of his Article 9 rights, among other claims. The court ruled unanimously in his favor on 12 February 2009, again using strong language to criticize the actions of the Russia authorities.

Russia has lost another case filed by an evangelical Christian group before the ECtHR. The group headed by Pastor Brankevich had been refused a permit to hold an outdoor service in a park in Chekhov in the Moscow region. The refusal was based on the grounds that most residents of the area were not of the same faith as Pastor Brankevich's group and that they would not approve of the use of the public park for such a meeting. The Pastor sought assistance from the courts but was not successful, and eventually filed a claim in 2003 with the ECtHR claiming a violation of Article 9 and 11 (freedom of assembly). The court ruled on 26 July 2007 unanimously against Russia, finding a violation of Article 11 interpreted in light of Article 9.

Conclusion

The records of France and Russia before the ECtHR are not, of course, fully representative of the original or the newer Member States of the COE. However, we suggest that these records are quite informative, and yield some evidence on the question of what sort of pattern of jurisprudence is being developed by the court. France, as one of the major original Member States, has traditionally enjoyed a very strong "margin of appreciation," with the court deferring to it on most claims that involve Article 9. The few exceptions regarding taxation of the Jehovah's Witnesses, Aumists, and Evangelical Church could be the beginning of a new approach to jurisprudence involving original Member States, but the facts of these cases were so egregious that the outcome could be viewed as predictable and also anomalous.[17] However, these cases are supportive of the theorizing of Garlicki and of Evans that the court does seek to defend the right of religious groups to exist.[18]

Compared to this recently dramatic change in Article 9 jurisprudence involving France, Russia has developed a unique record before the ECtHR on Article 9 cases, losing a number of cases involving all sorts of issues and with strongly worded and unanimous decisions. The majority of the cases support the Garlicki/Evans hypothesis, but there are exceptions as well, such as the UC member Nolan case that involved only one individual and his child. Thus it seems that the jury is still out on the question of the meaning of the pattern of Article

---

[17] Note that at the time of this writing these three cases are subject to appeal, given that the country against which a judgment is rendered has 90 days to file an appeal and seek a Chamber review of the case.

[18] Note, however, that the judgment (which favored one of the three only) in the recent United Kingdom case did seem to affirm individual religious freedom rights of employees to express their religious beliefs within a work setting. See *Eweida and Others v. United Kingdom.* See http://www.cjicl.org.uk/index.php/cjicl-blog/echr-chamber-judgment-eweida-and-others-v-united-kingdom-between-the-freedom-of-religion-and-the-prohibition-of-discrimination (accessed 2/8/2013) for a discussion of this interesting case.

9 cases that have flooded the court since the initial *Kokkinakis* case in 1993. The overall pattern seems to support the idea that the court has treated newer and original Member States (except for Greece) differently, but within the pattern are some decisions that also support the idea that the court is focusing more on protecting the right of religious groups to exist within the environment of the new Member States from Central and Eastern Europe. Note also that the pattern of cases from France is suggestive of the proposal of Meerschaut and Gutwirth (2009) that there is an anti-Islam (or anti-non-Christian) bias operating within the court's jurisprudence. Many of the French cases that were dismissed involved non-Christian religions and a number involved Islam in one way or another. As the court is forced to deal with more cases involving non-Christian faiths, perhaps the pattern will become more clear, but for now, we can only say that the case law pattern is disturbing, even if not fully clear.

Table 10.1   ECtHR Religious Freedom Cases Plaintiff v. France

Plaintiff	Case Number	Description	Ruling Year	Ruling
D.	10180/82	Applicant, who is Jewish, got divorced and did not want to hand over the guett after the divorce. Argued it was a manifestation of his religious right.	1983	No interference with Article 9, application rejected.
P.	11691/85	In prison. Argues violation of Article 9 because could not worship while there in addition to other claims.	1986	Declared inadmissible.
J.	15932/89	Arrested on suspicion of terrorism. Along with other claims, argues he was imprisoned because of his religion and beliefs under Article 9.	1990	Declared inadmissible.
Beldjoudi	12083/86	Deportation issue. Made claims under Article 9 among others, but with no further information.	1992	7 votes to 2 would be a violation of Article 8 if deported. Article 14 in conjunction with Article 8; Articles 3, 9, and 12 do not need to be considered.
Bouessel du Bourg	20747/92	Argues that paying funds towards abortions (through social security) is against his religious beliefs under Article 9.	1993	Declared inadmissible.

Plaintiff	Case Number	Description	Ruling Year	Ruling
Church of Scientology of Paris	19509/92	Applicant applied to view information collected by the intelligence department on its organization and was denied. Applicant claims that collecting information about its religious members is a violation of their right to Manifest their religion under Article 9 (in addition to other claims)	1995	Declared inadmissible.
Sivananda Yoga Vedanta	30260/96	Applicant organization teaches yoga and Hindu philosophy. Subject to a tax audit for yoga taxes. Applicant claims that taxing it as a company infringes on Article 9 and 10 rights. Additionally, nonprofit activities for other religions (e.g. Catholic) are recognized which is thus discriminatory against their organization under Article 14 (among other claims).	1998	Declared inadmissible.
Gluchowski and others	44789/98	The applicants are JWs. Claimed a violation of Article 9 and 11 over the creation of the UNADFI,* an association they felt went against many of their primary tenets.	1999	Declared inadmissible.
Pannulo et Forte	37794/97	The applicants' daughter died in the hospital, and an inquiry over the death then occurred. In addition to other claims, applicants state a violation of Article 9 because they were not able to bury and pray for child as Catholics due to the delay over the body's return.	1999	Admissible complaints regarding interference with public and family life. Remainder of application inadmissible with no separate examination in light of Article 9 needed.
Cha'are Shalom Ve Tsedek	27417/95	Claimed violation of Article 9 for not providing approval to access a slaughterhouse to ensure the ritual slaughter was done in accordance with ultra-orthodox Jewish beliefs.	2000	12 to 5 votes no violation of Article 9 alone, 10 to 7 votes no violation of Article 9 in conjunction with Article 14.

Plaintiff	Case Number	Description	Ruling Year	Ruling
Aumist (Mandarom)	62234/00	Statue of Cosmo-Planetary Messiah destroyed after blueprints had been approved.	2001	Inadmissible.
Aumist (Mandarom)	69867/01	Burial of founder of religion was stopped.	2001	Inadmissible.
Piss	46026/99	Applicant was not able to visit with children. Argues that part of the reason is due to his affiliation with the JWs under Article 9.	2001	Adjourns examination of complaint over not being able to access his children, remainder of application inadmissible.
Pichon and Sajous	49853/99	Applicants own a pharmacy and refused to sell contraceptives. The French court found them in violation. Appealed to ECtHR claiming it was a manifestation of their freedom of religion as it interfered with their religious beliefs.	2001	Declared inadmissible.
Aumist (Mandarom)	4084/02	A book published by a psychiatrist with no personal familiarity with the Aumist religion claimed brainwashing and was brought to the Medical Association.	2002	Inadmissible.
Aumist (Mandarom)	20373/02	Newspaper "France-Soir" slandered the Aumist founder.	2002	Inadmissible.
Aumist (Mandarom)	42684/02	Charges against France for causing the President of the Association of the Pyramid Temple to become insolvent.	2003	Inadmissible.
Aumist (Mandarom)	74759/01	Case against the About-Picard Law.	2004	Inadmissible.
Aumist (Mandarom)	28263/02	Suit against the RMC radio station for slandering the founder of the Aumist religion.	2004	Inadmissible.

Plaintiff	Case Number	Description	Ruling Year	Ruling
Palau-Martinez	64927/01	The applicant, a JW, argues that the court giving custody to her ex-husband violated Article 8, her private and family life in conjunction with Article 14, as well as Article 9 alone and in junction with Article 14 by infringing her freedom of religion.	2004	Violation of Article 8 in conjunction with Article 14, unnecessary to rule on Article 8 alone, no separate issue under Article 6 section 1 or Article 9 alone or in conjunction with Article 14.
Phull	35753/03	British national of the Sikh tradition, requiring the wearing of a turban. Argued that asking him to remove the turban at the airport as a security measure violated his freedom of religion under Article 9.	2005	Declared inadmissible.
Aumist (Mandarom)	74764/01	Two parliamentary reports of 1996 and 1999 claiming the religion to be a cult were discriminatory.	2005	Inadmissible.
F.L.	61162/00	Custody case. Applicant is part of the Raelian group, and the custody arrangement was such that no association with the movement was allowed for the children. Argues that not allowing contact with Raelian members violates Article 8 alone and in conjunction with Article 14 and also that she was discriminated against due to her religion under Article 9 alone and in conjunction with Article 14 in addition to other claims.	2005	Declared inadmissible.
Milan	7549/03	Applicant is a Muslim that sent a letter that was perceived as Anti-Semitic and a death threat linked to terrorism. Was arrested and claims was beaten during his arrest. Among other claims, argued that his arrest and torture were because of his religion under Article 9	2005	Adjourned examination of Article 3 and 13 complains. Remainder of complaints declared inadmissible.

Plaintiff	Case Number	Description	Ruling Year	Ruling
Cultural Office of Cluny	1002/02	The applicant organization, founded on developing man through beauty and art based on a Christian vision, was taken to court over not contributing to social security. Claimed under Article 9 and 14 that the role leaders in the organization took on was similar to that of a pastor and his congregation and volunteers paying social security inhibited this.	2005	Inadmissible.
Aumist (Mandarom)	8560/04	Suit against newspaper *l'Humanite* for slandering founder of the Aumist religion.	2006	Inadmissible.
Paturel	54968/00	Applicant was a JW that wrote a book titled *Sects, Religions, and Public Freedoms*. Convicted for defamation of character because of the book. Alleged his Article 9 and 10 rights were violated due to his conviction for writing the book.	2006	Violation of Article 10, rejects just satisfaction for remainder.
Deschomets	31956/02	Applicant and ex-husband were part of the Brethren movement. Ex left the movement and custody proceedings began. Applicant argues under Article 8 in conjunction with Article 14 that her right to respect for her family life was infringed on when the children changed residence and under Article 9 in conjunction with Article 14 that freedom of religion is a private domain, and she felt the court infringed on this right solely because of her religious beliefs as they were not "traditional" or "admissible."	2006	Declared inadmissible.
Aumist (Mandarom)	2169/03	Refusal to allow burial of founder of the religion and diversion of funeral convoy.	2006	Inadmissible.

Plaintiff	Case Number	Description	Ruling Year	Ruling
Vincent	6253/03	Applicant was in prison. In addition to other violations, alleged a violation of Article 9 because he could not practice his religion due to no worship space.	2007	Violation of Article 3 upheld, remaining claims rejected.
Aumist (Mandarom)	12248/06 15933/06	Regarded compensation to former religious members for damages occurring while members.	2007	Inadmissible.
El Morsli	15585/06	Was not allowed into France to be with her husband because she, a Muslim, would not remove her veil to allow confirmation of her identity	2008	Non-exhaustion of internal grounds for appeal – declared inadmissible.
E.D.	45605/05	Applicant was placed under involuntary hospitalization. Among other complains, argued that his Article 9 rights had been violated because the nurses would not contact a chaplain.	2008	Application struck from list.
Mann Singh	24479/07	Is a practicing Sikh. Driver's license was stolen and when a duplicate was requested, request was denied because in his photograph he wore a turban. Argued violation of religious freedom and privacy to appear bare-headed in the passport photograph.	2008	Declared inadmissible.
Dogru Kervanci	27058/05 31645/04	A Muslim student expelled from school for refusing to remove headscarves during Physical Education classes.	2009	No violation Article 9.
Association Solidarite des France	26787/07	Providing clothing and food to the poor; however, media claimed the food was primarily "pig soup" and therefore discriminatory towards certain religious groups. Claimant argued interference with helping the needy and discrimination was not established and prohibiting foods due to Muslim dietary regulations ignored the right of the applicant to not pursue a religion.	2009	Declared inadmissible.

Plaintiff	Case Number	Description	Ruling Year	Ruling
Aktas Bayrak Gamaleddyn Ghazal J. Singh R. Singh	43563/08 14308/08 18527/08 29134/08 25463/08 27561/08	Muslim students refused to remove headscarves or keski's and were denied entry to classrooms and later were expelled.	2009	Declared inadmissible.
S.A.S	43835/11	Muslim who freely wears a burqa and a veil over the face, covering everything but the eyes. Although the applicant does not always wear this full outfit, when it is a special occasion like Ramadan, the applicant will wear it in public, not as a nuisance, but to honor the Muslim faith. This is against the 2010-1192 act forbidding face concealment in public. Invoked Article 9, complaining violation of freedom of religion because not being able to wear the veil in public violates ability to manifest religion, in addition to other grievances.	2011	Questions posed to parties concerning claims that articles 8, 9, and 14 rights were violated.
Jehovah's Witnesses	8916/05	The parliamentary report on Sects in France labeled the JWs a sectarian movement and required a tax audit and later the JWs were notified of past-due notices from member gifts. JWs complained that as an association of worship they should be exempt from transfer taxes and gift taxes.	2012	Violation of Article 9.
Religious Association of the Pyramid Temple Association of the Knights of the Golden Lotus	50471/07 50615/07	Contributions towards the construction of a Pyramid Temple and toward the Association des Chevaliers du Lotus d'Or taxed by French government. Argued tax legislation deprived the new religion of funds by requiring gifts to be listed on a tax audit which were then "revealed" and could be taxed.	2013	Violation of Article 9.

Plaintiff	Case Number	Description	Ruling Year	Ruling
Evangelical Missionary Church and Salaûn	25502/07	Applicant is a religious organization that was audited and was required to pay taxes on hand-to-hand gifts as they did not meet exempt status.	2013	Violation of Article 9.
Sukyo Mahikar France	41729/09	The applicant association argues it is a religious organization but was labeled as a sect in the 1995 report on cults in France. In 1998 the association was audited because of concerns over it being engaged in for profit activities. After the audit, gifts to the organization were considered taxable at over a million Euros. The applicant paid, but challenged the taxes. Argued under Article 9 that being taxed at 60% of donations restricted its freedom of religion.	2013	Inadmissible.
Aumist (Mandarom)	43786/07	France's refusal to officially grant recognition to the Monastery of Mandarom for over 20 years	No further details	No further details.

*UNADFI is the National Union of Associations for the Defense of Family and Individual, recognized by the French government on 30 April 1996 as a public utility association. Its purpose "is to prevent and protect families and individuals against practices by groups, movements, or organizations in the nature of destructive cults and, whatever name and form they hold, adversely affect the human rights and fundamental freedoms set out in the Universal Declaration of Human Rights" (44789/98).

Table 10.2   ECtHR Religious Violation Cases Plaintiff v. Russia

Plaintiff	Case Number	Description	Ruling Year	Ruling
Nikishina	45665/99	Applicant had custody of son, with visits to the father on weekends. Applicant began to affiliate with the Jehovah's Witnesses and brought her son with her. Father spoke to the Committee for Rescuing Youth from Totalitarian Sects and a state agency to look into gaining custody of the child. The father refused to return the child and later gained custody.	1998	Application inadmissible.
Pitkevich	47936/99	Member of the Living Faith Church (part of the Russian Union of Evangelical Christian Churches) that ran for mayor in Noyabrsk. Opponents claimed she was a cultist. Did not win the election. Was a judge, and later it was found she had "misused her office to pursue religious activities in the interests of the Church." Argued under Article 6 section 1, Article 9, 10, and 14, and Article 1 of Protocol No. 1.	2001	Application declared inadmissible.
Patrikeyev	68493/01	In prison. In addition to other violations, invoked Article 9 claiming he was not allowed to correspond with Christians in the United States.	2004	Adjourned examination of length of proceedings, detention conditions, and censorship with Court. Remainder of application inadmissible.
Vatan	47978/99	The registered political party was founded to support the Tartar nation. After a regional ceremony honoring the 1350th anniversary of the founding of Sember, a prosecutor asked the court to suspend the organization's activities, claiming they incited violence. The applicant argued that suspending their activities violated their right to freedom to hold opinions, ideas, association, and its members' right to manifest their religion.	2005	Court unanimously held it could not consider the merits and accepted the government's preliminary objection.

Plaintiff	Case Number	Description	Ruling Year	Ruling
Khudoyorov	6847/02	In prison. Claimed Violation of Articles 6, 8, 9 13, and 14 with no details.	2005	Partially admissible. Violations 6, 8, 9, 13 and 14 were rejected.
Seredyuk	24984/02	The applicant was in prison and claims he was denied being able to attend the Orthodox Church within prison territory among other claims.	2006	Struck from the list.
Moscow Branch of the Salvation Army	72881/01	Salvation Army reapplied for official status in 1997, but application was rejected.	2007	Violation of Article 11 in conjunction with Article 9.
Barankevich	10519/03	Pastor of the evangelical Christian church "Christ's Grace" was refused permission for an outdoor service with claims it might cause discontent and public disorder.	2007	Violation of Article 11 in light of Article 9.
Church of Scientology Moscow	18147/02	COS, Moscow unsuccessfully attempted to re-register 10 times after the 1997 law was passed.	2007	Violation of Article 11 in conjunction with Article 9.
Kuznetsov and others	184/02	Various acts against JWs by the government, including denial of registration application, breaking up meetings, investigations into luring young children into their "sect," meeting at a school disbanded.	2007	Violation of Article 6 and 9.
Ismailova	37614/02	The applicant began to affiliate with the Jehovah's Witnesses at the same time as her marriage was dissolving. She took the children and later became a JW. The children went to visit the grandparents and were not returned to their mother. The husband filed for divorce and for custody of the children because of concern for moral conditions living with their mother and because they were being taken to religious meetings with the potential to convert to the JW faith. Applicant argued interference with freedom of religion and a breach of Article 8.	2008	4 votes to 3 there had been no violation of Article 8. Unanimously that no separate issue under Article 8 taken alone and Article 9 taken alone or in conjunction with Article 14.

Plaintiff	Case Number	Description	Ruling Year	Ruling
Avilkina and others	1585/09	Applicants were JWs that refused blood transfusions for medical conditions. All medical institutions were asked to submit a report for refusals for transfusions. Additionally, the Committee for the Salvation of Youth from Destructive Cults lodged multiple complaints regarding the actions of the JWs. The applicant argued under Article 9 and 11 that the investigation into its activities were abusive and excessive. Under Article 9 and 14, that other religions were not subject to the same type of abuse, and to Article 6, 8, and 14; 13, and 4 additionally.	2008	Questions posted to parties.
Sabanchiyeva and others	38450/05	The applicants were relatives of people who died in Nalchik in October of 2005. Complained under Article 3 that refusal to return bodies of relatives violated rights of the deceased, under Article 6 that the deceased's rights to being presumed innocent and have a fair trial, under Article 3, 8, and 9 alone and in conjunction with Articles 13 and 14.	2008	Declares admissible the applicant's complaints under Article 3, 8, and 9 alone and in conjunction with 13 and 14.
Maskhadova and others	18071/05	Applicants were the widow and children of a suspected terrorist. Charged that Russian authorities used excessive lethal force in arresting the deceased, and that they would not return the body.	2008	Holds unanimously no violation of Article 2 or 14 (in conjunction with Article 8). Dismisses government's objection that applicants had failed to exhaust domestic remedies under Article 8, Holds by 5 to 2: Violation of Article 8, and Article 13 (taken together with Article 8). Holds unanimously in light of findings under Article 8 and 13 no separate examination needed under Article 9.

Plaintiff	Case Number	Description	Ruling Year	Ruling
Nolan and K.	2512/04	The applicant is a member of the Unification Church in Russia. He was allowed to stay in Russia on a yearly basis through the Ministry of Foreign Affairs via invitations through the Unification Church and the Family Federation for World Peace and Unification (FFWPU) to help with their activities. In 2001 Rostov police stamped his passport to indicate his registration was terminated after the FFWPU had been dissolved by court order. In 2002 he traveled to Cyprus, leaving his son in the care of a nanny in Russia and was not allowed to re-enter and was detained by border control for 9 hours. He then got a new visa and was again denied entry.	2009	Violation of Article 9, 8, 5§1; 5§5, 1 of Protocol 7, and a failure to comply with Article 38 § 1 (a).
Sharkunov and Mezentsev	75330/01	Applicants were in prison. Among other issues, the first applicant requested visits by an Orthodox priest and were denied.	2009	Article 9 complaint declared inadmissible.
Faizov	19820/04	The applicant was a Jehovah's Witness that requested alternative civilian service due to his religion and was charged under draft evasion. Complained under Article 9 and Article 14 read in conjunction with Article 6 Section 1 and Article 9.	2009	Struck from the list.
Skugar and others	40010/04	The Orthodox Church applicants requested their taxpayer ID be cancelled because the number was a mark of the Antichrist referencing Revelation 13. The request was denied. The applicant complained their rights had been impaired under Article 9.	2009	Court declared application inadmissible.
Sevastyanov	75911/01	The applicant was convicted of selling drugs. He argued under Article 3 that the conditions of his imprisonment were inhuman, under Article 5 that his detention was unlawful, under Article 9 that he had been denied his request to see a priest, and under Article 14 for discrimination because of his drug addiction.	2010	Holds there was a violation of Article 6 § 1 of the Convention on account of the unlawful composition of the court which convicted the applicant. Remainder of application inadmissible.

Plaintiff	Case Number	Description	Ruling Year	Ruling
Jehovah's Witnesses of Moscow	302/02	Attempted to re-register as a religious organization five times unsuccessfully. The community was court ordered to dissolve and banned all activities.	2010	Unanimous violation of Article 11 in light of Article 9.
Pylnev	3038/03	The applicant was charged on tax evasion. Along with many other Articles, he claims he was denied visits by his priest under Article 9.	2010	Unanimously decides to discontinue the application of Article 29 section 3. Declares application inadmissible.
Kimlya and others	76836/01 32782/03	Both applicants are members of the Church of Scientology. Registration in Surgut and Nizhnekamsk was refused.	2010	Violation of Article 9 in light of Article 11.
Alibayev	27325/06	Applicant was incarcerated and complained under Articles 7, 9, 10, and 14. The government responded but no further response came from the applicant.	2011	Application struck out of the list.
Kraczkiewicz and others	15120/10 17883/10 13626/11	Applicants were relatives of Polish Army servicemen killed during communist occupation of Eastern Poland in 1940. Applicants complain under Article 2 that Russian authorities had not investigated adequately into the case, a breach of Article 3 for the government's response, Article 8 because the names of the deceased were not cleared, and Article 9 that they had not been able to pay respects in accordance with their religion.	2011	Declared inadmissible.
Boyko	42259/07	While in detention, the applicant claims the investigator did not allow him to visit with his Russian Orthodox pries,t and as such, there was a violation of Article 9.	As of 2012	Communicated Case with Questions to Parties.
Vasilyev and others	38891/08	Five Muslim Russian nationalists currently imprisoned for affiliation with a banned religious extremist (terrorist) organization Hizb ut-Tahrir. Applicants complain that conviction is a violation of Article 9 and that not allowing the activities of Hizb ut-Tahrir in Russia also violates their right to assembly.	As of 2012	Communicated Case with Questions to Parties.

References

Beckford, J.A. 1985. *Cult Controversies: The Societal Response to the New Religious Movements.* London: Tavistock Publishers.

Beckford, J.A. 2004. "'Laicité,' 'Dystopia,' and the Reaction to New Religious Movements in France." In *Regulating Religion: Case Studies from around the Globe*, edited by J.T. Richardson. 27–40. New York: Kluwer.

COE 2010. *Protocol 14: The Reform of the European Court of Human Rights.* Online: 15 May 2010. https://wcd.coe.int/ViewDoc.jsp?Ref=FS+28&Language=lanEnglish&Ver=original&BackColorInternet=F5CA75&BackColorIntranet=F5CA75&BackColorLogged=A9BACE, accessed 7 January 2013.

COE/ECtHR 2011. *Practical Guide on Admissibility Criteria.* Online: Council of Europe/ European Court of Human Rights. http://echr.coe.int/Documents/Admissibility_guide_ENG.pdf, accessed 7 January 2013.

Cumper, P. 1999. "The Rights of Religious Minorities: The Legal Regulation of New Religious Movements." In *Minority Rights in the 'New Europe,'* edited by P. Cumper and S. Wheatley. 165–83. New York: Kluwer.

Dumper, P. and T. Lewis. 2012. *Religion, Human Rights, and Secular Society.* Cheltenham, U.K.: Edward Elgar, Ltd.

Duvert, C. 2004. Anti-cultism in the French Parliament: Desperate Last Stand or an Opportune Leap Forward? A Critical Analysis of the June 2001 Act." In *Regulating Religion: Case Studies from around the Globe*, edited by J.T. Richardson. 41–52. New York: Kluwer.

ECtHR 2010. *50 Years of Activity: The European Court of Human Rights Some Facts and Figures.* Online: European Court of Human Rights. http://echr.coe.int/Documents/Facts_Figures_1959_2009_ENG.pdf, accessed: 7 January 2013.

ECtHR 2011a. *Filtering Section Speeds up Processing of Cases from Highest Case-Count Countries.* Online: European Court of Human Rights. http://www.echr.coe.int/Documents/Filtering_Section_ENG.pdf, accessed: 7 January 2013.

ECtHR 2011b. *The General Practice Followed by the Panel of the Grand Chamber when Deciding on Requests for Referral in Accordance with Article 43 of the Convention.* Online: European Court of Human Rights. http://www.echr.coe.int/Documents/Note_GC_ENG.pdf, accessed: 7 January 2013.

ECtHR 2012a. *Overview 1959–2011.* Online: European Court of Human Rights. http://www.echr.coe.int/Documents/Overview_2011_ENG.pdf, accessed: 14 January 2013.

ECtHR 2012b. *HUDOC User Manual*. Online: European Court of Human Rights. http://www.echr.coe.int/Documents/HUDOC_Manual_2012_ENG.pdf, accessed: 9 February 2013.

Evans, C. 2001. *Freedom of Religion under the European Convention on Human Rights*. Oxford: Oxford University Press.

Evans, C. 2010. Individual and Group Religious Freedom in the European Court of Human Rights: Cracks in the Intellectual Architecture." *Journal of Law and Religion* 26: 321–43.

Garlicki, L. 2007. "Collective Aspects of the Religious Freedoms: Recent Developments in the Case Law of the European Court of Human Rights." In *Censorial Sensitivities: Free Speech and Religion in a Fundamentalist World*, edited by A. Sajo. 217–33. Utrecht: Eleven International Publishing.

Gomien, D. 1991. *Short Guide to the European Convention*. Strasbourg: COE Publishing.

Introvigne, M. 2004. "Holy Mountains and Anti-cult Ecology: The Campaign against the Aumist Religion in France." In *Regulating Religion: Case Studies from around the Globe*, edited by J.T. Richardson. 73–83. New York: Kluwer.

Luca, N. 2004. "Is There a Unique French Policy on Cults? A European Perspective." In *Regulating Religion: Case Studies from around the Globe*, edited by J.T. Richardson. 53–72. New York: Kluwer.

Meerschaut, K. and S. Gutwirth. 2009. "Legal Pluralism and Islam in the Scales of the European Court of Human Rights: The Limits of Categorical Balancing." In *Conflicts between Fundamental Rights*, edited by E. Brems. 431–65. Mortsel: Intersentia.

Palmer, S.J. 2011. *The New Heretics of France*. Oxford: Oxford University Press.

Richardson, J.T. 1985. "Minority Religions, Religious Freedom, and the Pan-European Political and Judicial Institutions." *Journal of Church and State* 37: 39–60.

Richardson, J.T. 2006. "Religion, Constitutional Courts, and Democracy in Former Communist Countries." *The Annals of the American Academy of Political and Social Science* 603: 129–38.

Richardson, J.T. and A. Garay. 2004. The European Court of Human Rights and former communist states, in *Religion and Patterns of Social Transformation*, edited by D.M. Jerolimov, S. Zrinscak, and I. Borowik. 223–34. Zagreb: Institute for Social Research.

Richardson, J.T. and V.A. Lykes. 2011. "France and the Tax Cases against the Jehovah's Witnesses and the Aumists." Presented at biannual conference of the International Society for the Sociology of Religion, Aix en Provence, France, July.

Richardson, J.T. and B. van Driel. 1994. "New Religions in Europe: A Comparison of Developments and Reactions in England, France, Germany, and the Netherlands." In *Anti-Cult Movements in Cross-Cultural Perspective*, edited by A. Shupe and D. Bromley. 129–70. New York: Garland Publishing.

Richardson, J.T., and J. Shoemaker. 2008. "The European Court of Human Rights, Minority Religions, and the Social Construction of Religious Freedom." In *The Centrality of Religion in Social Life: Essays in Honour of James A. Beckford*, edited by E. Barker. 103–16. Surrey, England.

Richardson, J.T., G. Krylova, and M. Shterin. 2004. "Legal Regulations of Religion in Russia: New Developments." In *Regulating Religion: Case Studies from around the Globe*, edited by J.T. Richardson. 247–57. New York: Kluwer.

Sadurski, W. 2005. *Rights before the Courts: A Study of Constitutional Courts in Postcommunist States of Central and Eastern Europe*. Dordrecht: Springer.

Sadurski, W. 2009. "Partnering with Strasbourg: Constitutionalization of the European Court of Human Rights, the Accession of Central and East European States to the Council of Europe, and the Idea of Pilot Judgments." *Human Rights Law Review* 9: 397–453.

Shterin, M.S. and J.T. Richardson. 1998. "Local Laws Restricting Religion in Russia: Precursors of Russia's New National Law." *Journal of Church and State* 40: 319–41.

Shterin, M.S. and J.T. Richardson. 2000. "The Effects of Western Anti-cult Sentiment on the Development of Laws concerning Religion in Post-communist Russia." *Journal of Church and State* 42: 247–71.

Shterin, M.S. and J.T. Richardson. 2002. "The *Yakunin v. Dworkin* Trial and the Emerging Religious Pluralism in Russia." *Religion in Eastern Europe* 22: 1–38.

PART IV
Minority Religious Groups in Court: Experimental Evidence

Chapter 11

Cults in Court:
Jury Decision-Making and
New Religious Movements

Jeffrey E. Pfeifer[1]

Introduction

Although the United States, like a number of countries throughout the world, attempted to ensure the separation of church and state through constitutional means, it may be argued that this delineation has done little to stem the flow of legal challenges (Murray 2008). Historically, these challenges revolve around one's First Amendment right to freedom of religion and involve a judicial determination of the extent to which this guarantee should prevail when placed in conflict with other constitutional rights, such as freedom of expression and assembly (Blakeman and Greco 2004). These constitutionally based challenges expanded over the years to include a significant number of criminal and civil cases involving the intersection of religion and a variety of diverse issues including education (Moshman 1990), the right to refuse medical treatment (Anderson 1983), and mental health (Behnke 2012).

Although there is an extensive legal history in the U.S. relating to freedom of religion, it may be argued that until fairly recently the preponderance of these cases involved assessing the degree to which the views and practices of those from traditional religions fell within constitutional protection (e.g., the right to prayer in school, the right to proselytize in public venues). However, during the latter half of the twentieth century, a new and distinctive trend began to emerge as the popularity and notoriety of non-traditional religions (i.e., NRMs,

[1]   Correspondence should be addressed to the author at Swinburne University of Technology, Psychological Sciences and Statistics, PO Box 218, H24, Hawthorn, Victoria, Australia 3122 (email: jpfeifer@swin.edu.au). Appreciation is extended to Justin Trounson for assistance with this manuscript.

'cults', etc.) increased, bringing with it a marked increase in legal attention (see Barker 1989 for a detailed review of the modern history of NRMs). For example, Wybraniec and Finke (2001) examined over 2,000 U.S. court cases involving religion from 1981–96 and concluded that religious sects and cults were significantly more likely to be the focus of the legal action than traditional religions. In addition, further multivariate analyses indicated that cases involving sects and cults were more likely to receive unfavourable rulings when compared to cases involving more traditional religions. This trend was also noted by Pfeifer and Ogloff (1992: 1) who suggested that

> although ratification of the First Amendment in 1791 sought to establish a clear boundary between church and state in the United States, the proliferation of new religious movements (or cults) ... has served to cloud that boundary almost beyond recognition. The popularity of new religious movements throughout the 1970s and 1980s was matched only by the apprehensiveness which ultimately led to a number of legal confrontations on constitutional, criminal and civil levels.

In addition to the above, it may be argued that closer examination of the legal cases involving NRMs indicates an interesting pattern which closely parallels public concerns regarding the alleged practices of these groups (Pfeifer and Ogloff 1992). For example, the increasing popularity of NRMs during the 1970s and early 1980s brought with it numerous claims that these groups were employing brainwashing techniques to recruit and maintain their membership (Barker 1989). These claims, in turn, led to a scientific debate regarding the degree to which 'brainwashing' and coercive persuasion may be employed by groups to control the thoughts and actions of their members (Kent 2008; Young and Griffith 1992). Not surprisingly, these concerns also eventually made their way to courtrooms across the U.S. as well as elsewhere and resulted in a cluster of legal challenges (Anthony and Robbins 1992; McPherson 1992; Richardson 1991a, 1993, 1996; Richardson and Introvigne 2001; Van Hoey 1991).

Although the issues of 'brainwashing' and coercive persuasion continue to be present with regard to NRMs and the law, the mid-1980s brought with it a significant shift in focus toward 'satanic' cults and their alleged involvement in illegal activities (Malcarne and Burchard 1992; Ogloff and Pfeifer 1992). According to a number of researchers, this shift in focus was largely due to a media-driven moral panic regarding the involvement of NRMs in satanic practices such as human sacrifice and child molestation (Richardson 1991b). This negative public perception was also heavily influenced through a spate of allegations made by psychotherapists and their clients, religious fundamentalists, and law enforcement personnel (deYoung 1994).

The result of this negative attention was a significant increase in criminal and civil cases involving the alleged activities of satanic cults and their members, including a number of high-profile trials such as those involving the McMartin family in California (Fukurai et al. 1994) and the Little Rascals Day-Care Center in North Carolina (see e.g., Shopper 2009). This increase was also documented by a number of researchers including Reichert and Richardson (2012), who conducted a review of civil and criminal proceedings during the late 1980s and early 1990s. The results of this review indicated that not only was there a significant increase in satanic cult cases during the 'satanic panic' era, but that that there was evidence that the negative public perceptions may have biased the decisions of both jurors and judges involved in these cases. According to these authors, the examination of these cases also indicated that the negative bias of judges and jurors toward defendants associated with satanic cults continues to the present-day, despite the fact that the moral panic relating to this issue has subsided in recent years.

Jury Decision-Making and Religion

The assertion of researchers such as Reichert and Richardson (2012) that jurors may be negatively impacted by trial information involving NRMs, suggests the importance of empirically examining this possibility. Yet, despite the fairly comprehensive literature on jury decision-making as it relates to issues such as race (Mitchell et al. 2005; Pfeifer and Bernstein 2003; Pfeifer and Ogloff 1991) and gender (see e.g., Campbell et al., 1992; Swystun and Pfeifer, 1994), there is comparatively little research on jury decision-making as it relates to NRMs.

Even though there is a paucity of empirical studies on how a trier of fact such as a juror may be impacted by evidence indicating an NRM association, there is at least some indication that, like race and gender, religion in general may play a role in the decisions of jurors. For example, Miller et al. (2008), suggest that one's religious orientation may have a significant impact on a number of trial aspects specifically related to jury decision-making such as jury selection, presentation of evidence, and jury deliberations. A review of the literature indicates some support for this contention, including a study on jurors and death penalty sentencing which found that the use of religion as part of a defence strategy significantly impacted the verdicts of mock jurors as well as the assessments of aggravating and mitigating evidence (Miller and Bornstein 2006).

Similarly, a recent study examining jury decision-making and cross-religious relationships found that the verdicts of mock jurors were significantly impacted by the religious orientation of the defendant and victim in a murder trial involving a claim of battered spouse syndrome (Pfeifer et al. 2012). In this study, participants were presented with a trial in which a wife was accused of killing her husband as he slept. Although the evidence clearly indicated that the wife committed the act, the defence argued that she was a victim of physical and emotional abuse at the hands of her husband and that this contributed to her actions (i.e., she was suffering from battered spouse syndrome). In order to assess the impact of religious orientation on juror decisions, the husband and wife were portrayed as either Muslim or Christian. Results indicated that jurors were significantly more likely to reject a claim of battered spouse syndrome and subsequently rate the defendant (i.e., wife) guiltier in the Muslim wife and Christian husband condition compared to the Christian wife/Muslim husband condition. The authors suggest that these results demonstrate that jurors hold prejudicial attitudes toward individuals characterized as Muslim and that these prejudicial attitudes are employed within a trial context, especially one in which there is a cross-relationship between the individuals involved in the trial.

Jury Decision-Making and New Religious Movements

In addition to research findings such as those described above indicating that mock jurors may be significantly impacted by religious information within a trial context, there is at least some indication that a similar impact may be found when there is a connection to an NRM (Pfeifer 1999). Although the existing literature on jury decision-making and NRMs is limited, it may be argued that a close examination of these studies indicate a number of interesting trends which may have implications for trials involving NRMs.

It is suggested that the most effective approach for assessing the impact of NRM involvement on jury decision-making is to examine the issue through the concept of psychological framing (Tversky and Kahneman 1981). This theory suggests that our decisions about others are sometimes based on the presence of a cognitive anchor which subsequently activates a schematic representation (e.g., stereotype, belief) of the person or group. It is further suggested that this process is most likely to occur in situations where the cognitive anchor is bizarre, salient, and/or negative and the individual has very little firsthand experience with the target. This would certainly appear to be reflective of research on NRMs with regard to anchors such as 'satanic panic' as well as research indicating that individuals hold negative schematic representations about NRMs and that these are seldom based on firsthand experience (Ogloff and Pfeifer 1992).

Empirical support for this contention is provided by at least one study which found that perceptions of an indoctrination process were significantly impacted by the name of the group involved (Pfeifer 1992). Specifically, participants in this study were provided with a summary of the indoctrination process experienced by an individual named Bill. Depending on the condition, the name of the group was either the Moonies (i.e. Unification Church), the U.S. Marines or the Catholic Church. It is important to note that the description of the process remained exactly the same across conditions; the only variable altered was the label of the group. After reading a summary of the indoctrination process, participants were asked a number of questions relating to the process as well as about Bill. Responses to these questions provided a number of interesting trends. First, participants were more likely to support the idea that the process they read should be labelled 'brainwashing' if the group was identified as the Moonies. In contrast, the process was more likely to be labelled as 'resocialization' if it was the Catholic Church and 'conversion' if it was the Marines. Perhaps more interesting was the fact that participants rated the process as significantly less fair if it was imposed by the Moonies than if imposed by the Catholic Church or Marines. It is noteworthy that these ratings were obtained despite the following instruction to participants to objectively assess the process regardless of the group and its philosophies (Pfeifer 1992: 536):

> Think about the process Bill has undergone, and try to separate the process from the specific message of the (Moonies, Marines, Catholic Church). That is, you may or may not agree with the philosophy of the (Moonies, Marines, Catholic Church), but try to put aside your disagreement with that philosophy. As such, solely in terms of the process, was Bill treated fairly by the (Moonies, Marines, Catholic Church)?

In addition to the above, participants also rated Bill as significantly less positive on a number of personality traits if he were portrayed as joining the Moonies rather than the Marines or the Catholic Church. Included among these perceptions was the view that Bill was less happy, less intelligent, and less responsible, as well being more likely to have been coerced into joining the group. According to the author of this article, the results provide clear evidence for the framing theory as it relates to NRMs. Specifically, the term 'Moonie' appears to have acted as a cognitive anchor for participants leading to the activation of a number of negative schematic representations. These representations were then employed by participants as a basis for making their judgments and were so salient that even an instruction directing them to ignore their perceptions of the group could not counteract the impact.

When applied to the issue of jury decision-making and NRMs, the above findings suggest that one's religious orientation, like other demographic trial information (e.g., race, gender), may be employed by jurors as a basis for their decision (see e.g., Pfeifer 1992), especially if that orientation is perceived as an NRM. As such, it is suggested that any comprehensive understanding of jury decision-making and NRMs be nested within a psychological framing theory that identifies the three related components that might result in a biased verdict: (1) the schematic representations jurors hold toward NRMs and their members,[2] (2) how and when these biases are most likely to be triggered (i.e., cognitive anchors and activation) within a trial context, and (3) what procedures or practices may be employed within a trial context to block the expression of these biases (i.e., behavioural constraints).

Component 1: Schematic Representations Related to NRMs

As stated above, any assessment of decision-making bias (be it with regard to juries or otherwise) begins with an understanding of the schematic representations that decision makers may hold toward the target group and its members (Alcock et al. 2001). In terms of gaining a more comprehensive understanding of the role which schematic representations play in terms of NRMs and jury decision-making, it is important to examine both the source of these representations as well as specifying the specific attributes that these representations comprise.

To begin with, a review of the literature on NRMs suggests that the negative schematic representations held by the general public toward these groups are overwhelmingly based on vivid media reports which highlight both the alleged practices of the organizations as well as the impact that these practices have on followers (Woodberry 1989). MacHovec (1992), for example, suggests that the extensive and detailed print and television media coverage of a number of high-profile legal cases involving cults and child abuse in the late 1980s contributed to the development of numerous negative stereotypes toward these organizations. According to McHovec (1992: 32), the negative stereotypes promoted by media reports revolve around a number of common themes: 'Writers who describe harmful and destructive cults report certain common negative characteristics including: a charismatic leader, an exclusivist group separated from or opposing

---

[2]   A schematic representation is a cognitive concept (such as a schema) that is employed by an individual when evaluating others and is based on the psychological framing theory developed by Tversky and Kahneman (1981). The concept includes a myriad of other social psychological terms employed to describe one's beliefs about a person, object or event (e.g., bias, stereotypes, prototype, etc.).

mainstream or traditional values, isolation of cult members from family, friends, school or career, and *deviant behavioral norms and lifestyle*' (emphasis added). Similar claims regarding the impact of media on perceptions of NRMs have been put forward by a number of other authors (Passas and Castillo 1992; Reichert and Richardson 2012; Szimhart 2004), including a longitudinal examination of print media conducted by Van Driel and Richardson (1988).

There is at least some empirical evidence that the volume and intensity of the media coverage described above has translated into negative beliefs relating to NRMs and their members. For example, in their paper on perceptions of cults, Bromley and Breschel (1992) reported the results from a number of public opinion polls which indicated an increase in negative sentiments toward NRMs from the early 1980s to the latter half of the decade. Based on these findings, the authors conducted their own survey and found evidence that the negative perceptions of the general public toward cults continued into the 1990s and that these beliefs included support for governmental and legal restraints to be put in place to control NRMs. Evidence regarding negative public perceptions of specific NRMs has also been documented, including Scientology (Passas and Castillo 1992) and the Unification Church and its leadership (Richardson 1992).

In order to gain a more detailed description of the specific beliefs held toward cults and satanic cults by the general public, Ogloff and Pfeifer (1992) distributed a survey to individuals from Canada as well as the United States asking them to provide information regarding: (1) their belief in the existence of cults and satanic cults, (2) their personal experiences with these groups, and (3) their beliefs as to the practices carried out by these groups. The results of the survey provided a number of interesting insights. To begin with, participants overwhelmingly indicated their belief in the existence of cults (97.5%) and satanic cults (97%), despite the fact that comparatively few of the respondents reported having any personal knowledge regarding the existence of these entities. This finding certainly appears to corroborate the findings reported above regarding the role played by the media in the process of impacting NRM knowledge and negative beliefs. Perhaps even more telling is the data relating to respondents beliefs about the specific practices that these groups engage in. When asked to list these practices, a significant percentage of respondents indicated a belief that cult and satanic cult members engaged in a variety of practices including ritualistic worship, animal sacrifice, human sacrifice, brainwashing, sex, deviant sex, and illegal activity and deviant behaviour.

Despite suggestions that media coverage of NRMs has significantly decreased in the last decade (Reichert and Richardson 2012), it appears that the negative perception of these groups and their members remain. For example, Olson

(2006) recently conducted a study in the United States assessing attitudes toward cults, NRMs and New Christian Churches. In order to empirically demonstrate the attitudes held toward NRMs, participants were asked to provide their level of agreement to the following two questions: (1) 'How comfortable would you be if your neighbour joined a (cult, NRM, New Christian Church)', and (2) 'How much would you agree with the following statement? The government should have the right to regulate the activities and practices of (cults, NRMs, New Christian Churches)'. The results of the survey clearly indicated a negative bias toward cults and NRMs when compared to New Christian Churches. Specifically, respondents were significantly more likely to report feeling 'very comfortable' should their neighbour join a New Christian Church (59.9%) as opposed to an NRM (28.4%) or a cult (5.2%). A similar pattern emerged regarding public perceptions toward government control of these groups with only 12.4% in agreement (i.e., strongly agree and agree) that there was a need to regulate the activities of New Christian Churches compared to NRMs (25.6%) and cults (56.2%).

Component 2: Cognitive Anchors and Activation

The above section clearly indicates that the general public continues to hold a variety of negative schematic representations regarding NRMs and that these representations are heavily based on mass media portrayals rather than personal experience. There is also some indication that these representations may have had a subsequent impact on a number of criminal and civil trials such as the tax evasion trial of Reverend Moon (Richardson 1992), child abuse trials (Fukurai et al. 1994; Shopper 2009), and a variety of allegations involving satanic cults and their membership (deYoung 1994; Richardson 1991b). In order to more effectively assess the role that these schematic representations may play in the domain of jury decision-making it is important to review the empirical evidence which exists to date with a view to identifying the circumstances under which these negative schematic representations are likely to be activated.

One of the first empirical studies investigating the impact of NRM involvement within an experimental jury decision-making paradigm was conducted by Pfeifer in 1999. The purpose of this study was to investigate the degree to which the term 'satanic cult' would adversely impact the guilt determinations of mock jurors in homicide and child sexual assault scenarios. In order to accomplish this, participants were asked to read a summary of either a homicide or child sexual assault trial. The summary itself included information regarding the defendant in the case and, depending on the experimental condition, described the defendant as having no religious affiliation, admittedly being a member of a satanic cult, or allegedly being a member of a satanic cult.[3] After reading the trial information, participants were asked to rate the guilt of the defendant as well as how confident they were in their verdict.

Results indicated that for both the homicide and child sexual assault trials, the defendant was rated as significantly more guilty if he was portrayed as admitting to be a member of a satanic cult than if no mention of religious orientation was made. Interestingly participants were just as confident in their verdict regardless of the condition they were in. Further analyses indicated that participants rated the defendant equally high in guilt regardless of whether he admitted to being a member of a satanic cult or whether this information was simply alleged by the prosecution without any corroboration other than the evidence of a neighbour who stated that they 'thought' the defendant might be in a satanic cult. Importantly, the bias against the satanic cult defendant persevered even when participants were provided with instructions explicitly directing them to avoid any inclusion of religious prejudice or discrimination in their judgment. Overall it may be argued that, among other things, the results of this study indicate the pervasiveness and depth of schematic representations regarding satanic cults as well as the ease with which these representations may be activated. These findings led the author to conclude (Pfeifer 1999: 417):

> The increased media and academic attention paid to satanism in recent years has indeed culminated in a public belief in the reality of a 'satanic panic' or 'satanism scare' that is both widespread and dangerous. The strength of this perception is illustrated by the results of this study, and if left unchecked, may lead to increased biases toward individuals allegedly involved with satanic cults.

More recently, Pfeifer, Naidoo and Katapodis (2012) conducted a study in order to examine whether the negative schematic representations toward NRMs might be extended to additional legal decision-making paradigms. Specifically, these authors sought to examine the degree to which the decisions of participants would be adversely affected by religious affiliation when asked to decide whether a mother should be allowed to regain custody of her child. In order to examine this question, participants were asked to read a summary of a case in which a mother was petitioning to regain custody of the child which was taken from her

---

[3] It is important to note that although the religious orientation of the defendant was varied to include an admitted or alleged membership in a satanic cult, the trial evidence itself did not suggest any religious basis for the acts alleged to have occurred.

and put into care two years earlier. The case itself included a fairly positive report from a social services caseworker which indicated that the mother had made significant life improvement strides in the past three years (e.g., had addressed her drug addiction, completed a college program, gained employment, and was in a stable relationship).

In addition to the above, some participants were also informed that the mother had a slight affiliation with a local religious organization through attending a weekly meeting which she claimed helped her to cope and stay on a positive path. The report also emphasized that the affiliation consisted solely of attending the weekly meeting and did not extend to any other affiliation with the organization or its members. The organization itself was described as a church, a new age church, a cult or a satanic cult. The methodology also included a manipulation with regard to the provision of a set of instructions specifically indicating that the participant should not employ any information regarding religion or religious affiliation when making their decision. The overarching design, therefore, resulted in 10 conditions through the manipulation of two variables: affiliation (i.e., no affiliation, church, new age church, cult or satanic cult) and instruction (i.e., no instructions, inclusion of instructions). Once participants had read the summary they were asked to indicate whether the mother should regain custody of her child as well as to rate the mother on a number of traits such as competence, strength, rationality and stability. Finally, participants were asked to indicate the degree to which their decision was influenced by the mother's religious affiliation.

The findings of this study provide insight into the question of NRM affiliation on decision-making in a legal context and, as such, bear a somewhat detailed description. To begin with, results indicate that participants were inclined to view the mother as significantly more negative on a variety of personality traits if she were portrayed as having an affiliation with a cult or satanic cult. Specifically, participants rated the mother as significantly less competent, weaker, less rational, and less stable if she was associated with a cult or satanic cult than if she had no religious affiliation or was affiliated with a church or new age church. This finding appears to support the argument made above that individuals hold negative schematic representations about NRMs and their members and that these representations can be activated through the mere mention of an NRM affiliation no matter how tenuous the association may be.

In addition to the above, analysis of the responses also indicated that the religious affiliation had a significant impact on the subsequent custody decisions made by participants. Interestingly, participants were most likely to support the mother's bid for custody in the church affiliation condition, followed by the no affiliation and new age church affiliation conditions, and were significantly less likely to support the mothers request in the cult and satanic cult conditions. This trend maintained itself even when participants were provided with instructions specifically directing them to avoid any information regarding religion in their decision. As above, this finding demonstrates that the activation of negative schematic representations can directly result in biased decision-making within a legal context. It may also be argued that these negative representations are so deeply ingrained that they are impervious to attempts to constrain them through explicit instructions. This finding is of even more interest when viewed in conjunction with participant ratings on the degree to which they employed the mother's religious affiliation in their decision (i.e., participants indicated no significant differences across conditions). In other words, participants appear to clearly be employing religious affiliation evidence in their perceptions of the mother as well as their custody decision while at the same time claiming that they are not doing so.

Although the above two studies appear to provide empirical evidence that decision-makers within a legal context may be negatively impacted by an individual's affiliation with an NRM, there has been little attention given to examining the impact of NRM affiliation with regard to other related aspects of the trial process, such as the testimony of experts (see e.g., Shinn 1992). One notable exception is a study conducted by DeWitt, Richardson and Warner (1997). As with the two studies described above, the DeWitt et al. paper also sought to empirically demonstrate that individuals holding negative schematic representations about NRMs are likely to employ these biases within a jury decision-making paradigm. In this case, however, there was a focus on the impact these representations would have when assessing evidence related to so-called brainwashing. Specifically, the study sought to examine the degree to which the presence of expert testimony and participant's need for cognition would interact with negative representations toward NRMs and ultimately impact verdicts. In order to accomplish this, participants were presented with a scenario in which a plaintiff who was a former member of an NRM claimed that he had been brainwashed by the church, resulting in accusations of (1) intentional infliction of emotional distress and (2) false imprisonment.

Analysis of participant responses indicated a main effect for all three independent variables investigated (i.e., pre-existing juror bias, need for cognition and expert testimony) with regard to the two dependant variables (emotional distress and false imprisonment). That is, participants who held pre-existing biases toward NRMs were more likely to agree that the church had falsely imprisoned the plaintiff and had also intentionally caused him emotional distress. Similarly, those participants who demonstrated lower need for cognition scores were more likely to find in favour of the plaintiff than those scoring higher on need for cognition. Finally, participants who were exposed to conditions which included expert testimony on brainwashing and NRMs were also more likely to agree that the plaintiff had suffered at the hands of the church than were participants who were not exposed to expert testimony.

This study adds to our knowledgebase regarding NRMs and jury decision-making in a number of ways. To begin with, it may be argued that this research both replicates and extends the findings of the other two jury decision-making studies discussed above (Pfeifer 1999; Pfeifer et al. 2012). Specifically, it not only demonstrates that participants holding negative schematic representations about NRMs tend to employ these biases in their verdicts (as did the participants in the other two studies), but also empirically demonstrates that participants who do not hold these representations are not impacted by the NRM affiliation (i.e., the cognitive anchor). This in itself is an important demonstration in that it empirically compares the verdicts of those holding negative representations about NRMs with the verdicts of those not holding negative representations about NRMs, something which had none been done in previous studies.

The findings presented by Dewitt, Richardson, and Warner (1997) also opens up the possibility that the presence of negative beliefs about NRMs may not always lead directly to biased decision-making, especially when combined with other cognitive factors such as need for cognition. Finally, the study also demonstrates that, in addition to the personal factors (e.g., biases, need for cognition) that a juror may bring to the table when assessing a case with NRM overtones, there are also a number of other important aspects of the trial that may interact with these factors (i.e., expert testimony). At the very least, the findings of this study demonstrates the need for additional, and more detailed, empirical examinations of this phenomenon.

Though limited in number, it may be argued that when combined with the information presented in Component 1 (i.e., Schematic Representations Related to NRMs) the three studies described above provide us with at least a modicum of information regarding the cognitive anchors that may play a role in the activation of negative schematic representations toward NRMs and their members. For example, these studies indicate that there are a number of specific terms which individuals equate with a negative religious organization and therefore act as a cognitive anchor which subsequently activates a variety of negative schematic representations. Included among these are terms relating to the organization itself (e.g., cult, satanic, NRM), terms relating to the alleged activities of these organizations (e.g., brainwashing, sacrifice, mind control, deprogramming), as well as names of specific groups (e.g., Unification Church, Church of Scientology). In addition, the results of these studies also indicate that terms such as 'new age church' (Pfeifer et al. 2012) and 'new Christian church' (Olson 2006) may also act as cognitive anchors yet appear to activate fewer negative cognitions than terms such as cult or NRM.

Interestingly, the above studies also suggest that these cognitive anchors may be activated based on the merest suggestion of association. Specifically, the Pfeifer (1999) study found that mock jurors were just as likely to employ their negative schematic representations in cases where an individual was alleged to be involved in an NRM as they were in cases where the association with an NRM was admitted. This finding parallels the work of Reichert and Richardson (2012) who reported that their analysis of jury decision-making in civil and criminal cases indicated a bias toward organizations both allegedly and admittedly involved in satanic practices. According to Pfeifer (1999: 417) this state of affairs may eventuate in a situation in which 'social justice concerns may be overwhelmed in cases involving unpopular religious groups, even if the ties with such groups are tenuous or unfounded'.

Component 3: Identifying and Implementing Behavioural Constraints

According to the above findings, it appears clear that people hold a number of specific negative schematic representations about NRMs and that these representations may be activated (through a variety of cognitive anchors) in a jury decision-making context, potentially disadvantaging those associated with the NRM. Given this situation, it is worthwhile to examine whether there are any potential avenues for counteracting this bias within a legal context.[4] There certainly appears to be some support for this contention from a variety of sources, including jury instructions, jury selection and the deliberation process.

Jury Instructions

It may be argued that one avenue for behaviourally constraining the negative beliefs of jurors toward NRMs may be through jury instructions. Support for this contention may be gleaned from the research on juror racism. For example, Pfeifer and Ogloff (1991) were able to empirically demonstrate that the racial

---

[4]   This contention is based on the importance placed on the distinction between an attitude (i.e., prejudice) and a behaviour (i.e., discrimination) in both psychology and the law (see Pfeifer, 1990, for a more detailed discussion with regard to jury decision-making).

biases held by white mock jurors toward black defendants could be constrained by the inclusion of standard jury instructions. This finding was particularly noteworthy given that it seemingly contradicted a series of studies demonstrating the impact of racially based biases toward black defendants, especially in rape and murder cases (Gerbasi, Zuckerman and Reis 1977; Klein and Creech 1982; Pfeifer 1990). According to the authors, the majority of these earlier studies were flawed in that the methodology did not include jury instructions, and as a result, white participants were able to more freely express their biases. It was further suggested that the inclusion of instructions not only resulted in a methodology more accurate in reflection of a legal context, but also served to constrain the racially based beliefs of white mock jurors. The study concluded that

> jurors asked to make a decision about a situation without any guiding factors tend to fall back on stereotypical characterizations of the defendant.... However, specific jury instructions give mock jurors something to 'anchor' on to make their decisions. This allows jurors to make decisions which rely less upon their stereotypes and more upon factors that are important in formulating a legal decision; factors that are specified in the jury instructions. (Pfeifer and Ogloff 1992:1721)

Given that the publication of this study prompted a series of articles highlighting the importance of instructions in jury decision-making studies for constraining potential biases (Mitchell et al, 2005; Pfeifer and Ogloff 2003), there is a clear need to investigate whether a similar pattern can be found with relation to jury studies on NRMs. That is, it may be argued that, like racism, negative views toward NRMs may be constrained in a jury decision-making paradigm if the methodology includes the instructions.

Although few studies have been conducted to date regarding this possibility, those which do exist appear to indicate that the inclusion of standard jury instructions in NRM cases does not have the same impact as that found in cases involving racial issues. For example, in a study on jury decision-making and cults, Pfeifer (1999) found that the inclusion of instructions had no impact on the verdicts of jurors with regard to a defendant who was associated with a cult or satanic cult. Similarly, the Pfeifer et al. (2012) study on child custody and religious orientation also found that instructions failed to constrain the negative biases of participants toward those associated with a NRM – even when the instruction included a specific directive to jurors to not employ any information regarding religion when making their decision.

Although it appears that, unlike racial bias, bias toward NRMs and their members is not able to be constrained by standard instructions, it is important to note that further empirical investigations should be carried out in this area before it is abandoned. For example, it may be that although the bias held toward NRMs is seemingly impervious to standard jury instructions, other types of instruction may have more of an impact. In addition, it may be possible that standard instructions are not effective in this context due to the fact that bias toward NRMs, unlike racial bias, is still viewed as acceptable and therefore not perceived as being prejudicial or discriminatory by jurors. This is an important consideration given that standard instructions implore jurors to not be prejudicial or discriminatory in their role. Future research may provide additional insight into these possibilities.

Jury Selection

In addition to the possibility that instructions may play a role in constraining bias toward NRMs, there is also some evidence that jury selection may be of assistance in counteracting this bias through the use of both challenge for cause as well as through peremptory challenges. In terms of employing challenge for cause as a mechanism for the removal of a juror, it is imperative that the judge be presented with compelling evidence that a juror has a clear bias and that he or she would be unable or unwilling to ignore this bias when assessing the evidence (see Pfeifer, 1996, for an overview of these concept as applied to jury decision-making research). This may be more difficult in cases involving NRMs than those involving other issues such as race or gender as exemplified by Passas and Castillo (1992) who suggest that many presiding judges themselves hold negative views toward NRMs and their members. Despite this situation however, it is suggested that future research may aim at identifying what type of evidence may be considered as compelling by judges with regard to supporting a challenge for cause in NRM-related cases. In addition, research is also needed to identify how biases toward NRMs may be demonstrated by potential jurors. This research may be informed by the literature examining how racial bias may be demonstrated and employed as a challenge for cause (Marder 2012).

In terms of the use of peremptory challenges to constrain potential biases toward NRMs and their members, the literature indicates a number of potential possibilities. To begin with, the study conducted by Bromley and Breschel (1992) appears to suggest that attitudes of America's institutional elite (i.e., industry and finance leaders, academics, government representatives) toward NRMs are much more positive than the attitudes of the American general public. According to the data presented by the authors, this differential culminates in those in the institutional elite sample espousing significantly less rigorous restrictions on NRMs than those in the general public (i.e., less likely to support laws and regulations specifically censuring NRMs and their members). It may be argued that this finding takes on even more importance when combined with the study conducted by DeWitt, Richardson and Warner (1997), which found that mock jurors who were identified as high in need for cognition were less likely to support a claim of brainwashing by an NRM than mock jurors who were identified as low in need for cognition.

Taken together, the above results indicate that jurors with higher levels of formal education, higher need for cognition, and/or higher levels of professionalization may be less likely to allow their verdicts to be negatively impacted by evidence of an NRM association. Future research may assist in corroborating this supposition as well as identifying the additional psychological factors that may elicit a similar response in jurors such as flexible thinking styles (Goclowska et al. 2013).

Deliberations

One final element of the trial process that may potentially serve to constrain the negative perceptions of jurors toward NRMs may be found in the deliberation phase. Although the impact of deliberations has yet to be empirically examined with regard to NRMs specifically, there is some indication that religion can play a role in the process (Miller et al. 2011; Miller, Singer, and Jehle 2008). Specifically, it is suggested that religion may play a significant role in the deliberations of jurors in a number of ways (e.g., reliance on the Bible, views on punishment, imposition of the death penalty) and that this impact may be explained through a variety of social psychological theories such as social judgment theory and reactance theory. Although the literature to date on this topic is sparse, the initial indicators regarding religion and deliberations, combined with an increasing literature on the social psychology of deliberations (Adams, Bryden and Griffith 2011; Patry 2008) suggests that the area is one that deserves future attention.

Future Directions

At the very least, the above review indicates a need for additional empirical examinations of how NRM involvement may impact jury decision-making. It may also be argued that although the extensive literature examining other variables such as race and gender may provide some insight into this issue, there are clearly a number of important distinctions to be made when it comes to

NRMs (e.g., lack of impact regarding instructions, activation even in situations where NRM association is only alleged). In addition to the specific suggestions made above with regard to future research, there are a number of other possible avenues for investigation.

For example, Miller et al. (2008) suggest that there are four specific stages that are ripe for the study of religion and jury decision-making, including voir dire, the trial phase, closing arguments and the deliberation phase. To date, it appears that the bulk of the research conducted on NRMs has been limited to examining the impact during the trial phase (e.g., defendant affiliation, expert witnesses) with comparatively little research effort directed at the other phases. Certainly, the above discussion regarding potential behavioural constraints on the expression of NRM bias would suggest that additional research on the voir dire phase would be a useful addition to the literature. A similar argument may be made for investigations into the deliberation phase as well as the closing argument phase.

In addition to the above, it may be argued that there is a need for additional research examining the cognitive representations that people hold about NRMs and their members, especially with regard to the strength (Krosnick and Petty 1995) and basis of these representations (Eagly and Chaiken 1992). For example, future research might better identify which attitudes or beliefs about NRMs are least salient and, as such, most likely to be countered by trial evidence. Similarly, it would be helpful to have additional empirical evidence regarding whether the attitudes held by jurors toward NRMs are affectively, behaviourally or cognitively based.

Future research may also be directed toward gaining a greater understanding of the specific terms which are used by jurors as cognitive anchors, subsequently activating the negative representations they have toward these groups. Certainly the work of DeWitt, Richardson and Warner (1997) indicates that activation of beliefs regarding NRMs may be impacted by a number of activation models including the Elaboration Likelihood Model. It may be that future research in this area can provide greater insight into the how and when the cognitive representations regarding NRMs may be activated or constrained.

References

Adams, L.T., M.W. Bryden, and J.D. Griffith. 2011. 'Middle Eastern Racial Bias and the Impact of Jury Deliberation'. *American Journal of Forensic Psychology* 29: 41–59.

Alcock, J.E., D.W. Carment, and S.W. Sadava. 2001. *A Textbook of Social Psychology*. Toronto, Ontario: Pearson.

Anderson, G.R. (1983). 'Medicine vs. Religion: The Case of Jehovah's Witnesses'. *Health and Social Work* 8: 31–8.

Anthony, D., and T. Robbins. 1992. 'Law, Social Science and the "Brainwashing" Exception to the First Amendment'. *Behavioral Sciences and the Law* 10: 5–29.

Barker, E. 1989. *New Religious Movements: A Practical Introduction*. London: Her Majesty's Stationary Office.

Behnke, S.H. 2012. 'Constitutional Claims in the Context of Mental Health Training: Religion, Sexual Orientation, and Tensions between the First Amendment and Professional Ethics'. *Training and Education in Professional Psychology* 6: 189–95.

Blakeman, J.C., and D.E. Greco. 2004. 'Federal District Court Decision Making in Public Forum and Religious Speech Cases, 1973–2001'. *Journal for the Scientific Study of Religion* 43: 439–49.

Bromley, D.G. and E.F. Breschel. 1992. 'General Population and Institutional Elite Support for Social Control of New Religious Movements: Evidence from National Survey Data'. *Behavioral Sciences & the Law* 10: 39–52.

Campbell, E., D. Pierre-Trettel, H. Koenig, J.E. Pfeifer, and K. Gabriel. 1992. 'Gender and Presentational Style: When the Verdict of the Trial is Unaffected by an Attorney's Personal Characteristics and Behavior, Justice is Served'. *Washburn Law Journal* 31: 415–54.

Dewitt, J.S., J.T. Richardson, and L.G. Warner. 1997. 'Novel Scientific Evidence and Controversial Cases: A Social Psychological Examination'. *Law and Psychology Review* 21: 1–27.

deYoung, M. 1994. 'One Face of the Devil: The Satanic Ritual Abuse Moral Crusade and the Law'. *Behavioral Sciences and the Law* 12: 389–407.

Eagly, A.H., and S. Chaiken. 1992. *The Psychology of Attitudes*. Fort Worth, Texas: Harcourt Brace Jovanovich.

Fukurai, H., E. Butler, and R. Krooth. 1994. 'Sociologists in Action: The McMartin Sexual Abuse Case, Litigation, Justice, and Mass Hysteria'. *The American Sociologist* 25: 44–71.

Gerbasi, K.L., M. Zucherman, and H.T. Reis. 1977. 'Justice Needs a New Blindfold: A Review of Mock Jury Research'. *Psychological Bulletin* 84: 323–45.

Goclowska, M.A., R.J. Crisp, and K. Labuschagne, K. 2013. 'Can Counter-stereotypes Boost Flexible Thinking?' *Group Processes & Intergroup Relations* 16: 217–31.

Kent, S.A. 2008. 'Contemporary Uses of the Brainwashing Concept: 2000 to Mid-2007'. *Cultic Studies Review* 7: 99–128.

Klein, K., and B. Creech. 1982. 'Race, Rape and Bias: Distortion of Prior Odds and Meaning Changes'. *Basic and Applied Social Psychology* 3: 21–33.

Krosnick, J.A., and R.E. Petty. 1995. 'Attitude Strength: An Overview'. In *Attitude Strength: Antecedents and Consequences; Ohio State University Series on Attitudes and Persuasion*, edited by R.E. Petty and J.A. Krosnick, 1–24. Mahwah, New Jersey: Lawrence Erlbaum Associates.

MacHovec, F. 1992. 'Cults: Forensic and Therapeutic Aspects'. *Behavioral Sciences and the Law* 10: 31–7.

Malcarne, V.L., and J.D. Burchard. 1992. 'Investigations of Child Abuse/Neglect Allegations in Religious Cults: A Case Study in Vermont'. *Behavioral Sciences and the Law* 10: 75–88.

Marder, N.S. 2012. 'Batson Revisited'. *Iowa Law Review* 97: 1585–612.

McPherson, S.B. 1992. 'Death Penalty Mitigation and Cult Membership: The Case of the Kirtland Killings'. *Behavioral Sciences and the Law* 10: 65–74.

Miller, M.K., and B. Bornstein. 2006. 'The Use of Religion in Death Penalty Sentencing Trials'. *Law and Human Behavior* 30: 675–84.

Miller, M.K., J. Maskaly, M. Green, and C.D. Peoples. 2011. 'The Effects of Deliberations and Religious Identity on Mock Jurors' Verdicts'. *Group Processes and Intergroup Relations* 14: 517–32.

Miller, M.K., J.A. Singer, and A. Jehle 2008. 'Identification of Circumstances under which Religion affects Each Stage of the Trial Process'. *Applied Psychology in Criminal Justice* 4: 135–71.

Mitchell, T.L., R.M. Haw, J.E. Pfeifer, and C.A. Meissner. 2005. 'Racial Bias in Juror Decision-making: A Meta-analytic Review of Defendant Treatment'. *Law and Human Behavior* 29: 621–37.

Moshman, D. 1990. 'Equal Access for Religion in Public Schools? An Empirical Approach to a Legal Dilemma'. *Developmental Review* 10:184–99.

Murray, B.T. 2008. *Religious Liberty in America: The First Amendment in Historical and Contemporary Perspective*. Amherst, Massachusetts: University of Massachusetts Press.

Ogloff, J.R.P., and J.E. Pfeifer. 1992. 'Cults and the Law: A Discussion of the Legality of Alleged Cult Activity'. *Behavioral Sciences and the Law* 10: 117–40.

Olson, P.J. (2006). 'The Public Perception of 'Cults' and 'New Religious Movements.'" *Journal for the Scientific Study of Religion* 45: 97–106.

Passas, N., and M.E. Castillo. 1992. 'Scientology and its "Clear" Business'. *Behavioral Sciences and the Law* 10: 103–16.

Patry, M. 2008. 'Attractive but Guilty: Deliberation and the Physical Attractiveness Bias'. *Psychological Reports* 102: 727–33.

Pfeifer, J.E. 1990. 'Reviewing the Empirical Evidence on Jury Racism: Findings of Discrimination or Discriminatory Findings?' *Nebraska Law Review* 69: 230–50.

Pfeifer, J.E. 1992. 'The Psychological Framing of Cults: Schematic Representations and Cult Evaluations'. *Journal of Applied Social Psychology* 22: 531–44.

Pfeifer, J.E. 1996. 'Social Psychology in the Courtroom'. In *Applied Social Psychology*, edited by S.W. Sadava and D.R. McCreary, 157–84. New York: Prentice Hall.

Pfeifer, J.E. 1999. 'Perceptual Biases and Mock Juror Decision Making: Minority Religions in Court'. *Social Justice Research* 12: 409–19.

Pfeifer, J.E., and D. Bernstein. 2003. 'Mock Juror Decision Making and Modern Racism: Examining the Role of Task and Target Specificity on Judgmental Evaluations'. *Social Behavior and Personality* 31: 749–66.

Pfeifer, J.E., T.S. Naidoo, and N. Katapodis. 2012. 'Child Custody and Cults: Assessing the Role of Religious Orientation and Perceptions of Parental Fitness'. Paper presented at the Australian Association for the Study of Religion Conference. Sydney, Australia.

Pfeifer, J.E., and J.R.P. Ogloff. 1991. 'Ambiguity and Guilt Determinations: A Modern Racism Perspective'. *Journal of Applied Social Psychology* 21: 1713–25.

Pfeifer, J.E., and J.R.P. Ogloff. 1992. 'New Religious Movements and the Law: Past Interactions and New Directions'. *Behavioral Sciences and the Law* 10: 1–3.

Pfeifer, J.E., & Ogloff, J.R.P. (2003). 'Mock Juror Ratings of Guilt in Canada: Modern Racism and Ethnic Heritage'. *Social Behavior and Personality* 31: 301–12.

Pfeifer, J.E., J.S. Trounson, and K. Nathan. 2012. 'Juror Decision-making and Battered Spouse Syndrome: Examining the Impact of Cross-religious Relationships'. Paper presented at the Australian Association for the Study of Religion Conference. Sydney, Australia.

Reichert, J. and J.T. Richardson. 2012. "Decline of a Moral Panic: A Social Psychological and Socio-Legal Examination of the Current Status of Satanism. *Nova Religio* 16: 47–63.

Richardson, J.T. 1991a. 'Cult/brainwashing Cases and Freedom of Religion'. *Journal of Church and State* 33: 55–74.

Richardson, J.T. 1991b. 'Satanism in the Courts: From Murder to Heavy Metal'. In *The Satanism Scare*, edited by J.T. Richardson, J. Best and D.G. Bromley, 205–17. New York: Aldine de Gruyter.

Richardson, J.T.1992. 'Public Opinion and the Tax Evasion Trial of Reverend Moon'. *Behavioral Sciences and the Law* 10: 53–63.

Richardson, J.T. 1993. 'A Social Psychological Critique of 'Brainwashing' Claims about Recruitment to New Religions'. In *The Handbook of Sects and Cults in America*, edited by D.G. Bromley and J.K. Hadden, 75–97. Greenwich, CT: JAI Press.

Richardson, J.T. 1996. '"Brainwashing" Claims and Minority Religions outside the United States: Cultural Diffusion of a Questionable Legal Concept'. *Brigham Young University Law Review* 1996: 873–904.

Richardson, J.T., and M. Introvigne. 2001. '"Brainwashing" Theories in European Parliamentary and Administrative Reports on "Cults" and "Sects"'. *Journal for the Scientific Study of Religion* 40: 143–68.

Shinn, L.D. 1992. 'Cult Conversions and the Courts: Some Ethical Issues in Academic Expert Testimony'. *Sociological Analysis* 53: 273–85.

Shopper, M. 2009. 'What I Learned from the Edenton "Little Rascals" Sex Abuse Trial'. *Psychoanalytic Inquiry* 29: 513–27.

Swystun, J., and J.E. Pfeifer. 1994. 'Gender Stereotypes and Physical Spousal Abuse: Investigating Perceptual Biases in Mock Juror Evaluations'. *Journal of Psychology and the Behavioral Sciences* 8: 129–37.

Szimhart, J.P. 2004. 'Persistence of "Deprogramming" Stereotypes in Film'. *Cultic Studies Review* 3: 202–25.

Tomkins, A.J., and J.E. Pfeifer. 1991. 'Modern Social Scientific Theories and Data Concerning Discrimination: Implications for Using Social Science Evidence in the Courts'. In *Handbook of Psychology and Law*, edited by D.K. Kagehiro and W.S. Laufer, 385–407. New York: Springer-Verlag.

Tversky, A., and D. Kahneman. 1981. 'The Framing of Decisions and the Psychology of Choice'. *Science* 211: 453–8.

Van Driel, B., and J.T. Richardson. 1988. 'Print Media Coverage of New Religious Movements: A Longitudinal Study'. *Journal of Communication* 38: 37–61.

Van Hoey, S. 1991. 'Cults in Court'. *Cultic Studies Journal* 8: 61–79.

Woodberry, R. 1989. 'Cult of the Red-Haired Devil'. *Time*, April 24: 30.

Wybraniec, J., and R. Finke. 2001. 'Religious Regulation and the Courts: The Judiciary's Changing Role in Protecting Minority Religions from Majoritarian Rule'. *Journal for the Scientific Study of Religion* 40: 427–44.

Young, J.L. and E.E. H. Griffith. 1992. 'A Critical Evaluation of Coercive Persuasion as Used in the Assessment of Cults'. *Behavioral Sciences and the Law* 10: 89–101.

Chapter 12

Parents' Use of Faith Healing for Their Children: Implications for the Legal System and Measuring Community Sentiment

Monica K. Miller

Introduction

When Brandi and Russel Bellew's son Austin became ill in 2011, they decided not to seek medical care but instead to pray for his healing. After he died, the Oregon couple was charged and eventually pled guilty to negligent homicide in September 2012 and lost custody of their six other children. As members of the General Assembly Church of the First Born, they believed in faith healing. Many such religious groups practice various forms of faith healing rather than traditional medical procedures. Such cases are controversial because they pit the state's right to protect children against parents' rights and religious freedoms. Parents who practice faith healing typically claim that the government cannot force them to seek medical care for their children because of their religious rights that are protected under the First Amendment's Free Exercise Clause (Williams 2012). This clause states that "Congress shall make no law respecting an establishment of religion, or prohibiting the free exercise thereof" (U.S. Constitution, First Amendment). While this Amendment protects many religious activities from government intervention, the Supreme Court has made it clear that there are many exceptions, such as child labor and polygamy (Williams 2012).

In the mid-1970s, nearly all states had faith healing exemptions that protected parents who chose not to seek traditional medical treatment; in the 1980s, some states began repealing their exemptions, with Oregon being the latest to do so. Two cases involving the death of Oregon children who were Followers of Christ prompted Oregon legislators to pass Or. Rev. Stat. §163.115(4) in 2011. This law forbids parents from using their reliance on spiritual treatment as a defense to crimes against children under 18. This statute represents a shift away from protecting religious parents. Despite this shift, as of 2012, nearly 40 states had faith healing exemptions (Darby Howell 2012; Loue 2012; Williams 2012). Because of the changing legal landscape, it is important to study community sentiment about this issue because it helps instill a belief in legitimacy of the government and promotes compliance with the legal system in general (Tyler 2006b).

This chapter briefly traces the history and evolution of legal cases and legislation involving religious faith healing in lieu of traditional medical treatment. It also reports on a study which measures community sentiment for faith healing and the legal actions that surround it.

Faith Healing

Loue (2012) provides a long list of religious groups that practice various forms of faith healing, including, "Christian Science Church, the Church of the First Born, End Time Ministries, Faith Tabernacle, Followers of Christ Church, Bible Believers' Fellowship, Christ Assembly, Christ Miracle Healing Center, Church of God Chapel, Church of God of the Union Assembly, Holiness Church, Jesus Through Jon and Judy, "No Name" Fellowship, Northeast Kingdom Community Church, and The Source" (399). These groups are predominately Christian groups who rely on passages from the Bible which describe how Jesus healed the ill and cured ailments ranging from mental illness to leprosy—and even raised people from the dead (see Darby Howell 2012 for review). Further, some Biblical passages suggest that Jesus' followers were able to heal ailments as well. Believers practice various rituals or procedures as a sign of their belief and faith in Jesus. While such groups claim that faith healing is successful (and deaths are infrequent), these claims have not been well researched.

"Faith healing" is a concept that encompasses a wide variety of practices and procedures, which include praying, anointing the injured or sick person with oils, performing an exorcism, meditating, and speaking in tongues (Loue 2012; Williams 2012). Not all of the groups listed above practice all of these procedures, and not all of them rely exclusively on faith healing or reject traditional medical practices completely. Further, these groups use different terms for the procedures (e.g., faith healing, spiritual healing). For the purposes of this chapter, the term "faith healing" will be used to refer to any religious-based procedure that is used in lieu of more traditional medical procedures.

Although statistics are difficult to come by, it has been estimated that between the years of 1975 and 1995, 172 children died because their parents chose faith healing rather than traditional medical care (Asser 1998). Of these children, 140 would likely have survived if they would have been treated, as most died of common and treatable ailments such as diabetes, appendicitis, or bowel obstructions. Some scholars suggest that this number of deaths may be much higher (Williams 2012). When such cases come to light, they often receive a great deal of publicity and occasionally prompt legal action.

Legal History in the United States

Typically, parents can be charged with child abuse or neglect for failing to provide medical care for their children, however there are exceptions. The Christian Science Church prompted a nationwide movement for faith healing exemptions in 1967 after a member of the church was convicted of manslaughter for failing to seek medical treatment for her five-year-old, who died of pneumonia (Williams 2012). The Christian Science Church lobbied legislatures for exemptions, beginning with Massachusetts's child neglect laws which stated that a child would *not* be considered neglected if the only evidence of neglect is that medical care was being withheld in favor of religious treatments (Ciullo 2007).

Supporters of these exemptions won a major victory in 1974, when the Child Abuse Prevention and Treatment Act (CAPTA) was passed. CAPTA was a federal legislation with the goal of providing funding for states to develop and carry out child abuse and prevention education programs. As a result of a lobby by the Christian Science Church, CAPTA contained a regulation that states must provide a religious exemption to their child abuse and neglect statutes in order to receive funding. Not wanting to forfeit federal funds, nearly every state adopted an exemption which limited parents' liability for harm to their child resulting from their failure to seek medical care in favor of faith healing. Prior to this time, laws specified that it was child abuse or neglect to withhold medical treatment, and courts had generally refused to allow a "faith healing defense." Thus, the exemptions required to get CAPTA funding represented a departure from legal tradition (Williams 2012).

The exemption regulation found in the federal CAPTA was reversed in 1983, when federal regulations defined failure to provide medical care as child abuse; this was in part due to several high profile cases of Christian Science children who died because their parents chose faith healing over traditional medicine (see Richardson and Dewitt 1992). This federal change allowed states to eliminate exemptions; however, most states still have exemptions (Hamilton 2005; Williams 2012). While some exemptions seem to provide blanket protection for parents, other exemptions only allow parents to refuse medical care for their children if the child is not at risk of death or permanent disability. Some exemptions protect parents against charges of manslaughter or murder, while other exemptions only protect parents from charges of child abuse or neglect (Darby Howell 2012; Hamilton 2005; Williams 2012). To provide an example, Ohio's statute (Ohio Rev. Code Ann. § 2919.22(A)) reads:

> No person, who is the parent ... of a child ... shall create a substantial risk to the health or safety of the child, by violating a duty of care, protection, or support. It is not a violation of a duty of care, protection, or support under this division when the parent ... treats the physical or mental illness or defect of the child by spiritual means through prayer alone, in accordance with the tenets of a recognized religious body.

Some states specify that, if a child dies, the parents can use their religion as an affirmative defense to claim that they should not be held accountable for the harm they caused their child by refusing them medical care. The Arkansas capital murder statute (Ark. Code Ann. § 5-10-10(a)(9) (2006)) provides the following language:

> It is an affirmative defense to any prosecution ... arising from the failure of the parent ... to provide specified medical or surgical treatment, that the parent ... relied solely on spiritual treatment through prayer in accordance with the tenets and practices of an established church or religious denomination of which he or she is a member.

Some less lenient exemptions allow a state to intervene and force the parents to get medical services for the child (Loue 2012). Alabama's statue (Ala. Code § 26-14-7.2(a) (2011)) reads:

> When an investigation of child abuse or neglect by the Department of Human Resources determines that a parent or legal guardian legitimately practicing his or her religious beliefs has not provided specific medical treatment for a child, the parent or legal guardian shall not be considered a negligent parent or guardian for that reason alone. This exception shall not preclude a court from ordering that medical services be provided to the child when the child's health requires it.

While most states have some sort of exemption and/or affirmative defense available to protect parents, other states are moving toward the removal (or reduction) of these protections for parents. Oregon is the most recent state to remove an exemption. In 2011, Oregon legislature passed a law, Or. Rev. Stat. §163.115(4), which removed the faith healing exemption for harm caused to children. It now forbids parents from using a faith healing defense in homicide cases resulting from the death of a child because the parents chose faith healing over medical treatment. The law still contains an exemption for parents of people over 18 years old who die because of lack of medical treatment.

As this brief review of U.S. law illustrates, states have taken a variety of approaches to protecting (or not protecting) parents who use faith healing rather than traditional medical treatment. There is no federal standard, resulting in a variety of laws (see Darby Howell 2012 for a complete review of statutes in each state).

Legal Situation Outside the United States

The issue has received less attention outside the U.S. Under the U.N. Convention on the Rights of the Child, the medical decisions for children are left up to the parents unless the child is deemed capable of making the decision. The document does not clearly address whether a parent's refusal of treatment for a child can be overruled. In contrast, the fiftieth World Medical Assembly adopted the Declaration of Ottawa on the Right of the Child for Health Care in 1998. The declaration states that a parent can refuse treatment for their child, but a physician should obtain judicial or legal assistance to perform a treatment that, without which, would put the child in grave danger or risk of death.[1]

Most European nations are silent on the issue; while most give parents the right to consent or refuse medical treatment for their children, many countries' laws do not address whether this right is absolute or whether doctors and legal professionals can intervene (see Boele-Woelki, Braat, and Sumner 2005 for a review). A few notable exceptions include Germany, Bulgaria, and the Czech Republic. In Germany, the parent has the right to consent or refuse medical treatment for the child, but the family court can intervene and substitute their own consent for the parents' consent if the child is perceived to be in danger. Similarly, the Bulgarian Law on Health, adopted in 2005, allows the parent

---

[1]   The declaration can be found at http://www1.umn.edu/humanrts/instree/ottawa.html.

to refuse treatment for their child, except when it is life-threatening. Giving the child treatment against the parents' wishes is not possible unless the law stipulates (Article 91). Although the Articles provide for the possibility of terminating the parental rights of the parent who refuses life-saving treatment for their children, there is no case law on the matter. In a slightly different approach, the Czech Act No. 20/1966 Coll. On Care of People's Health, as amended, allows a doctor to decide about medical care if the parent refuses medical care for a child. None of these legal documents, however, mention exemptions for religious beliefs. Thus, the legal landscape in the U.S. is unique on this issue.

Influencing Sentiment

As with many controversial issues, there are many individuals and groups trying to influence the sentiment and actions of others. For instance, the Christian Science Church lobbied for the exemptions in the original federal CAPTA legislation. They frequently still lobby legislators, make their presence known at public hearings, and express their sentiments through correspondence with legislators (Williams 2012). Christian Science Church—and other religious groups that practice faith healing—are vocal advocates of exemptions and actively fight the removal of statutory exemptions. In contrast, groups such as the American Academy of Pediatrics (AAP), American Medical Association, and National Committee for the Prevention of Child Abuse have openly opposed faith healing exemptions (Williams 2012). Such groups publically advocate for the removal of statutory exemptions.

Even legislatures, in adopting statutes, try to change sentiment and behavior. The stated goals of removing the exemption from the Oregon law include influencing churches that practice faith healing to seek medical treatment for their children (Williams 2012).

Such individuals or groups attempt to influence sentiment of certain people (e.g., legislators, church members) or the community in general. Community sentiment is important because it can influence both legislative and judicial decisions (McGuire and Stimson 2004; Zgoba 2004). Indeed, legislators are often called "representatives," reflecting the notion that they should represent the wishes of their constituents. Often, if legislators do not represent the wishes of their constituents, they will not be in office long (Finkel 1995). Community sentiment is an important part of upholding the democratic principles of the U.S., and thus, legal actors often heed the wishes of the general population.

From a social science perspective, studying community sentiment is important because legal actions that agree with community sentiment help instill a belief in the legitimacy of the government (Tyler 2006b). Legitimacy is a "psychological property of an authority, institution, or social arrangement that leads those connected to it to believe that it is appropriate, proper and just" (Tyler 2006b). When individuals have a sense that the authority is legitimate, they are more likely to comply with the legal system in general (Tyler 2006b). As such, it is important to understand the community's sentiment about legal issues.

Measuring Community Sentiment

Community sentiment is often quite complex, especially concerning issues requiring the balancing of interests and rights of multiple parties, as does the issue of parental refusal of medical care for children due to religious beliefs. Asking one simple question (e.g., "On a scale of 1 to 10, do you think parents should be legally required to seek medical care for their children?") is not going to provide a very robust representation of community sentiment. Participants might have difficulty answering this question because they may feel they support legal requirements in some situations, but not in others, and thus, it is difficult to circle a number on a scale. Overly general questions fail to capture the complexity of a participant's sentiment (Miller and Thomas, forthcoming). Asking participants multiple questions can better measure sentiment.

In addition, overly general questions might provide an incomplete and possibly inaccurate measure of sentiment. Participants might only base their answer on the first image that comes to mind. Exemplars tend to be extreme and rare examples rather than more mundane and common examples (Finkel 1995; Miller and Thomas, forthcoming). In the current study, participants might think of a news article in which they read about an infant death that could have been prevented had the parents sought medical care instead of faith healing for a life threatening but easily curable ailment. This extreme example is likely to evoke more different responses than the more typical situation in which a parent refuses medical care for an older child's non-life threatening ailment, but the child survives (a situation which is unlikely to make it into the news). Thus, to control what images come to mind, it is helpful to ask participants to respond to a specific scenario.

Care should be taken to decide what scenarios are presented and what questions are asked. At times, two different studies ask starkly different questions or provide very different scenarios to respond to, resulting in the two studies finding seemingly different results (Finkel 1995). In the current study, it is possible that participants would give significantly different responses to the question about refusal of medical treatment if the child was suffering from a curable ailment than if he was suffering from an incurable ailment. Participants might believe it is futile to force a parent to seek medical treatment for a child with an incurable ailment. Further, asking participants whether they support criminal sanctions might garner different results than asking participants if they support legally requiring parents to seek medical care for their children. Participants might be more supportive of ensuring the child got care than they are with punishing parents criminally. Thus, asking multiple questions about multiple scenarios is essential to gather a more complete representation of community sentiment.

At times, community sentiment is best gauged using multiple measures. One method is to use a repeated measures design (Miller and Thomas, forthcoming). Asking the same participants multiple questions can provide a clearer representation of sentiment about this complex issue. In the current study, participants are asked their sentiment about many different scenarios.

First, scenarios used in this study vary the characteristic of the child's ailment. Community sentiment might vary based on the characteristics of the ailment (e.g., is it curable? Is it life-threatening?) and the medical treatment available (e.g., is it risky?). The law sometimes recognizes these caveats as being relevant. For instance, some laws only allow parents to refuse medical treatment in non-life threatening situations while others have no such limitation. The community might be more supportive of parental freedom when the child's ailment is less serious or non-life threatening. Judges deciding whether to force medical treatment for a child against the parents' wishes also balance issues such as the severity of the ailment, risk of the procedure, success of the parents' proposed treatment, and the overall welfare of the child (*In re Custody of a Minor* 1978, *In re Sampson* 1970). Thus, participants might be more supportive of legal actions (1) when the procedure is risky rather than not risky, (2) when the ailment is curable rather than not-curable, and (3) when the ailment is life threatening rather than non-life threatening.

Second, multiple questions are asked about each scenario. Specifically, participants are asked whether parents should be legally required to seek medical treatment for the child, whether the parent should lose custody of the child, and whether the parent should be charged with child abuse. These various questions further probe sentiment about each scenario. Participants might be supportive of some legal actions (e.g., forcing parents to seek treatment), but less supportive of other legal actions (e.g., prosecuting the parent for child abuse). As noted in the review of legislation above, laws vary as to whether they force the parent to seek treatment, whether it is considered abuse, and thus could lead to criminal sanctions or loss of custody of the child.

Third, questions ask participants their sentiment about allowing parents to use their religion as a defense or to get a lighter sentence. Some states allow parents to use their religions as an affirmative defense, while others, such as the new Oregon law, strictly forbid using ones religion as a defense.

Finally, questions are asked that will allow for comparison of sentiment toward exemptions for child abuse and exemptions for murder. States differ in the amount of protection afforded parents. For instance, Arkansas allows absolute immunity—even from murder—while Alabama's statute only protects parents in child abuse and neglect cases. Just as states apparently support different levels of immunity and exemptions, the community might support one type of immunity or exemption over another, for instance, believing that parents should not be held legally responsible for child neglect; however, if the child dies, the parents should be held legally responsible.

In sum, community sentiment can be quite complex. Asking participants multiple questions about multiple scenarios allows for a deeper understanding of community sentiment. This is the goal of the current study.

Overview of Study

In a within-subjects design, participants were given a variety of scenarios which measure their agreement that parents should be charged with criminal child abuse, be legally required to get medical care for the child, and lose custody of the child. Scenarios varied the type of illness (curable, incurable; life threatening or not life threatening), and the level of risk involved in the medical treatment. Four research questions were posed:

Research Question One: How supportive are participants of legal actions (i.e., requiring parents to get medical treatment for the child, removing the child from the parents' custody, and charging parents with criminal child abuse)?

Research Question Two: Does support for these legal actions vary depending on the characteristics of the medical situation (e.g., risk of procedure, life-threatening nature of the illness)?

Research Question Three: Do participants equally support actions that treat a parent's failure to seek medical care as *child abuse* and actions that treat such failure as a *homicide*?

Research Question Four: Do participants support allowing parents to use their religion as a defense or allowing parents to get a lighter sentence because of their religious beliefs?

Methods

Participants were 601 University of Nevada, Reno students.[2] Participants completed an online survey for partial course credit. Participants were presented with an introduction that stated,

> Some religions do not believe in traditional medical treatments. For instance, the Jehovah's Witnesses believe that blood is sacred and a person should not receive a blood transfusion, even in order to save one's life. A person who receives a transfusion could be shunned by other followers and will face eternal damnation after death. They often claim they have the right to do so because of their First Amendment right to freedom of religion.

Then, participants all read six scenarios concerning religious reasons for parents to refuse medical treatment for their children. The six scenarios included: (1) The "Prayer" scenario, which read, "Some groups who do not believe in traditional medical treatments instead use faith healing and prayer when they are ill. Sometimes parents decide not to get medical care for their children for religious reasons," (2) The "Incurable/Not Life Threatening" scenario, which read, "If the child has an incurable illness that is NOT life threatening, such as Crohn's disease (chronic inflammation of the intestinal tract)," (3) The "Treatable/ Life Threatening" scenario, which read, "If the child has a life threatening but treatable illness, such as cancer, (4) The "Incurable/LifeThreatening" scenario, which read, "If the child has an incurable illness that will eventually kill the child, such as Tay-Sachs (deterioration of mental and physical abilities which

---

[2]   They were majors in criminal justice (31%), psychology/sociology (14%), and other majors (36%). They ranged in age from 17–51 ($M = 20.85$). They were 61% female, and they were 65% White, 10% African American, and 13% Hispanic. They were 29% Catholic, 13% Protestant, and 24% believe in God but do not have a particular religion. They were 30% democrats, 25% republicans, 13% independents, and 27% had no political affiliation.

causes death, usually by the age of four)," (5) The "Transfusion" scenario, which read, "If the treatment for the illness is a blood transfusion," (6) The "Risky Treatment" scenario, which read, "If the treatment for the illness is a complicated or risky surgery." The "Prayer" scenario intentionally did not give any description of the illness or treatment so that this scenario can act as a baseline for the other five scenarios.

For each of the six scenarios, participants were asked three questions: (1) Should the parents be legally required to get treatment for the child? (2) Should the parents lose custody of their child? (3) Should the parent be prosecuted for criminal child abuse? Each question was answered on a Likert scale from 1 (no, strongly disagree) to 5 (yes, strongly agree).

Then, participants were asked to imagine that the parents refuse medical treatment for their child and the child dies. They were asked three questions: (1) Should the parents be charged criminally for the death (e.g., charged with homicide)? (2) If the parents are charged with homicide, should the parents be allowed to use their religious beliefs as a defense at trial? (3) Should the parents get a lesser sentence because of their religious beliefs? Each question was answered on a Likert scale from 1 (no, strongly disagree) to 5 (yes, strongly agree). Finally, participants completed a demographics questionnaire.

Results of Research

Analyses were conducted to answer each research question.

Research Question One: How Supportive are Participants of Legal Actions?

The first analyses were descriptive in nature, designed to measure support for legal actions such as requiring parents to get medical treatment for the child, removing the child from the parents' custody, charging parents with criminal child abuse, and charging parents with homicide if the child dies.

Results indicate that participants are generally supportive of all of these measures. See Table 12.1 for means, medians, and standard deviations for every variable. The item receiving the greatest support[3] was legally requiring treatment when the child has a treatable disorder and the ailment is life-threatening. The least support[4] was for removing the child from the parents' custody when the

---

[3] $(M = 4.09)$.

[4] $(M = 2.53)$.

procedure was risky. Importantly, means for every question for every scenario was over the mid-point (2.5 out of 5), indicating a moderate or high level of support for all of the legal actions for each of the scenarios. Participants were also quite supportive of charging parents with homicide if their child dies because they opted to use faith healing rather than medical care.[5]

Table 12.1: Descriptive statistics for all dependent variables

	n	Mean	Median	Std. Dev.
Faith healing				
Legally required treatment	598	3.64	4.00	1.03
Lose custody	598	2.85	3.00	1.06
Prosecuted for child abuse	599	3.10	3.00	1.09
Incurable, Non- Life threatening				
Legally required treatment	599	3.42	4.00	1.04
Lose custody	597	2.58	2.00	.990
Prosecuted for child abuse	593	2.74	3.00	1.07
Treatable/ Life Threatening				
Legally required treatment	601	4.09	4.00	.98
Lose custody	599	3.21	3.00	1.17
Prosecuted for child abuse	598	3.34	3.00	1.19
Incurable/Life Threatening				
Legally required treatment	601	3.54	4.00	1.31
Lose custody	599	2.78	3.00	1.17
Prosecuted for child abuse	595	2.87	3.00	1.20
Transfusion				
Legally required treatment	599	3.84	4.00	.99
Lose custody	598	2.98	3.00	1.09
Prosecuted for child abuse	596	3.07	3.00	1.11
Risky				
Legally required treatment	596	3.06	3.00	.99
Lose custody	595	2.53	2.00	.96
Prosecuted for child abuse	592	2.55	2.00	.98
Charged with homicide if child dies	597	3.40	3.00	1.13
Religious beliefs as defense	594	2.94	3.00	1.16
Lighter sentence	590	2.55	3.00	1.09

Note: n's differ for each variable because of missing data

---

[5]   ($M = 3.40$).

Research Question Two: Does Support for These Legal Actions Vary Depending on the Medical Situation?

Three within-subjects repeated measures analyses were performed, one for each dependent variable.

Legally Required Treatment
The first analysis tested whether participants' responses to the dependent variable "Should the parents be legally required to get treatment for the child?" differed depending on the scenario they had just read. A test of within-subjects effects reveals that the differences were significant.[6] The Incurable/Life Threatening scenario did not differ from the Prayer scenario and only marginally differed from No Threat scenario.[7] The means indicated that participants gave the lowest level of agreement in the Risky Treatment condition, followed by the Incurable/ Not Life Threatening, Incurable/Life Threatening, Prayer, Transfusion, and Treatable/Life Threatening conditions, in that order. Notably, only the Transfusion and Treatable/Life Threatening garnered more support than the Prayer scenario, which serves as the baseline scenario because it provides no details of the ailment or treatment. This indicates that risky treatments or incurable ailments reduce the amount of support for requiring parents to seek treatment. On the other hand, a relatively simple procedure like a blood transfusion or a treatable life threatening ailment increases support for requiring parents to seek medical treatment, compared to the baseline.

Custody of Child
The second within-subjects analysis tested whether participants' responses to the question "Should the parents lose custody of their child?" depended on the details of the scenario. A test of within-subjects effects revealed that the differences were significant.[8] The Incurable/Life Threatening scenario did not differ from the Prayer scenario.[9] Otherwise, every scenario differed significantly from every other scenario.[10] The exact same patterns of means emerged as with the "Legally Required Treatment" dependent variable just discussed. That is, the lowest level of agreement was in the Risky Treatment condition, followed

---

[6]   (F $(5, 2652)$ = 152.61, $p < .001$), using Huynh-Feldt correction for sphericity.
[7]   Planned contrasts using the Bonferroni method ($p = .078$).
[8]   (F $(5, 2770)$ = 75.27, $p < .001$), using Huynh-Feldt correction for sphericity.
[9]   Planned contrasts using the Bonferroni method.
[10] ($ps < .05$).

by the Incurable/Not Life Threatening, Incurable/Life Threatening, Prayer, Transfusion and Treatable/Life Threatening conditions.

Child Abuse

The third within-subjects measures analysis tested whether participants' responses to the question "Should the parent be prosecuted for criminal child abuse?" depended on the details of the scenario. The test of within-subjects effects revealed that the differences were significant.[11] The Transfusion condition did not differ from the Prayer scenario, and Incurable/Not Life Threatening scenario did not differ from the Incurable/Life Threatening scenario.[12] Otherwise, every scenario differed significantly from every other scenario.[13] A similar pattern emerged from the other two dependent variables (the "Legally Required Treatment" question and the "Custody of Child" question); the pattern of means was identical, except that the Prayer and Transfusion scenarios traded places on the list. However, the Prayer scenario mean was not significantly higher than Transfusion scenario mean, indicating that they are statistically the same.

In sum, all three dependent variables had the same general pattern of means. Participants were less supportive of legal actions when the treatment was a risky surgery or treatment than when it was a less risky blood transfusion. They were less supportive of legal actions when the condition was incurable than when it was treatable. They were less supportive when it was not life threatening than when it was life threatening.

Research Question Three: Do Participants Equally Support Actions that Treat a Parent's Failure to Seek Medical Care as Child Abuse and Actions that Treat Such Failure as a Homicide?

A repeated measures analysis was conducted with the responses to the question "Should the parent be prosecuted for criminal child abuse?" for each of the six scenarios, and the question "If the child dies ... should the parents be charged criminally for the death (e.g., charged with homicide)?" A test of within-subjects effects reveals that the differences were significant.[14] The Homicide support scenario differed from every one of the six scenarios except the Treatable/ Life Threatening scenario.[15] This indicates that, although participants are at least

---

[11] $(F\,(5, 2701) = 85.48, p < .001)$, using Huynh-Feldt correction for sphericity.

[12] Planned contrasts using the Bonferroni method.

[13] $(ps < .05)$.

[14] $(F\,(6, 3227) = 96.37, p < .001)$, using Huynh-Feldt correction for sphericity.

[15] Planned contrasts using the Bonferroni method.

moderately supportive of treating a parent's refusal to seek medical treatment for the child as child abuse, they are significantly more supportive of treating it as a crime, e.g., homicide, when the child dies. See Table 12.1 for means for each question.

Research Question Four: Do Participants Support Allowing Parents to Use Their Religion as a Defense or Allowing Parents to Get a Lighter Sentence because of Their Religious Beliefs?

Participants were only moderately supportive of allowing parents to use their religious beliefs as a defense if they are charged with homicide for failing to give their child medical care ($M = 2.94$ on a scale from 1 to 5). Nevertheless, participants were on average neutral on whether parents should get a lesser sentence because they acted because of religious beliefs ($M = 2.55$).

Discussion and Implications of Research

The issue of parental refusal to seek medical treatment for a child because of religious beliefs has many legal and policy and health consequences that are beyond the scope of this chapter (for broader reviews, see Darby Howell 2012; Loue 2012; Williams 2012). This issue also has implications for community sentiment, which is the focus of this chapter. Results of this study generally show that community sentiment varies depending on the scenario (i.e., the medical situation), and a "one size fits all" law is unlikely to find the support of the community. Laws and court rulings that recognize factors such as the risk of the treatment and the severity of the illness are more likely to find favor in the community. This has implications for policy development and adoption within legislatures and the judiciary. Specifically, if legislators and judges listen to community sentiment, they will craft laws or rulings that recognize the characteristics of each particular case.

Another implication arises from the finding that participants are more supportive of legal actions that recognize a parent's failure to seek medical care for the child as homicide than as child abuse. Some state laws reflect this sentiment and provide parents an exemption, but only for abuse and not for homicide. Such laws have been criticized because of the "catch-22" they create. Specifically, parents are protected as long as the child does not die—once the child dies, they are not protected. Thus, the parent might withhold medical treatment up to the point the child is near death. At that point, it may be too late for medical professionals to do anything, or serious harm may have already occurred even if the child lives. Legislators should carefully consider this dilemma and the public health consequences that such statutes create.

A third implication stems from the finding that participants are moderately supportive of allowing parents to use a religious defense and get a lighter sentence because of their religious beliefs. Thus, participants likely recognize that religious beliefs are important and protected legally, and they believe that parents deserve to voice their concerns. Perhaps participants are concerned that parents will have procedural justice (Tyler 2006a). When people feel like they have had a voice, they are more pleased with the process and more likely to follow the laws in the future. Thus, legislators should consider allowing such affirmative defenses—or at least allowing the religious beliefs as mitigating factors in sentencing.

Finally, this study—like Richardson and Dewitt (1992)—revealed more support for protecting children than prosecuting parents. On each of the six scenarios, the mean for the item measuring support for requiring parents to seek medical treatment was higher than the means for removing the child from the parent's custody and prosecuting the parents for child abuse. These results imply that lawmakers should focus on protecting children over punishing parents.

Lawmakers have difficult decisions to make concerning this issue. They must weigh parents' religious rights with public health concerns, concerns for the child's wellbeing, and the state's interest in protecting its citizens. Community sentiment is also an important consideration, as the community might develop negative perceptions of the government's legitimacy if legal actions are not in agreement with their sentiment. Ultimately, when people feel a government is not a legitimate authority, they may be less likely to obey laws (Tyler 2006b). Thus, community sentiment is an important consideration for legal actors.

Limitations and Future Research Directions

This study has several notable limitations. First, this study used a sample of University of Nevada, Reno students. Because community sentiment could vary based on age, state of residence, socio-economic status, or education level, the study's external validity is a weakness of the study. Simply put, this study might not reflect the general population's sentiment. Second, the study's methodology presents some limitations. All participants read the scenarios and answered the questions in the same order. When this occurs, earlier responses might affect later responses because participants have been primed by reading about earlier scenarios. For example, reading the scenario about a life-threatening ailment first might affect later responses to the non-life threatening scenario. Thus, responses to each question might not be independent.

To address these limitations, future research should measure community sentiment using a nationwide sample of participants from a variety of backgrounds. Additionally, future studies should use other methodologies, such as an experiment in which participants only read one scenario and thus could not be affected by reading other scenarios. Alternately, a within-groups study could be conducted with counterbalancing, meaning that participants would read the questions in a random order—rather than every participant reading the scenarios in the same order. Even though these limitations exist, the study has important policy implications for legal actors who are addressing the issue of parental refusal to seek medical treatment for their children for religious reasons.

Conclusions

Parents have a duty to protect the health of their children, and both civil and criminal child abuse and neglect laws address parents' failure to do so. Many religious groups reject traditional medical treatment in favor of a variety of faith healing procedures or rituals. Lawmakers have adopted a variety of laws permitting or rejecting exemptions to laws ranging from child abuse and neglect to homicide.

Study results indicate that participants are overall supportive of legal actions addressing parents' refusal to seek medical care for their children. In addition, participants are differentially supportive of legal actions based on the characteristics of the medical situation. For instance, they are more supportive of legally requiring parents to provide medical treatment when the treatment is a routine blood transfusion rather than a risky treatment; they are also more supportive when the condition is life-threatening rather than when it is not. These results indicate that participants are supportive of judges who take such cases on a case-by-case basis and consider case-specific factors, and that a "one size fits all" statute might not be met with uniform community support.

Understanding community sentiment regarding this issue is important if legal actors wish to adopt laws that are met with public approval. Doing so will increase perceived legitimacy of the government and, in turn, increase compliance with laws in general (Tyler 2006b). Future studies should further investigate the community's sentiment about this issue. This—coupled with input from experts in health, psychology, and law—will help develop legal responses with the most positive outcomes.

References

Asser, S.M. and R. Swan. 1988. "Child Fatalities from Religion-Motivated Medical Neglect." *Pediatrics* 101(4):625-629. http:// childrenshealthcare. org/wp-content/uploads/2010/07/Pediatricsarticle.pdf.t. Accessed: Jan 25, 2013.

Boele-Woelki, K., B., Braat, and I. Sumner. 2005. *European Family Law in Action: Parental Responsibilities*. Oxford: Intersentia.

Ciullo, A. 2007. "Prosecution without Persecution: The Inability of Courts to Recognize Christian Science Spiritual Healing and a Shift Towards Legislative Action." *New England Law Review* 42(1): 155–88.

Darby Howell, S. 2012. "Religious Treatment Exemption Statutes: Betrayest Thou Me with a Statute?" *Scholar: St. Mary's Law Review on Minority Issues* 14: 945–85.

Finkel, N. J. 1995. *Commonsense Justice: Jurors' Notions of the Law*. Cambridge, MA: Harvard University Press.

Hamilton, M.A. 2005. *God vs. The Gavel: Religion and the Rule of Law*. New York: Cambridge University Press.

In re Custody of a Minor, 375 Mass. 733 (Mass 1978).

In re Sampson, 317 N.Y.S.2d 641, 643 (NY Fain. C. 1970).

Loue, S. 2012. "Parentally Mandated Religious Healing for Children: A Therapeutic Justice Approach." *Journal of Law and Religion* 27: 397–420.

McGuire, K.T. and J.A. Stimson. 2004. "The Least Dangerous Branch Revisited: New Evidence on Supreme Court Responsiveness to Public Preferences." *The Journal of Politics* 66(4): 1018–35.

Miller, M.K., and A. Thomas. (forthcoming). "Understanding Changes in Community Sentiment about Drug Use During Pregnancy Using a Repeated Measures Design." In *Handbook of Community Sentiment,* edited by M. Miller, J. Blumenthal, and J. Chamberlain. New York: Springer.

Richardson, J.T., and J. Dewitt. 1992. "Christian Science Spiritual Healing, the Law, and Public Opinion." *Journal of Church and State* 34(3): 549–62.

Tyler, T.R. 2006a. "Restorative Justice and Procedural Justice: Dealing with Rule Breaking." *Journal of Social Issues* 62(2): 307–26.

Tyler, T.R. 2006b. "Psychological Perspectives on Legitimacy and Legitimation." *Annual Review of Psychology* 57: 375–400.

Williams, R. 2012. "Faith Healing Exceptions Versus Parens Patriae: Something's Gotta Give." *First Amendment Law Review* 10: 692–729.

Zgoba, K. 2004. "The Amber Alert: The Appropriate Solution to Prevent Child Abduction?" *Journal of Psychiatry and Law* 32: 71–88.

Chapter 13

Muslims and the Courtroom:
Legal Issues and Empirical Research

Evelyn M. Maeder and Jeffrey E. Pfeifer

Introduction

On April 22, 2013, a doctoral student at the Université de Sherbrooke named Chiheb Esseghaier was arrested on allegations of engaging in terrorist plotting (O'Toole et al. 2013). Despite the seriousness of the allegations made against him, the devout Muslim was unable to procure legal representation. Although he had successfully applied for legal aid, no lawyer had agreed to represent him due to his unusual request: Esseghaier insisted on counsel who would assist him in "chang[ing] the reference of his judgment" to the Qur'an, rather than the Criminal Code of Canada (Gillis 2013). Specifically, Esseghaier argued that he would not accept representation by any lawyer who would not agree that he had the right to be tried by 'the holy book', rather than a 'book written by humans'. At the time of the writing of this chapter, he is still searching for a lawyer who will take his case, yet most legal scholars agree that his request is an impossible one.

Among other things, the Esseghaier case highlights a number of important issues relating to the degree to which Islam may play a role in the courtroom. As such, this chapter seeks to provide an overview of these issues through (1) a discussion of the increasing number of trial-specific areas where evidence and/or information relating to the Muslim faith has been identified, (2) a review of the sparse empirical literature examining the confluence of law and the social sciences with regard to the role that religious orientation may play in trials with a Muslim connection, and (3) a discussion of the apparent disconnect between many of the legal issues and social scientific research as well as a review of potential future areas that require empirical analysis.

Islam in the Courtroom: Legal Issues

As stated above, it is clear that the past 15 years have brought with them a significant increase in the number of trials in both Canada and the United States involving issues related to Islam and the Muslim faith (Kruger et al. 2004; Zaman 2008).[1] Although a review of these trials indicates a wide range of legal questions, a number of specific trends have begun to emerge with regard to the role of Islam in issues such as jury selection, the wearing of religious attire during a trial, the defense of provocation, and child custody matters. Each of these issues is discussed in detail below.

Jury Selection

Unlike a challenge for cause, in which jurors are excused because of obvious bias, peremptory challenges are employed by lawyers to dismiss jurors for virtually any reason (Pfeifer 1996). In the United States, the ability to use peremptory challenges to exclude jurors on the basis of religion depends on the state in which the trial takes place, due to the fact that the United States Supreme Court has declined to provide a ruling on the issue. For example, in *State v. Hodge* (1999), a lawyer used a peremptory challenge to strike a Muslim from sitting on the jury panel, leading to an appeal on the basis that the challenge was unconstitutional according to the Equal Protection Clause of the Fourteenth Amendment. Despite the fact that the Supreme Court of Connecticut ruled that the striking of a potential juror solely on the basis of his or her religion was unconstitutional, the striking of the juror in this particular case was not considered to be unconstitutional due to the fact that the prosecution had other reasons for striking him (i.e., he had a criminal record). However, other courts have allowed for jurors to be struck solely on the basis of religion (e.g., *Minnesota v. Davis* 1993). Thus, it appears that some jurisdictions in the United States would allow for Muslim jurors to be removed on the basis of religious orientation via the use of peremptory challenges while others will not.

In order to make effective use of peremptory challenges, lawyers seek to glean information from potential jurors relating to their beliefs, experiences, and values. However, the courts may place limitations as to what types of questions may be asked; one such limitation may be the questioning of jurors as to their

---

[1]   Although legal issues involving Islam are worldwide (e.g., Dwyer and Meyer 1995; Thomas 2006), this chapter will focus predominantly on Canada and the United States, due largely to the fact that the majority of the empirical literature emanates from these countries.

religious beliefs. At least one court has considered this question. In the trial of Zacaraias Moussaoui (*Unites States v. Moussaoui* 2006), one of the men charged following 9/11, lawyers sought to ask jurors about their religious beliefs and attitudes toward Islam during *voir dire* (i.e., jury selection). The court ruled that the questions could be asked, and among other things, it may be argued that the tone and direction of the questions reflected a number of ingrained beliefs about Muslims and their faith that lawyers thought might lead to impartiality in the trial and subsequent verdict. Among the questions allowed by the court were the following: "Do you believe that Islam endorses violence to a greater or lesser extent than other religions?" "How knowledgeable are you about the history/ practices of Islam?" and "Do you have any negative feelings or opinions about Muslims?" A number of questions were also included that related to the potential jurors' degree of contact with Muslims. In addition to these questions being included in the jury questionnaire that each potential juror completed prior to *voir dire*, jurors were questioned further about religious beliefs during selection. It appears, therefore, that the courts will sometimes allow extensive questioning about jurors' religious beliefs, attitudes, and affiliations during jury selection.

Religious Attire in the Courtroom

Courts have long faced the question of whether to allow religious garb in the courtroom, with mixed results. For example, in *La Rocca v. Lane* (1975), a Roman Catholic priest was required to remove his clerical collar before appearing as a defense attorney in a criminal trial. Conversely, in *Close-It Enterprises, Inc. v. Weinberger* (1978), the Court of Appeals reversed a trial court's decision to prohibit a defendant from testifying while wearing a yarmulke, indicating that the defendant "should not have been required to choose between his legal interests and his religious beliefs." The question of whether to allow religious garb in the courtroom has implications for trials involving Muslims as well. For example, in *Spanks-El v. Finley* (1988), the plaintiff was a devout Muslim who indicated that he was required by his religion to wear a fez on his head at all times. As a result, he refused to remove the fez during a security search, and was subsequently prevented from entering the courtroom and testifying during the trial. The plaintiff argued that his free exercise rights had been violated. Upon appeal, the district court was faced with balancing the plaintiff's freedom of religion and the state's interest in a secure courtroom. The court argued that the quick removal of his fez for a security check was a limited burden in serving the compelling state interest of courtroom security, and that therefore the plaintiff's free exercise rights had not been violated.

One area that has received more recent attention in the legal arena is the permissibility of wearing Muslim veils (e.g., a *burqa* or *hijab*) while testifying in a civil or criminal courtroom (Williams 2008). Courts in both Canada and the United States have faced this issue and subsequently provided rulings on whether a Muslim woman must remove her face-covering veil prior to testifying at trial. In Canada for example, a judge asked N.S., a Muslim woman, to remove her *niqab* prior to testifying in a sexual assault trial. The defense lawyer had requested that she remove her veil so that the Court could observe her facial expressions, but N.S. maintained that she wanted to wear the veil for religious purposes. The judge at the original trial ruled that in order to testify, she must remove her veil, and in the ruling indicated that N.S.'s religious beliefs were "not that strong" and were "open to exceptions," stating that "wearing the veil was a matter of comfort" rather than religious obligation. The judge based this assumption on the fact that N.S. had posed for her driver's license photo without the veil. Following this ruling, critics remarked that "the forced removal of her niqab as a pre-requisite to testifying in a sexual assault prosecution turns the metaphor of re-victimization at trial into a literal reality" (Women's Legal Education and Action Fund 2010: 4).

Not surprisingly, the ruling was appealed and the subsequent higher court decision held that both the witness's freedom of religion and the accused's right to a fair trial were at stake, and if they could not be reconciled, that the witness may be ordered to remove her veil depending on the context *R. v. N.S.* (2009). The case was returned to the preliminary court, and N.S. appealed to the Supreme Court of Canada *R. v. N.S.* (2012), which ruled:

> An extreme approach that would always require the witness to remove her niqab while testifying, or one that would never do so, is untenable. The answer lies in a just and proportionate balance between freedom of religion and trial fairness, based on the particular case before the court. A witness who for sincere religious reasons wishes to wear the niqab while testifying in a criminal proceeding will be required to remove it if (a) this is necessary to prevent a serious risk to the fairness of the trial, because reasonably available alternative measures will not prevent the risk; and (b) the salutary effects of requiring her to remove the niqab outweigh the deleterious effects of doing so.

Subsequent to this ruling, the Supreme Court returned the case to the preliminary inquiry judge, ordering him to make a decision on the basis of these considerations. The case is presently being heard, and so at the time of writing this, it is unknown whether N.S. was permitted to wear her veil during testimony.

In the United States, a Michigan small-claims court had to decide on a similar issue when Ginnah Muhummad wanted to testify while wearing her *niqab* in a case she had brought against a rental car company. The judge informed her that she must remove her veil or her case would be dismissed, because he would need to see her face in order to properly evaluate her testimony (Gorchow 2006). When she refused this request, the judge dismissed her case, prompting Muhammad to bring a case against the judge for violating her First Amendment right to freedom of religion. The case this was eventually dismissed *Muhammad v. Paruk* (2008).

Given the above, it is evident that different courts (at least within Canada and U.S.) will vary in their decisions to allow Muslim women to wear veils while testifying at trial. It is likely that this issue will receive more attention as more trials involving Muslim parties in Canada and the United States take place.

Provocation

Provocation is a partial defense that typically reduces a murder conviction to manslaughter (Berman and Farrell 2011). In order to mount a claim of provocation, the defendant must show that he or she acted in the heat of passion and that a reasonable person in the same situation would have acted similarly. On occasion, a defendant will argue that his or her passion was inflamed as a result of an action of the victim being contrary to the tenets of his or her cultural or religious beliefs. For example, in one such case in England, *R. v. Mohammed* (2005), a devout Muslim man discovered his daughter in her bedroom with her boyfriend and stabbed her to death, claiming that the act was an honor killing. Despite the fact that the trial judge allowed the provocation defense, the jury ultimately found the defendant guilty as charged.

A year later in Canada, the issue was once again before the courts in *R. v. Humaid* (2006). In this case, a Muslim man killed his Muslim wife after she made a comment which he interpreted as an admission of infidelity. During the trial, an expert testified that infidelity was a very serious violation of the tenets of the defendant's religion and could therefore be perceived as a provocation. The trial judge allowed the provocation defense and indicated that the reasonable person *need not be one of the same cultural or religious background as the defendant*. This instruction was upheld on appeal, indicating that while the courts may allow for consideration of religious values in determining the seriousness of the insult involved in provocation, the jury need not consider the "reasonable person" to share the defendant's religious beliefs.

Child Custody Agreements

Child custody disputes are not a recent addition to the legal arena, and the question of how to best factor religious upbringing into child custody agreements has been considered by courts for decades (e.g., *Kendall v. Kendall* 1997; *Munoz v. Munoz* 1971; *Pater v. Pater* 1992). However, some scholars argue that child custody agreements involving a Muslim parent can be particularly complicated. For example, Camp (2011) argues that child custody disputes in American families with a Muslim parent or parents are markedly different from those involving other religious and cultural backgrounds. Of particular note is the unique situation of Muslim families leaving Arab and Western nations—nations in which attitudes toward the United States can be very negative. That is, many native-born Muslims will have children with non-Muslim partners upon settling in the United States and, as such, the possibility of child kidnapping following a separation or divorce is much higher, as relatives may wish to intervene to ensure the proper Muslim education of the child in the event that the parent winning custody does not have strong Muslim beliefs. Camp (2011) suggests that in order to minimize this possibility, courts ought to recognize the importance of the child's Muslim heritage and to subsequently ensure that draft custody agreements incorporate Islamic education.

Based on the above, it is clear that issues related to Islam have become increasingly prevalent within the Canadian and American legal systems. The intersection of religion and the law has been controversial for many different faiths, and Islam is no exception. Given this situation, it is clear that research is needed in order to determine how Islam is perceived in the courtroom in order to determine whether trials are proceeding fairly. Unfortunately, there is very little research in this area—the next section will discuss the extant literature investigating perceptions of Muslims in the courtroom.

Empirical Research on Muslims in the Courtroom

According to Miller, Singer and Jehle (2008), religious orientation may play a significant role in a number of specific trial aspects including jury selection, presentation of evidence, and jury deliberations. These authors also suggest that a variety of religious information may impact the decisions of jurors, including the presence of religious objects, the religious beliefs of jurors, the religious orientation of defendants and/or victims, expert testimony, and jury instructions. Despite this array of possible influences, it appears that the majority of empirical attention paid to Islam and the Muslim faith as it relates to the courtroom focuses almost exclusively on the impact of the defendant or victim orientation on jury decision-making.

It may be argued that the above situation may be a logical extension of the large body of existing research examining the influence of extralegal characteristics on jurors' decisions. Extralegal characteristics refer to any factor outside of the facts in evidence, or legal instructions, that influence a juror's decision in a trial. A significant amount of psycho-legal research to date has demonstrated that factors such as race (e.g., Mitchell, et al. 2005; Sommers and Ellsworth 2009), gender (Duke and Desforges 2007; Quas et al. 2002; Thompson, Merrifield and Chinnery 2011), attractiveness (Abel and Watters 2005; Patry 2008), and age (e.g., Higgins, Heath and Grannemann 2007; Loeffler and Lawson 2002; Tang and Nunez 2003) can affect jurors' processing of trial information, perceptions of trial parties, and ultimately, verdict decisions. One extralegal characteristic that has more recently begun to receive attention is that of religion. Although researchers have examined the influence of defendant religion (Pfeifer 1999), juror religion (Eisenberg, Garvey and Wells 2001; Miller 2006; Skeem and Golding 2001), and the use of religion in trials (Johnson 1985; Miller and Bornstein 2006), very few studies have examined the influence of Islam specifically. The following will discuss the small body of research examining perceptions of Muslim trial parties.

Muslim Defendants and Jury Decision-Making

In terms of gaining a more comprehensive understanding of the perceptions that jurors may have of Muslim defendants, it is important to examine the social psychological factors that may underpin these beliefs. Several researchers have argued that perceptions toward Muslims have changed substantially following the attack on the World Trade Center in New York City on September 11, 2001, with attitudes toward Islam and those who practice the religion becoming increasingly negative (e.g., Bleich 2011; Cashin 2010; Oswald 2005). For example, Raiya, Pargament, Mahoney and Trevino (2008) found an association between threatening assumptions about Muslims (e.g., that they oppose the teachings of Christ) and negative attitudes. Therefore, there is reason to suspect that Muslim defendants may be treated differently in the courtroom as a function of this bias. For example, jurors with negative attitudes toward Muslims may assume that a Muslim defendant is dangerous and therefore likely also to be a criminal, and as such, guilty of all charges. Similarly, jurors who feel threatened by Muslims may also be likely to recommend harsher sentences when consulted, fearing that these defendants are more likely to recidivate.

In terms of legal history, it is apparent that these attitudes have manifested themselves in the courtroom, especially with regard to a number of Muslim defendants who were tried post 9/11 on charges of terrorist involvement. In one such trial, the defendant entered a guilty plea, with his attorney remarking that "one has to question whether a fair and impartial jury could be found anywhere in America today that could sit in judgment of an Arab American in a case involving allegations of terrorism" (Vidmar 2003). It may be argued that examples such as this illustrate that negative perceptions of Muslims as a group have implications for individual defendants in a variety of ways. Vidmar (2003) for example, argues that policies such as automatic fingerprinting of male visitors to the U.S. from Muslim nations, and media representations of Muslims as terrorists, only worsened already-existing negative perceptions of Muslim Americans. He further suggests that when an Arab American defendant who identifies as Muslim is tried with charges involving terrorism, jurors' biased logic linking Islam and terrorism will result in prejudice even for those jurors who do not ordinarily feel negatively towards Arab Americans.

Despite a fairly comprehensive literature on a variety of social psychological concepts relating to bias (e.g., attitudes, attributions, prejudice), there is very little empirical research directly investigating perceptions of Muslim defendants in criminal trials. One study which may provide some level of insight into this issue examined the perceptions of Muslim versus non-Muslim alleged perpetrators of domestic violence outside of the courtroom context. In this study, De Castella et al. (2011) asked non-Muslim participants to recommend either retributive or restorative justice solutions after watching a video in which a woman described her experiences with domestic violence at the hands of an in-group (Anglo-Australian) or out-group (Muslim) abuser. The study also manipulated the religious/cultural background of the victim (Anglo or Muslim Australian), as is described in more detail below.

Results demonstrated that endorsement of retributive or restorative justice measures did not differ as a function of offender religious/cultural background; thus, participants were no more likely to prefer one justification for punishment over another when the offender was Muslim Australian compared to when he was Anglo Australian. However, the researchers did observe an interesting interaction between offender and victim religious/cultural background on perceived value violation, which refers to the degree to which the crime represented a violation of Australian principles. Specifically, participants rated domestic violence involving an Anglo defendant/Anglo victim or Muslim defendant/Muslim victim couple to be a more serious violation of societal norms than domestic violence involving a Muslim defendant/Anglo victim or

Anglo defendant/Muslim victim couple. De Castella et al. (2011) suggest that this unexpected finding may stem from Australian principles of egalitarianism, or the tendency to attribute the domestic violence to a power imbalance within the relationship to a greater extent in inter-group couples.

In contrast to the above, in another Australian study, Pfeifer, Trounson, and Nathan (2012) varied the religion of the defendant and victim in a battered spouse syndrome scenario—a trial in which a woman was charged with killing her abusive husband. These researchers manipulated the religion of each partner to be either Muslim or Catholic, and found that defendant and victim religion did affect mock jurors' perceptions and their subsequent trial decisions. Specifically, participants perceived the Muslim defendant more negatively, indicating that she was less intelligent, honest, sensitive, and trustworthy. Further, mock jurors rated the Muslim defendant as significantly guiltier than her Catholic counterpart, and were less likely to believe that she was suffering from battered spouse syndrome, particularly when her husband was portrayed as Catholic.

In a two study experiment, Miller, Maskaly, Green, and Peoples (2011) manipulated defendant religion to be either Muslim or Christian in a trial involving a stereotypically Muslim crime (bombing a transportation centre) in Study 1 and a stereotypically Christian crime (bombing an abortion clinic) in Study 2. Religion was manipulated using both stereotypical names, as well as the nature of the defendant's alibi: the alibi witness for the defendant claimed to have been with the defendant at the time of the crime, performing Christian prayers, Islamic prayers, or in the control condition, watching television. In Study 1, the results demonstrated that although not statistically significant, mock jurors were most likely to find the Muslim defendant guilty; however, these results disappeared following deliberation. In Study 2, participants were once again less likely to convict a Muslim defendant post-deliberation than they were prior to deliberating with other mock jurors. Thus, discussing the case with other jurors seemed to lessen the degree of bias faced by the Muslim defendant—the researchers posit that this may be due to an unwillingness to appear prejudiced in front of other jurors.

Taken together, the above results appear to indicate that perceptions of Muslim defendants in a jury decision-making context are mixed, demonstrating the need for additional studies. It is important to note, however, that although it appears that individual jurors demonstrate bias against Muslim defendants, the results of Miller and colleagues (2011) suggest that this effect may be mediated by deliberation. Research has demonstrated that racial bias can be reduced by deliberation (Sommers 2006), and so it is possible that this is true for bias as a function of religion as well. However, more research is needed in order to determine the reliability of this effect.

Muslim Victims and Jury Decision-Making

To our knowledge, only two empirical research papers have investigated perceptions of Muslim victims within a trial context. Maeder, Dempsey, and Pozzulo (2012) examined the influence of Muslim veils on jurors' perceptions of a victim in a sexual assault trial. Given the largely negative perceptions of religious veils in Canada (where this study took place; Angus Reid Public Opinion 2010), the authors hypothesized that jurors would assign more responsibility to the victim, and be less likely to find the defendant guilty, when she was wearing a Muslim veil (*burqa* or *niqab*) than when she was bare-faced. Interestingly, their findings revealed the opposite—mock jurors were significantly more confident that the defendant was guilty when the victim was described as wearing a *burqa* or *niqab* than when she was not described as wearing a veil. Given that this is the only study to directly investigate the influence of religious veils on juror decision-making, more research is needed in order to understand how veils are viewed in the courtroom.

Though not a courtroom study, De Castella and colleagues (2011) conducted research investigating perceptions of Muslim versus Anglo domestic violence victims in Australia. In this study, participants viewed a video blog recorded by a mock victim of domestic violence; in half of the conditions, she was depicted as Anglo (wearing a black tank top and calling herself "Emily"), and in the other half, she was depicted as Muslim (wearing a *hijab* and calling herself "Haseena"). In the video blog, she described her experiences as a victim of domestic violence. The abuser's cultural group was also manipulated; in half of the conditions the victim would refer to him as "Shaun" and indicate he was "a typical Aussie," and in the other half she called him "Rashid" and indicated that he was Muslim Australian. After watching the video blog, participants rating the severity of the abuse, their emotional reactions, and their support for either retributive or restorative justice measures to be taken in response to this situation. Results revealed that participants were more likely to endorse restorative justice measures, and less likely to endorse retributive justice measures, when the victim was Muslim Australian than when she was Anglo Australian. However, they perceived the crime to be more severe in conditions in which the victim was Anglo Australian.

Like the research on Muslim defendants, it appears there are also mixed findings with regards to the perceptions of Muslim victims in the courtroom. The contradictory findings may stem from the fact that the De Castella et al.

(2011) study did not involve an actual courtroom setting. This is an especially important consideration given research indicating that the inclusion of jury instructions and an objective legal rating of guilt can reduce racial bias (Pfeifer and Ogloff 1991; Pfeifer and Ogloff 2003). Many more studies are needed in order to determine how victims are viewed in light of their religious affiliation, making use of stronger and more salient manipulations of victim religion. The effects of Muslim veils should also be investigated further, including juror perceptions of victim credibility in a videotaped trial involving the presence and absence of face-covering veils, in order to determine whether jurors feel as though their ability to judge the veracity of a female Muslim victim's statement is hindered when her face is covered. In addition, future research should consider the effects of deliberation in this context.

Conflation of Race and Religion

Although the literature examining perceptions of Muslim trial parties is sparse, there is a separate body of research that may be informative with regards to perceptions of Islam in the courtroom. A number of studies have investigated bias against Middle Eastern and Arab persons, and there is evidence to suggest that the term Arab may be conflated with the term Muslim, such that those perceived to be Arab may also be automatically perceived to be Muslim. As such, the research investigating bias toward Arab and Middle Eastern targets may be applicable to our understanding of how Muslims may be affected in the courtroom.

It may be argued that following 9/11, "American Islam" emerged as a separate group in America's unofficial classification system and along with this categorization came the conflation of "Arab" and "Muslim," two groups that are neither mutually exclusive nor jointly exhaustive (Bakalian and Bozorgmehr 2011). This conflation extends to other countries, including Australia (Mason 2004) and Canada (Steuter and Wills 2009). For example, Mason (2004) reported a number of incidents in Australia following 9/11 in which Arab-Australians were attacked due to their perceived Muslim background—in particular, many Sikh individuals were targeted. Similarly, in Canada, researchers argue that the media presented Arabs and Muslims collectively as a "dehumanized other," supporting the already-existing confusion of racial and religious background (Steuter and Wills 2009). Chon and Arzt (2005) further argue that this categorization of Arab-Muslim reflects not only external pressure from other groups, but internal desire from those within the group to self-identify.

In the wake of 9/11, those who appeared to be of Arab descent became the target of negative responses, running the gamut from insult to hate crime (Gerstenfeld 2002). Racial profiling (again conflating race with religion) targeting Muslims emerged as a controversial area within the law (Chon and Arzt 2005). It may be argued that the common denominator was fear—following the attacks, people were afraid and targeted that fear towards what they perceived to be an easily identifiable group: Arab-Muslims (ironically, many of the targets of negative responses were neither Arab nor Muslim, Gerstenfeld 2002).

Some researchers have argued that negative perceptions of Arabs and Muslims is a function of media portrayal (particularly after 9/11), with Arabs and Muslims continually depicted as violent terrorists (e.g., Rehman and Dziegielewski 2004). Even prior to 9/11, research had uncovered negative portrayals of Arabs in both news and entertainment media. The work of Shaheen (1997, 2001) demonstrated that popular Hollywood portrayals of Arab Muslims include terrorists, sheiks with harems, and a variety of negative depictions, and that newscasts and documentaries painted a similar picture.

Unsurprisingly, then, attitudes toward Arabs have been found to be overwhelmingly negative. Even studies conducted prior to 9/11 demonstrated that participants held negative stereotypes toward Arabs, believing them to be radical Muslims who are either terrorist supporters or terrorists themselves (Johnson 1992). Following 9/11, attitudes appear to have become stronger and more salient. For example, Oswald (2005) demonstrated that prejudice, stereotyping and discrimination toward Arabs is a function of perceived threat, social dominance orientation and one's own identification as "American." Bushman and Bonacci (2004) found that bias toward Arab Americans was stronger than that facing other ethnic groups, including African Americans, Asian Americans, and Hispanic Americans.

In a study of stereotype content, Ghavami and Pelau (2013) asked participants to list attributes that are stereotypically associated with Middle Eastern individuals in general, as well as Middle Eastern men and Middle Eastern women (among other groups). Their results revealed some interesting differences in terms of perceptions of Middle Easterners in general, as well as gender-specific stereotypes. When asked to identify non-gender-specific attributes, the list for "Middle Eastern" included "terrorists" as the top attribute (i.e., this was the attribute most frequently listed for this group); other negative attributes such as "oppress women," "dangerous," "dirty," and "violent" also appeared in the list of top 15 attributes (it should be noted, however, that positive attributes such as "rich" and "intelligent" were also included). The fourth most common attribute listed was "Muslim," with "religious" as the seventh, suggesting again that race and religion are conflated by the general public. With regards to the gender-specific stereotypes, the pictures of Middle Eastern men and women are quite different. Middle Eastern men were assigned many of the same attributes as the general group, including "terrorists," "dirty," "Muslim," and "dangerous," but also included "anti-West" and "suspicious." For Middle Eastern women, participants listed "quiet" as the top attribute, with a number of other words related to passivity appearing in the top 15 (i.e., "covered," "oppressed," "submissive," "dependent," "petite"). These attributes may explain the findings from Maeder and colleagues (2012) described above, in that to the degree that participants associated the Muslim victim with a Middle Eastern woman, they may have viewed her as more passive and thus in more need of help, thus eliciting a guilty verdict for the defendant accused of assaulting her. However, the picture for Middle Eastern men, and Middle Easterners in general, is hardly a positive one.

Implicit attitudes toward Arabs have also been found to be negative. Nosek and colleagues (2007) used the Arab-Muslim Implicit Association Task (IAT) to compare Arab-Muslim names to "other people" and found that half of their participants implicitly preferred the general "other people" to Arab-Muslim names. In a more specific test, Park, Felix, and Lee (2007) compared Arab-Muslim names to white names and found a strong implicit preference for white names.

Behavioral measures have also shown that Arabs are a target of substantial bias. Bushman and Bonacci (2004) showed that participants were less likely to return a lost email informing a student of winning a scholarship if that student was of Arab descent rather than European descent. Derous, Nguyen, and Ryan (2006) found that participants rated resumes of Arab-sounding names as significantly worse than those of white-sounding names. Therefore, it appears that negative attitudes toward Arabs are also associated with negative behaviors toward group members. This suggests that negative attitudes toward Arab/Middle Eastern persons could carry over into jurors' perceptions of trial parties and verdict decisions.

Race and Jury Decision-Making

In terms of jury research and race, there are very few studies that have examined perceptions of Arab/Middle Eastern defendants in a mock courtroom setting. However, a great deal of research has examined the influence of race on jurors' decisions with regards to other target races, including black (Mitchell et al. 2005), Latino (Taylor and Hosch 2004), Aboriginal Canadian (Maeder and Burdett 2013; Pfeifer and Ogloff 2003), Native American (Struckman-Johnson, Miller, and Struckman-Johnson 2008), and Asian (Maeder, Mossiere, and Cheung 2013).

A number of studies have shown that race affects jurors' decisions (e.g., Foley and Chamblin 1982; Klein and Creech 1982; Ugwuegbu 1979). Most of this literature occurred in an American setting, comparing white and black defendants. Results have demonstrated that mock jurors find black defendants guilty more often than white defendants in rape and murder cases; this effect is heightened if the victim is white. Black defendants also tend to receive harsher sentences than do white defendants (see Sweeney and Haney 1992, for a meta-analysis). In addition, Gordon et al. (1987) found that mock jurors believe that black defendants are more likely to recidivate than a white defendant, and that mock jurors also make more situationally based attributions for white defendants but more dispositionally based attributions for black defendants. Sommers and Ellsworth (2000) also found that jurors who assign dispositional attributions to the defendant are more likely to vote guilty than are jurors who perceive the crime as a function of the defendant's situation. Therefore, black defendants are more likely to be found guilty as a result of being assigned more dispositional attributions. A recent meta-analysis (Mitchell et al. 2005) tied all of these findings together by demonstrating that a small but significant racial bias effect exists for both verdict and sentencing decisions.

Despite these findings, it has been suggested that a number of factors might moderate the effects of race on jury decision-making. Pfeifer and Ogloff (1988) found that studies using a dichotomous guilt scale and jury instructions may eliminate race effects in most jury decision-making. Type of crime also might influence guilt ratings for both black and white defendants, such that defendants are more likely to be found guilty of race-stereotypic crimes (Mazzella and Feingold 1994; Gordon et al. 1987).

Modern racism also might influence the race effect on verdicts. According to the theory of modern racism, many people are biased but wish to appear egalitarian for social desirability reasons (Sommers and Ellsworth 2000). When racial issues are made salient, most people will react in a non-prejudiced manner due to the lack of social desirability for overt racism. Discrimination emerges when situations are ambiguous, and the opportunity for bias to enter decision-making becomes greater (Sommers and Ellsworth 2000). For example, the inclusion of jury instructions might eliminate race effects because these instructions remove the ambiguity that allows jurors to be influenced by prejudices in their verdict decisions (Pfeifer and Ogloff 1991); this effect also might be explained by the higher task specificity of jury instructions (Pfeifer and Bernstein 2003). In addition, when racial issues are made salient, white mock jurors tend to provide non-biased verdicts because the racial issues alert these jurors to the possibility of prejudice (Sommers and Ellsworth 2000). In contrast, in cases where racial issues are not pertinent, but a defendant happens to be black, white jurors react with bias because they have not been alerted to the possibility of prejudice.

Finally, the Elaboration Likelihood Model also might help to explain how race influences jury decision-making. Sargent and Bradfield (2004) argued that the ELM suggests that jurors will give differential attention to certain pieces of evidence if a defendant is black than if he is white. When motivation is low (i.e., jurors have no incentive to be accurate), jurors are sensitive to the strength of the defendant's alibi if he is black, but not if he is white. When motivation is high (i.e., jurors are compensated only when accurate), on the other hand, jurors are equally sensitive to the strength of the defendant's alibi regardless of his race. Therefore, race does influence jurors' sensitivity to legally relevant information, at least when jurors are not particularly motivated.

Perceptions of Arab/Middle Eastern Defendants

Unfortunately, very few studies have directly tested the effects of defendant race in a trial involving an Arab defendant. One exception is a study by Adams, Bryden, and Griffith (2011) which presented 283 participants with a trial transcript involving a Caucasian or Middle Eastern defendant. In this study, eyewitness and victim race were also manipulated and will be discussed later. Defendant race was manipulated via names (Bob Sampson for the Caucasian defendant, Ahmad Gharani for the Middle Eastern defendant) and photographs (the same model was used, but was dressed in Middle Eastern garb for the Middle Eastern defendant conditions). The transcript dealt with an attempted murder case and was presented in both written and audiotaped format. Following the transcript, mock jurors provided a verdict and a sentence if applicable. They then deliberated in groups of 5 to 12 for 10 minutes, after which they presented a group verdict and each juror indicated how many times their personal verdict opinion had changed throughout the deliberation. Results indicated that although there was no overall main effect of defendant race, there were interesting findings in certain conditions involving Middle Eastern defendants—those in which the victim was white. In those conditions, pre-deliberation verdicts were predominantly guilty, but following deliberation, significantly more juries voted not guilty. Therefore, the effects of racial bias may have been mediated by deliberation. Indeed, this has been determined in other studies investigating the effects of deliberation in trials involving other-race defendants (Sommers 2006). However, in other conditions, deliberation did not have this mediating effect. In conditions in which the defendant and eyewitness were both Middle Eastern, deliberation did not reduce the number of guilty verdicts for the defendant. The authors suggest that this is because these conditions were most likely to activate an implicit stereotype of "terrorist collusion," and therefore deliberation could not overcome this effect. Again, however, it is important to note that there was no overall effect of defendant race in this study, suggesting that the effects of racial bias in trials involving Middle Eastern defendants may be more nuanced than originally anticipated.

In another study, Maeder and colleagues (2012) compared perceptions of a Middle Eastern defendant to those of a white defendant in a sexual assault trial and did not find a difference as a function of defendant race. In this study, however, photographs were not used, which may explain the lack of an effect. In addition, the sample in this study was diverse (approximately half of the participants identified as a race other than white, and about one-quarter were of Middle Eastern descent), and it is therefore possible that the effects were cancelled out. Unfortunately, the small cell sizes for other participant races did not allow for an analysis of this potential explanation.

Perceptions of Arab/Middle Eastern Witnesses

In terms of witness race, we found only one study that varied the race of a witness involving a Middle Eastern/Arab comparison group. Adams and colleagues (2011), in the study described above, manipulated the race of the eyewitness using names (Nick Jones or Rashid Asfar) and photos. There was no overall effect of eyewitness race, although there were interesting interactions with defendant race and deliberation as described earlier, suggesting that defendant-eyewitness race combinations that activate an implicit negative stereotype may be unaffected by deliberation.

Perceptions of Arab/Middle Eastern Victims

Some researchers have suggested that the race of the victim may be even more influential than the race of the defendant in the area of juror decision-making. Death penalty research in the United States has revealed that victim race is an extremely important factor in the decision to execute, such that defendants who kill white victims are much more likely to be sentenced to death (Baldus et al. 1998). In contrast, ForsterLee et al. (2006) demonstrated that Australian mock jurors were more punitive in a murder trial when the victim was Indigenous/black Australian as opposed to white. A. Marcus-Newhall, L.P. Blake, and J. Baumann (2002) found a similar result, in that white defendants who committed hate crimes against black victims were treated more severely than any other defendant-victim race pairing. Studies concerning sexual assault and the effect of victim and defendant race on mock juror decision-making have found that defendants (black/white) were treated most harshly and found guilty more often when their race differed from that of the victim (Hymes et al. 1993; Landwehr 2002). Thus, the literature on victim race appears to be somewhat contradictory.

With regards to Arab victims, only two known studies have examined the effect. Clark and colleagues (2012) compared perceptions of victims with Arab, African American, and Caucasian names in the context of an assault trial. This study involved 249 community participants who self-identified as Caucasian, African American, or Latin American. Participants read a vignette of an assault trial in which the defendant's race was held constant (Caucasian), but the victim's name was presented as Chris Jones (Caucasian), Jamal Jackson (African-American), or Mohammed Abdullah (Arabic). Following the vignette, they provided a verdict and completed a need for cognition scale, as well as perpetrator and victim blame measures. Results revealed a significant main effect of victim race, such that defendants accused of assaulting an Arabic victim were blamed significantly less than those who allegedly assaulted a Caucasian or African American victim. Interestingly, however, this effect was qualified by an interaction between victim race and participant race: the effect was driven entirely by jurors who self-identified as Latin American. These jurors also blamed the Arabic victim significantly more than the Caucasian or African American victim (there were no victim race differences for Caucasian or African American jurors). Need for cognition did not have an effect in this study. The researchers suggest that their findings of bias against Arabic victims, but not African American victims, may be due to the differing social acceptability of bias against these groups—racism against African Americans is clearly socially unacceptable, whereas the same might not yet be true for bias against Arab individuals.

Adams and colleagues (2011) also investigated the effects of victim race in their research described above. They manipulated the victim's race to be either Caucasian or Middle Eastern using both names (Thomas Norman or Hakim Ali) and photos. There was no overall effect for victim race in this study. However, there was an interesting effect following deliberation: after deliberating in groups, juries recommended longer sentences to defendants convicted of attempted murder of Middle Eastern victims. Although it did not reach statistical significance, the opposite was true prior to deliberations. Therefore, this study suggests that bias against Middle Eastern individuals may not be as socially acceptable as suggested by Clark and colleagues (2012)—at least in this study, participants were much less likely to reach a biased decision when forced to discuss the case and form a verdict in groups. However, at an individual level, the bias against Middle Eastern victims did occur, though not beyond a statistically significant threshold.

Therefore, overall it is apparent that although there are some conflicting findings in the literature, it can be argued that overall there exists bias against Arab and Middle Eastern persons, and that this bias may carry forward into the courtroom setting. Of course, it is necessary to again point out that more research is needed in this area in order to address the gaps in our understanding of these effects.

Beyond the Jury: Judge's Perceptions of Islam and Muslims

Although the empirical literature has focused on mock jurors' perceptions of Muslim trial parties, there is reason to suspect that judges may be similarly influenced by the presence of Muslims in the courtroom. First, there is substantial evidence to suggest that the rate of agreement between judges and juries is remarkably high. One of the pivotal examinations of jury decision-making, the Chicago Jury Project, investigated the correspondence between judges' and juries' decisions in criminal cases from the 1950s (Kalven and Zeisel 1966). This research found a rate of agreement of 75–80%, suggesting that judges and juries are quite similar in terms of their final decisions. More recent research attempted to replicate this benchmark study in order to determine whether the rate is consistent more than 35 years later (Eisenberg et al. 2005), discovering very similar rates of overall agreement between judges and juries. Other research has supported the finding that judges and jurors share a high agreement rate (Hannaford, Hans, and Munsterman 2000; Heuer and Penrod 1994), suggesting that judges' decisions are highly comparable to those of juries.

Furthermore, although research has not yet examined judges' decisions as a function of defendant religion, there is a small body of research investigating the effects of extralegal factors on judicial decision-making in the criminal courtroom. This literature demonstrates that judges may be influenced by defendant gender (Mann 1984; Meeker, Jesilow and Aranda 1992; Turner and Johnson 2006), defendant age (Wooldredge 2010), defendant race (Lichtenstein 1982; McCarter 2009; Meeker et al. 1992; Turner and Johnson 2005), and the interactions between these variables (Wooldredge 2010). Therefore, it is very possible that judges will be influenced by the extralegal factor of religion. As a result, the effects described above with regards to perceptions of Muslim trial parties could easily translate to bench trials and countries that do not make use of the jury system.

Research specifically examining judicial perceptions of Muslim trial parties is necessary, but based on the literature comparing juridical decisions to judicial decisions, and the literature describing the effects of extralegal characteristics on judges, there is certainly empirical evidence to suggest that judges will be influenced by the presence of Muslim trial parties.

Conclusions

From the above, it is obvious that much more research is needed in order to determine how Islam, and specifically Muslim trial parties, are viewed in the courtroom. Researchers should also be cognizant of the conflation of race and religion. Although it is clear that Islam has been considered in the legal arena, the body of empirical research investigating its influence is woefully small. More attention must be paid to this vastly understudied topic so that we can determine best practices for reducing or eliminating bias in the courtroom.

References

Abel, M. H. and H. Watters. 2005. "Attributions of Guilt and Punishment as Functions of Physical Attractiveness and Smiling." *The Journal of Social Psychology* 145(6): 687–702.

Adams, L. T., M.W. Bryden, and J.D. Griffith. 2011. "Middle Eastern Racial Bias and the Impact of Jury Deliberation." *American Journal of Forensic Psychology* 29(3): 41–59.

Angus Reid Public Opinion (2010). "Four-in-five Canadians Approve of Quebec's Face Veil Legislation." http://www.visioncritical.com/category/global-opinions-and-trends.

Bakalian, A. and M. Bozorgmehr. 2011. "Middle Eastern and Muslim American Studies Since 9/11." *Sociological Forum,* 26: 714–28.

Baldus, D.C., G. Woodworth, D. Zuckerman, N.A. Weiner and B. Broffitt. 1998. "Racial Discrimination and the Death Penalty in the Post-Furman Era: An Empirical and Legal Overview, with Recent Findings from Philadelphia." *Cornell Law Review* 83: 1638–821.

Bleich, E. 2011. "What is Islamophobia and How Much Is There? Theorizing and Measuring an Emerging Comparative Concept." *American Behavioral Scientist* 55(12): 1581–600.

Berman, M. and I. Farrell. 2011. "Provocation Manslaughter as Partial Justification and Partial Excuse." *William & Mary Law Review* 52: 1027–109.Bushman, B.J. and A.M. Bonacci. 2004. "You've Got Mail: Using E-mail to Examine the Effect of Prejudiced Attitudes on Discrimination against Arabs." *Journal of Experimental Social Psychology* 40: 753–9.

Camp, W.D. 2011. "Child Custody Disputes in Families of Muslim Tradition." *Family Court Review* 49(3): 582–90.

Cashin, S. 2010. "To Be Muslim or Muslim-looking in America: A Comparative Exploration of Racial and Religious Prejudice in the 21st Century." *Duke Forum for Law & Social Change* 2: 125–39.

Chon, M. and D.E. Arzt. 2005. "Walking While Muslim." *Law and Contemporary Problems* 68(2): 215–54.

Clark, J.W., R.J. Cramer, A. Percosky, K.A., Rufino, R.S. Miller and S.M. Johnson. 2012. "Juror Perceptions of African American-and Arabic-named Victims." *Psychiatry, Psychology and Law*, (ahead-of-print), 1–14.

Close-It Enterprises, Inc. v. Weinberger (1978). 407 N.Y.S.2d 587 (App. Div. 1978).

De Castella, K., M.J. Platow, M. Wenzel, T. Okimoto and N.T. Feather. 2011. "Retribution or Restoration? Anglo–Australian's Views towards Domestic Violence Involving Muslim and Anglo–Australian Victims and Offenders." *Psychology, Crime & Law* 17(5): 403–20.

Derous, E., H.H. Nguyen and A.M. Ryan. 2006. "Identifiers of Ethnicity and Discrimination against Arabs." Presented at the 21stAnnual Conference of the Society of Industrial and Organizational Psychology, Dallas, TX.

Duke, L. M. and D.M. Desforges. 2007. "Mock Juror Decision-making in Sexual Abuse Cases." *Applied Psychology in Criminal Justice* 3(2): 96–116.

Dwyer, C. and A. Meyer. 1995. "The Institutionalisation of Islam in the Netherlands and in the UK: The Case of Islamic Schools." *Journal of Ethnic and Migration Studies* 21(1): 37–54.

Eisenberg, T., S.P. Garvey and M.T. Wells. 2001. "Forecasting Life and Death: Juror Race, Religion, and Attitude toward the Death Penalty." *The Journal of Legal Studies* 30(2): 277–311.

Eisenberg, T., P.L. Hannaford-Agor, V.P. Hans, N.L. Waters, G.T. Munsterman, S.J. Schwab and M.T. Wells. 2005. "Judge-jury Agreement in Criminal Cases: A Partial Replication of Kalven and Zeisel's *The American Jury*." *Cornell Law Faculty Publications*. Paper 343.

Foley, L.A. and M.H. Chamblin. 1982. "The Effect of Race and Personality on Mock Jurors' Decisions." *Journal of Psychology* 112: 47–51.

ForsterLee, R., L. ForsterLee, I.A. Horowitz and E. King. 2006. "The Effects of Defendant Race, Victim Race, and Juror Gender on Evidence Processing in a Murder Trial." *Behavioral Sciences & the Law* 24(2): 179–98.

Gerstenfeld, P.B. 2002. "A Time to Hate: Situational Antecedents of Intergroup Bias." *Analyses of Social Issues and Public Policy* 2(1): 61–7.

Ghavami, N. and L.A. Peplau. 2013. "An Intersectional Analysis of Gender and Ethnic Stereotypes Testing Three Hypotheses." *Psychology of Women Quarterly* 37(1): 113–27.

Gillis, W. 2013. "Terror Train Plot: Chiheb Esseghaier's Qur'an Demand Reveals Law/Religion Collision." Retrieved July 20, 2013 from http://www.thestar. com/news/crime/2013/06/08/terror_train_plot_chiheb_esseghaiers_ quran_demand_reveals_lawreligion_collision.html.

Gorchow, Z. 2006. "Veil Costs Her Claim in Court—Judge: Face Key in Deciding Truth." Published in *Detroit Free Press*, October 22.

Gordon, R.A., T.A. Bindrim, M.I. McNicholas and T.L.Walden. 1987. "Perceptions of Blue-collar and White-collar Crime: The Effect of Defendant Race on Simulated Juror Decisions." *The Journal of Social Psychology* 128(2): 191–7.

Hannaford, P. L., V.P. Hans and G.T. Munsterman. 2000. "Permitting Jury Discussions During Trial: Impact of the Arizona Reform." *Law and Human Behavior* 24(3): 359–82.

Heuer, L. and S. Penrod. 1994. "Trial Complexity: A Field Investigation of its Meaning and Its Effects." *Law and Human Behavior* 18(1): 29–51.

Higgins, P.L., W.P. Heath, and B.D. Grannemann. 2007. "How Type of Excuse Defense, Mock Juror Age, and Defendant Age Affect Mock Jurors' Decisions." *The Journal of Social Psychology* 147(4): 371–92.

Hymes, R.W., M. Leinart, S. Rowe, and W. Rogers. 1993. "Acquaintance Rape: The Effect of Race of Defendant and Race of Victim on White Juror Decisions." *The Journal of Social Psychology* 133: 627–34.

Johnson, S.D. 1985. "Religion as a Defense in a Mock-jury Trial." *The Journal of Social Psychology* 125(2): 213–20.

Johnson, S.D. 1992. "Anti-Arabic Prejudice in 'Middletown.'" *Psychological Reports* 70: 811–18.

Kalven, H. and H. Zeisel. 1966. *The American Jury.* Boston: Little Brown.

Kendall v. Kendall (1997). 426 Mass. 238, 687 N.E.2d 1228.

Klein, K. and B. Creech. 1982. "Race, Rape, and Bias: Distortion of Prior Odds and Meanings Changes." *Basic and Applied Social Psychology* 3: 21–33.

Kruger, E., M. Mulder and B. Korenic. 2004. "Canada after 11 September: Security Measures and 'Preferred' Immigrants." *Mediterranean Quarterly* 15(4): 72–87.

Landwehr, P.H., R.K. Bothwell, M. Jeanmard, L.R. Luque, R. Brown and M.A. Breaux. 2002. "Racism in Rape Trials." *The Journal of Social Psychology* 142: 667–69.

La Rocca v. Lane (1975). 37 NY 2d 575.

Lichtenstein, K.R. 1982. "Extra-legal Variables affecting Sentencing Decisions." *Psychological Reports* 50(2): 611–19.

Loeffler, R.L. and T.J. Lawson. 2002. "Age and Occupational Status of Defendant in Relation to Mock Juror Sentencing Recommendations." *Current Psychology* 21(3): 289–92.

Maeder, E.M. and J. Burdett. 2013. "The Combined Influence of Defendant Race and Gang Affiliation on Mock Juror Decision-making." *Psychiatry, Psychology, and Law* 20: 188–201.

Maeder, E.M., A. Mossiere and L. Cheung. 2013. "Canadian Mock Juror Attitudes and Decisions in Domestic Violence Cases involving Asian and White Interracial and Intraracial Couples." *Journal of Interpersonal Violence* 28: 667–82.

Maeder, E.M., J. Dempsey and J. Pozzulo. 2012. "Behind the Veil of Juror Decision-making: Testing the Effects of Muslim Veils and Defendant Race in the Courtroom." *Criminal Justice and Behavior* 39: 666–78.

Mann, C.R. 1984. "Race and Sentencing of Female Felons: A Field Study." *International Journal of Women's Studies* 7(2): 160–72.

Marcus-Newhall, A., L.P. Blake and J. Baumann. 2002. "Perceptions of Hate Crime Perpetrators and Victims as Influenced by Race, Political Orientation, and Peer Group." *American Behavioral Scientist* 46: 108–35.

Mason, V. 2004. "Strangers within the "Lucky Country": Arab-Australians after September 11." *Comparative Studies of South Asia, Africa and the Middle East* 24(1): 233–43.

Mazzella, R. and A. Feingold. 1994. "The Effects of Physical Attractiveness, Race, Socioeconomic Status, and Gender of Defendants and Victims on Judgments of Mock Jurors: A Meta-analysis." *Journal of Applied Social Psychology* 24(15): 1315–38.

McCarter, S.A. 2009. "Legal and Extralegal Factors affecting Minority Overrepresentation in Virginia's Juvenile Justice System: A Mixed-method Study." *Child & Adolescent Social Work Journal* 26(6): 533–44.

Meeker, J.W., P. Jesilow and J. Aranda. 1992. "Bias in Sentencing: A Preliminary Analysis of Community Service Sentences." *Behavioral Sciences & the Law* 10(2): 197–206.

Miller, M. K. 2006. *Religion in Criminal Justice*. New York: LFB Publishing.

Miller, M.K. and B. H. Bornstein. 2006. "The Use of Religion in Death Penalty Sentencing Trials." *Law and Human Behavior* 30(6): 675–84.

Miller, M.K., J. Maskaly, M. Green and C.D. Peoples. 2011. "The Effects of Deliberations and Religious Identity on Mock Jurors' Verdicts." *Group Processes & Intergroup Relations* 14(4): 517–32.

Miller, M.K., J.A. Singer and A. Jehle. 2008. "Identification of Circumstances under which Religion Affects Each Stage of the Trial Process." *Applied Psychology in Criminal Justice*, 4: 135–71.

Minnesota v. Davis (1993). 504 N.W.2d 767.

Mitchell, T.L., R.M. Haw, J.E. Pfeifer and C.A. Meissner. 2005. "Racial Bias in Mock Juror Decision-making: A Meta-analytic Review of Defendant Treatment." *Law and Human Behavior* 29: 621–37.

Muhammad v. Paruk (2008). 553 F. Supp. 2d 893.

Munoz v. Munoz (1971). 79 Wash.2d 810.

Nosek, B. A., F.L. Smyth, J.J. Hansen, T. Devos, N.M. Lindner, K.A. Ranganath, C.T. Smith, K.R. Olson, D. Chugh, A.G. Greenwald, and M.R. Banaji. 2007. "Pervasiveness and Correlates of Implicit Attitudes and Stereotypes." *European Review of Social Psychology* 18: 36–88.

Oswald, D. L. 2005. "Understanding Anti-Arab Reactions Post-9/11: The Role of Threats, Social Categories, and Personal Ideologies." *Journal of Applied Social Psychology* 35(9): 1775–99.

O'Toole, M., S. Bell and A. Humphreys. 2013. "'I Don't Want a Book Written by Humans': VIA Terror Plot Accused Again Rejects Criminal Code." *National Post*, May 24.

Park, J., K. Felix, and G. Lee. 2007. "Implicit Attitudes toward Arab-Muslims and the Moderating Effects of Social Information." *Basic and Applied Social Psychology* 29: 35–45.

Patry, M.W. 2008. "Attractive but Guilty: Deliberation and the Physical Attractiveness Bias." *Psychological Reports* 102: 727–33.

Pfeifer, J.E. 1996. "Social Psychology in the Courtroom." In *Applied Social Psychology*, edited by S.W. Sadava and D.R. McCreary, 157–84. New York: Prentice Hall.

Pfeifer, J.E. 1999. "Perceptual Biases and Mock Juror Decision Making: Minority Religions in Court." *Social Justice Research* 12(4): 409–19.

Pfeifer, J.E. and D.J. Bernstein. 2003. "Expressions of Modern Racism in Judgments of Others: The Role of Task and Target Specificity on Attributions of Guilt." *Social Behavior and Personality* 31: 749–66.

Pfeifer, J.E., and J.R. Ogloff. 1988. "Prejudicial Sentencing Trends of Simulated Jurors in Canada." In *Law and Psychology in Canada: The Need for Training and Research*. Symposium presented at the Annual Meeting of the Canadian Psychological Association, Montreal. Ogloff, J.R.P. (Chair).

Pfeifer, J.E., and J.R. Ogloff. 1991. "Ambiguity and Guilt Determinations: A Modern Racism Perspective." *Journal of Applied Social Psychology* 21: 1713–25.

Pfeifer, J.E. and J.R. Ogloff. 2003. "Mock Juror Ratings of Guilt in Canada: Modern Racism and Ethnic Heritage." *Social Behavior and Personality* 31(3): 301–12.

Pfeifer, J.E., J.S. Trounson and K. Nathan. 2012. "Juror Decision-making and Battered Spouse Syndrome: Examining the Impact of Cross-religious Relationships." Paper presented at the Australian Association for the Study of Religion Conference. Sydney, Australia, September.

Quas, J.A., B.L. Bottoms, T.M. Haegerich and K.L. Nysse-Carris. 2002. "Effects of Victim, Defendant, and Juror Gender on Decisions in Child Sexual Assault Cases." *Journal of Applied Social Psychology* 32: 1993–2021.

Raiya, H.A., K.I. Pargament, A. Mahoney and K. Trevin. 2008. "When Muslims Are Perceived as a Religious Threat: Examining the Connection between Desecration, Religious Coping, and Anti-Muslim Attitudes." *Basic and Applied Social Psychology* 30(4): 311–25.

R. v. Humaid (2006). O.J. No. 1507.

R. v. Mohammed (2005). EWCA Crim 1880.

R. v. N.S. (2009). O.J. No. 1766.

R. v. N.S. (2012). SCC 72.

Rehman, T.F., and S.F. Dziegielewski. 2003. "Women Who Choose Islam: Issues, Changes and Challenges in Providing Ethnically Diverse Practice." *International Journal of Mental Health* 32(3): 31–50.

Sargent, M.J. and A.L. Bradfield. 2004. "Race and Information Processing in Criminal Trials: Does the Defendant's Race Affect how the Facts are Evaluated?" *Personality and Social Psychology Bulletin* 30: 995–1008.

Shaheen, J.G. 1997. *Arab and Muslim Stereotyping in American Popular Culture*. Washington DC: Georgetown University Center for Muslim-Christian Understanding.

Shaheen, J.G. 2001. *Reel Bad Arabs: How Hollywood Vilifies a People*. New York: Olive Branch Press.

Skeem, J.L. and S.L. Golding. 2001. "Describing Jurors' Personal Conceptions of Insanity and Their Relationship to Case Judgments." *Psychology, Public Policy, and Law* 7(3): 561.

Sommers, S.R. 2006. "On Racial Diversity and Group Decision Making: Identifying Multiple Effects of Racial Composition on Jury Deliberations." *Journal of Personality and Social Psychology* 90(4): 597–612.

Sommers, S.R. and P.C. Ellsworth. 2000. "Race in the Courtroom: Perceptions of Guilt and Dispositional Attributions." *Personality and Social Psychology Bulletin* 26: 1369–79.

Sommers, S.R. and P.C. Ellsworth. 2009. "'Race Salience' in Juror Decision-making: Misconceptions, Clarifications, and Unanswered Questions." *Behavioral Sciences and the Law* 27: 599–609.

Spanks-El v. Finley (1988). No. 85-C9259, 1987 U.S. Dist. LEXIS 3374 (N.D. Ill. Apr. 23, 1987), *affd, 845* F.2d 1023 (7th Cir. 1988).

State v. Hodge, 726 A.2d 531 (Conn. 1999).

Steuter, E. and D. Wills. 2009. "Discourses of Dehumanization: Enemy Construction and Canadian Media Complicity in the Framing of the War on Terror." *Global Media Journal: Canadian Edition* 2(2): 7–24.

Struckman-Johnson, C., M.G. Miller and D. Struckman-Johnson. 2008. "Effects of Native American Race, Intoxication, and Crime Severity on Judgments of Guilt." *Journal of Applied Social Psychology* 38: 1981–92.

Sweeney, L.T. and C. Haney. 1992. "The Influence of Race on Sentencing: A Meta-analytic Review of Experimental Studies." *Behavioral Sciences and the Law* 10: 179–95.

Tang, C.M. and N. Nunez. 2003. "Effects of Defendant Age and Juror Bias on Judgment of Culpability: What Happens When a Juvenile Is Tried as an Adult?" *American Journal of Criminal Justice* 28(1): 37–52.

Taylor, T.S. and H.M. Hosch. 2004. "An Examination of Jury Verdicts for Evidence of a Similarity-leniency Effect, an Out-group Punitiveness Effect, or a Black Sheep Effect." *Law and Human Behavior* 28 (5): 587–99.

Thomas, E.R. 2006. "Keeping Identity at a Distance: Explaining France's New Legal Restrictions on the Islamic Headscarf." *Ethnic and Racial Studies* 29(2): 237–59.

Thompson, S.B., A. Merrifield and H.L. Chinnery. 2011. "Are Mock Jurors Influenced by the Defendants Gender, Socio-economic Status and Emotional State in Forensic Medicine?" *Forensic Medicine* 2. Retrieved from http://www.webmedcentral.com/article_view/1632.

Turner, K.B. and J.B. Johnson. 2005. "A Comparison of Bail Amounts for Hispanics, Whites, and African Americans: A Single County Analysis." *American Journal of Criminal Justice* 30(1): 35–53.

Turner, K.B. and J.B. Johnson. 2006. "The Effect of Gender on the Judicial Pretrial Decision of Bail Amount Set." *Federal Probation* 70(1): 56–62.

Ugwuegbu, D.C.E. 1979. "Racial and Evidential Factors in Juror Attribution of Legal Responsibility." *Journal of Experimental Social Psychology* 15: 133–76.

United States v. Moussaoui (2006). Jury Questionnaire. Retrieved on July 28, 2013, from news.findlaw.com/cnn/docs/moussaoui/juryquestionnaire.pdf.

Vidmar, N. 2003. "When All of Us Are Victims: Juror Prejudice and Terrorist Trials." *Chicago-Kent Law Review* 78: 1143.

Williams, A.J. 2008. "The Veiled Truth: Can the Credibility of Testimony Given by a Niqab-wearing Witness be Judged without the Assistance of Facial Expressions?" *University of Detroit Mercy Law Review* 85: 273–291.

Women's Legal Education and Action Fund (LEAF). 2010. "Factum of the Intervener." Presented to the court in *R. v. N.S.* (2010), Court of Appeal for Ontario.

Wooldredge, J. 2010. "Judges' Unequal Contributions to Extralegal Disparities in Imprisonment." *Criminology: An Interdisciplinary Journal* 48(2): 539–67.

Zaman, S. 2008. "Amrikan Shari'a: The Reconstruction of Islamic Family Law in the United States." *South Asia Research* 28(2): 185–202.

Zummo v. Zummo (1990). 394 Pa. Super. 30, 574 A.2d 1130.

Index